KW-471-155

The European Community and its Mediterranean Enlargement

les absents ont toujours tort

The European Community and its Mediterranean Enlargement

Loukas Tsoukalis

St Catherine's College, Oxford

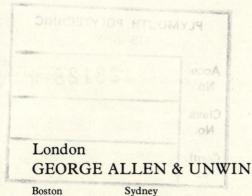

PLYMOUTH POLYTECHNIC
LIBRARY

Accn No

Class No.

Cont.

London
GEORGE ALLEN & UNWIN
Boston   Sydney

First published in 1981

This book is copyright under the Berne Convention. All rights are reserved. Apart from any fair dealing for the purpose of private study, research, criticism or review, as permitted under the Copyright Act, 1956, no part of this publication may be reproduced, stored in a retrieval system, or transmitted, in any form or by any means, electronic, electrical, chemical, mechanical, optical, photocopying, recording or otherwise, without the prior permission of the copyright owner. Enquiries should be sent to the publishers at the undermentioned address:

GEORGE ALLEN & UNWIN LTD
40 Museum Street, London WC1A 1LU

© Loukas Tsoukalis, 1981

British Library Cataloguing in Publication Data

Tsoukalis, Loukas
    The European Community and its Mediterranean
    enlargement.
    I. Title
    338.91'4'041   HV241.25.M/

    ISBN 0-04-382030-1 ✓
    ISBN 0-04-382031-X Pbk

PLYMOUTH POLYTECHNIC
LIBRARY

Accn. No.	128128-9
Class. No.	337·142 TSO
Contl. No.	0043820301

Typeset in 10 on 11 point Plantin by
Servis Filmsetting Ltd, Manchester,
and printed in Great Britain
by Billing and Sons Ltd.,
Guildford, London and Worcester

Contents

Inapicable freedom with 'Med', Spain, Pt, Greece
(France), Italy. Impact of C/S, 1 on CAP
for 33st Study.

Enlargement only occur when deep pressure.

Preface

This book goes to the printers at a time when the Community of Ten is almost a *fait accompli*, while serious doubts are developing about an early accession of the two Iberian countries. Greece's Treaty of Accession was signed in May 1979 and later ratified by all ten national parliaments. Thus Greece should become a full member by January 1981. In the meantime, Portugal and Spain have been negotiating their own accession which is not expected to take place before 1983 at the earliest. Although few people would doubt the eventual completion of the second round of enlargement with the entry of the two Iberian countries, many feel that the time interval between the Community of Ten and the Community of Twelve is likely to be more than two years. These lines are written while President Giscard d'Estaing has asked for a 'pause' in the enlargement negotiations; a 'pause' which according to the French president is necessary for the Community to resolve its internal problems.

Here I shall assume and indeed hope that the Community's second enlargement will not end with the accession of Greece. The object of this book is to study the entry of Greece, Portugal and Spain into the Community and what this membership means for the three Mediterranean countries as well as the future development of the Community of Twelve. I use the term Mediterranean to cover all three countries although strictly speaking Portugal may not qualify as such. From a Braudelian point of view I should not have to justify myself. For historical, cultural and economic reasons Portugal undoubtedly forms part of the wider Mediterranean area. The alternative I had was to use the term 'Southern enlargement'. But for somebody who was born in one of the old cities on the Mediterranean coast and who was taught that Mediterranean means the centre of the earth, the word 'Southern' has rather unpleasant connotations, especially in its current use. At times he would like to believe that the Mediterranean enlargement confirms a shift in the centre of gravity towards the old cultures and civilisations of Europe rather than a process of incorporating three peripheral countries into the European core. Illusions of grandeur, the reader may retort, totally unjustified!

I expressed the hope that the Community's second enlargement will not end with the accession of Greece. Indeed one cannot even say with confidence that the Mediterranean enlargement will be over with the accession of Portugal and Spain. Before the military *coup* in September 1980, Turkey's last civilian prime minister had stated the intention of

[handwritten notes in top margin: "applicant countries & relations to Community? do Community? is it separate &"]

his government to apply for membership of the Community. The issue can re-emerge in the future, assuming that Turkey's military do not stay in power indefinitely. Who knows? Cyprus, Malta, or even Yugoslavia might also follow. Thus the Mediterranean enlargement could become an open-ended process although the number of potential candidates is finite, given the condition set by the Rome Treaty that member countries have to qualify as European. In this book only a few references have been made to Turkey's relations with the Community and Turkey has not been included in this Mediterranean enlargement of the European Community. The reasons are many and, I think, obvious. First of all, there is now no prospect of a Turkish application in the immediate future. If and when it comes, it is likely to be followed by a relatively long period before any serious negotiations can start between the two sides. Thus it is virtually impossible for an eventual Turkish application to be linked with the applications lodged back in 1977 by the Portuguese and Spanish governments. Furthermore, given the size of the problems involved and the level of Turkey's economic development, full membership is not a realistic proposition for the foreseeable future unless it is accompanied by infinite transitional periods. Last but not least, the issues raised by a possible Turkish application are so different in kind and magnitude from those discussed in this book in relation to the three other Mediterranean countries that a global approach to the second enlargement would have lost any meaning whatsoever.

Part One of this book contains a comparative study of the recent economic development of the three applicant countries and their relations with the Community. The main objective has been to identify important factors behind their development and especially those which will be directly affected by accession and the new international economic environment. Part Two is a study of the interaction between the Three and the Nine during the enlargement negotiations; the political and economic interests behind the three applications for membership, the response of member governments; and the reactions of the various political forces and pressure groups in all the countries concerned. Finally, Part Three is an attempt to look into the future and discuss likely effects, possible internal reforms for the enlarged Community and its role in an ever-changing international environment. Separate chapters are devoted to industrial and agricultural policies. In the final chapter the discussion is broadened to include Community institutions and external relations. I am not sure whether the approach adopted in this book is sufficiently dialectical. To the author it seemed a logical way of dealing with the subject.

Although this book studies the interaction between the Three and the Nine and the possible outcome of the marriage, which is in fact more akin to polygamy on both sides, more emphasis has been laid on the problems of the three applicant countries. There are two main justifications for this relative imbalance. Enlargement will be an important factor in the development of the Community of Twelve and each individual member country. However, it is surely true that its impact will be more strongly felt in each of the three entrants than in any of the existing members. In addition, there is already an extensive bibliography on various aspects of Community policies and institutions, while this does not hold in the case of the three applicant countries. There is a particular shortage of literature dealing with the new dimension of Community membership. But this book is not only concerned with Greece, Portugal and Spain as future members of the European Community. Enlargement is seen as an opportunity to examine critically common policies and institutions and the political and economic prospects for internal reforms. The second round of enlargement takes place at a time when the Community is faced with serious internal crises and external challenges. If enlargement were to act as a catalyst for change it would perform a valuable service to the cause of European integration.

I have relied on a large number of primary and secondary sources written in the main Community languages as well as in Greek, Portuguese and Spanish. For the comparative study of the economic development of the Three I worked mainly with secondary sources and was often astonished by the dearth of material available. A great deal of statistical data was also collected for this purpose. Much of it had to be left out in the final draft. The analysis in Part Two of the book is based essentially on press cuttings and interviews with government and party officials, as well as representatives of the main pressure groups. Numerous interviews were conducted in Athens, Barcelona, Brussels, Lisbon, London, Madrid and Washington. Sometimes I was also allowed access to internal working documents. As for Part Three of the book, extensive use has been made of all the above-mentioned sources.

I received my initiation to enlargement issues at a Federal Trust study group which met in London in 1976. I was later persuaded by William Wallace and Geoffrey Edwards to share the work and responsibility for a long article published in *Europa Archiv*. Since then I have written numerous – probably too many – articles on various aspects of enlargement in different books and periodicals. I benefited a great deal from my work as a specialist adviser to the European Communities Committee of the House of Lords. In the course of the last four years I also had the opportunity of testing my ideas with many colleagues and students in conferences and seminars held in various European countries and the United States.

This book appears as the work of one individual. It owes, however, a great deal to many people. I have benefited enormously from the ideas, support and generosity of many colleagues and friends and I should like to apologise to all those who will remain unnamed. First of all, I owe a debt of gratitude to my colleagues at St Catherine's College, Oxford, for having given me the chance to work in such a pleasant and stimulating environment. I should also like to thank them for the tolerance they have shown towards a colleague who, while enjoying all the privileges of a Fellow of the College, offered very little in return and spent most of his time on his own research. I should like to mention especially Lord Bullock, the retiring Master of the College, and Wilfrid Knapp for their unfailing encouragement and support, and most of all for their friendship.

The British Social Science Research Council (SSRC) offered me a generous grant which enabled me to form a small research team which assisted with the preparatory work for this book. The SSRC also provided the financial support for our travel expenses. An invitation from the Institute on Western Europe of Columbia University in New York gave me the opportunity of exchanging ideas with many American colleagues and of interviewing Administration officials in Washington DC.

Agne Pantelouri has helped me with the background work on the Greek internal debate and Greece's negotiations with the Community. She has also made this book more readable with her valuable editorial comments and advice. Various people have participated in the research team and assisted with the collection and analysis of data. I should like to acknowledge the assistance of Claude Rosenfeld, who is responsible for all the statistical tables for Chapter 5 (with the exception of Table 5.14 which was done by Patrick Shea) and for much of the background work on Mediterranean agriculture; and António da Silva Ferreira for his work on industry and for some of the tables which appear in Chapter 1. I should also like to mention Panayiotis Perroulakis, Surojit Ghosh, Peter Hermann and Maaike Linkenhout who contributed in different ways in the preparation of the book.

I am grateful to all those who read and commented on particular chapters. Their criticisms and suggestions enabled me to improve considerably on earlier drafts although, needless to say, no one but the author is responsible for any remaining mistakes. I should like to mention Andrea Boltho, Charles Cavanagh, João Cravinho, Nikiforos Diamantouros, Jürgen Donges, François Duchêne, Rui Feijò, Rosemary Fennell, Tassos Giannitsis, Kostas Papageorgiou, John Pinder, Alan Swinbank and William Wallace. Special thanks are also due to Pamela Thomas and Audrey Hiscock who typed and retyped successive drafts, showing remarkable patience and endurance.

This book is an exercise in international political economy. It is probably overambitious in the sense that it attempts to provide a fairly comprehensive study of the Community's Mediterranean enlargement. In so doing I had to cover a wide range of different areas for some of which I have never claimed any specialist knowledge. However, I found that a good number of specialised studies on particular aspects of enlargement already existed and no doubt there is more to come. What was missing was a more global approach in which one would attempt to tackle simultaneously the various political and economic aspects of the problem and try to build this into a coherent whole. I have therefore taken a calculated risk and it is now up to the reader to pronounce on the final outcome of this enterprise.

As with other works on current affairs, this book has many limitations. I believe that it could have been considerably improved if I had had more time and space at my disposal. I could have then gathered more information, reflected at leisure on various problems and developed some ideas which as it is have been left suspended in the air. With regard to more space, I would have needed greater powers of persuasion to convince my publisher who is naturally very conscious of rising costs. The time factor is even more important. As this book goes to the printers, enlargement is still a live issue. Moreover, new ideas and policies are being put forward. My objective is not to write a history of the second round of enlargement but rather to contribute to the ongoing discussion. Accession to the Community will have a major impact on the political and economic systems of the three Mediterranean countries. It will also be an important factor in the Community's future development. This book will have served its purpose if it contributes in a very modest way to the development of new ideas and policies which help to strengthen the Community and the new democratic institutions in the three Mediterranean countries.

LOUKAS TSOUKALIS

Part One

THE THREE APPLICANT COUNTRIES

1

Three 'Economic Miracles' – Government Policies and the External Environment

Whether we look at GDP figures, economic structure or trade between Greece, Portugal and Spain and the Community of Nine, we cannot fail to notice the considerable differences that exist between the two sides. The three countries are usually referred to as semi-industrialised or 'newly industrialising countries' (NICs)[1] in order to distinguish them both from other developing countries – the word 'developing' is often used only as a euphemism – and the group of advanced industrialised countries which includes all existing members of the European Community (EC). In the case of Ireland, however, its inclusion in the privileged group seems to be almost entirely by virtue of its membership of the Community since the stage of its economic development is not substantially different from that reached by the three Mediterranean countries.

The NICs are a very disparate group of countries comprising the three future members of the Community as well as Yugoslavia, Brazil, Mexico, South Korea, Hong Kong, Singapore and Taiwan. But one characteristic they all have in common is a very rapid process of industrialisation during the last two decades, which has also been translated into a growing share of the world industrial production and world exports of manufactured goods. This process of industrialisation has inevitably brought about a major economic transformation in all the countries concerned.

Greece, Portugal and Spain now find themselves on the Community's doorstep, ready to join a group of advanced industrialised countries and accept a set of common rules of economic behaviour. In order to be able to make some projections into the future and draw a few tentative conclusions about the possible effects of accession on the three countries we first need to study their recent economic development and try to assess the importance of selected variables which will be directly affected by accession. On the other hand a study of the history of relations between each applicant country and the Community – how this relationship has developed and why – as well as the degree of economic dependence/interdependence already reached will enable us to examine critically the economic justification of the three applications. In the next chapter we will see how economic arguments have been used in the internal debate about membership in each of the three countries.

We certainly do not propose to make an exhaustive analysis of the recent economic development of the three Southern European countries. This would be an enormous and highly rewarding task which would justify a separate volume. The approach adopted in this chapter is only a partial one and can be explained in terms of the dual objective mentioned above. We therefore propose to concentrate on the study of two main variables in economic development, namely, government policies and the external environment. The former are important in providing the institutional framework as well as specific measures which can influence decisions made by private economic actors. Alternatively the state can choose to play the role of entrepreneur in specific sectors or subsectors of the economy. Government policies take the form of macroeconomic or regional and industrial policies as well as the form of external protection *vis-à-vis* the outside world. It is clear that such policies depend on the internal political balance of power and on external pressures. Accession to the Community will have a considerable effect on government policies by virtue of the simple fact that the three countries will have to adopt the *acquis communautaire*. On the other hand the external environment can influence internal economic developments through the international movement of goods and factors of production. Here again accession to the Community will have a major impact on the relation between the external environment and the domestic economy, although this does not exclude the possibility that exogenous changes can be more important.

We propose to concentrate on the period since 1960, which starts with significant changes in the internal and external economic policies of the three countries and then coincides with fast rates of growth and the gradual opening of the three economies. The timing of those changes was certainly not unrelated to developments in the rest of Western Europe. The 1960s and early 1970s was a period of uninterrupted growth and economic prosperity for the whole of the industrialised West. Since then the picture has changed radically. The three applications for membership have coincided with a prolonged international recession which manifests itself in high rates of unemployment and inflation – *pace* Phillips and his curve – and low rates of growth. This period is also characterised by a world energy crisis, international monetary instability and a growing challenge of the existing economic order coming from the Third World. One can therefore see the years after 1973 as a separate subperiod. As far as the three Mediterranean countries are concerned the international economic crisis has coincided with the return to parliamentary democracy which, in turn, has had a significant effect on the domestic economy. This varied between Portugal, Spain and Greece, very much depending on the form taken by the transition to democracy. Accession to the Community will bring about yet another change to the environment within which the economic development of the 1960s and early 1970s took place.

Some General Comparisons

All three applicant countries have relatively low GDPs per capita. The difference from the Community average varies considerably depending on whether GDP is measured at current prices and exchange rates or on the basis of some form of purchasing power parity. In 1977 GDP per capita in Spain, at current prices and exchange rates, was 51·6% of the Community average. The corresponding figures were 46·4% for Greece and 27·4% for Portugal (OECD data). According to calculations made by the Commission for 1976, using purchasing power parities, the figures obtained were considerably more favourable for the three countries, namely, 65·3% for Greece, 64·5% for Spain and 41·9% for Portugal.[2] Greece and Spain are therefore at about the same level as Ireland and only a small distance behind Italy, while the third applicant country lags far behind. National income statistics, however, give only a very broad indication of the level of welfare in different countries. Leaving aside the problem of exchange rate variability, we are still faced with another variable factor, the so-called 'hidden economy', which seems to have acquired increasing importance in the course of the recent economic recession.

During the period 1960–73 all three countries enjoyed higher rates of growth than the Community of Six or Nine (Table 1.1) or even any individual member country. The figures in this table also suggest that fast growth was mainly industry-induced (at least as far as the manufacturing sector is concerned). Since 1973 growth rates have slowed down in all Western European countries and indeed in the whole of the industrialised West. It is however interesting to note that some of the relatively less developed countries, namely, Greece, Ireland and Spain, continued to register the highest rates of economic growth (Table 1.2).

Table 1.1 **Annual Growth Rates**

	1960–5	1965–70	1970–3
Greece			
GDP/capita (volume)	7·3	6·7	7·2
GDP (volume)	7·9	7·3	7·8
Manufacturing	9·1	10·0	12·1
Agriculture	6·4	2·4	1·9
Portugal			
GDP/capita (volume)	5·7	6·6	8·9
GDP (volume)	6·3	6·2	8·6
Manufacturing	9·1	8·3	11·5
Agriculture	2·2	1·3	0·0
Spain			
GDP/capita (volume)	7·5	5·3	6·0
GDP (volume)	8·6	6·4	7·2
Manufacturing	12·1	7·8	11·0
Agriculture	2·9	3·5	3·8
EC*			
GDP/capita (volume)	3·8	4·0	3·8
GDP volume	4·8	4·7	4·5

* Data for the EC until 1973 cover only the six original members. This will also apply subsequently unless otherwise mentioned.

Sources: OECD, *National Accounts* (Paris: OECD, various issues); OECD, *Main Economic Indicators* (Paris: OECD, various issues).

Table 1.2 **Annual Growth Rates (GDP volume)**

	1973–8
Belgium	2·3
Denmark	1·7
France	3·0
Germany	1·9
Ireland	3·5
Italy	2·1
Luxembourg	0·7
Netherlands	2·6
UK	1·1
Greece	3·6
Portugal	2·2
Spain	3·0

Source: OECD data.

The relatively low rates of growth for agriculture should not also be taken to imply slow growth in productivity rates. As data in Table 1.3 show, there has been a radical transformation in the distribution of the labour force, particularly in Greece and Spain which both lost more than half of their farming population in the course of seventeen years. In the case of Portugal, the sudden reversal of the downward trend which appears in 1977 can be attributed to the 1974 revolution and various economic events which followed it, but also to a revision of the Portuguese statistics. Nevertheless the three countries still have a much higher percentage of their labour force engaged in agriculture than is the case for the Community as a whole and for any individual member country, with the exception of Ireland.

Table 1.3 **Distribution of the Labour Force**

	1960	1965	1970	1973	1977
Greece					
Agriculture	57·0	52·4	47·2	35·1	28·4
Industry	17·8	19·7	22·4	28·0	30·3
Other activities	25·2	27·9	30·5	36·9	41·3
Portugal					
Agriculture	42·8	37·1	33·0	27·0	32·5
Industry	29·5	33·4	35·7	34·4	33·1
Other activities	27·7	29·5	31·2	38·5	34·4
Spain					
Agriculture	42·3	33·6	29·6	24·3	20·7
Industry	32·5	35·9	37·4	36·7	37·6
Other activities	25·7	30·6	33·0	39·0	41·7
EC					
Agriculture	21·0	16·4	10·6	9·3	8·2
Industry	42·2	44·2	43·1	42·0	39·8
Other activities	36·8	39·4	46·3	48·7	51·9

Source: OECD, *Labour Force Statistics* (Paris: OECD, various issues).

During the 1960s Greece achieved a remarkable combination of fast rates of growth and price stability (Table 1.4). Since 1970 Greece has climbed up many steps of the inflation ladder and has now caught up with the fastest inflating countries of the Community, namely, the UK, Ireland and Italy. On the other hand Spain has been consistently running at faster rates of inflation than those experienced by Community countries. The same applies to post-1974 Portugal where the various governments formed after the revolution proved unable to

Table 1.4   **Consumer Prices (averages of annual rates)**

	1961–70	*1971–9*
Belgium	3·0	7·5
Denmark	5·9	9·5
France	4·0	9·2
Germany	2·7	5·1
Ireland	4·8	13·2
Italy[a]	3·9	13·0
Luxembourg	2·6	6·7
Netherlands	4·1	7·4
UK	4·1	13·2
EC–9[c]	3·7	9·0
Greece	2·1	13·2
Portugal[a, b]	3·9	18·8
Spain[a]	6·0	15·3

[a] Break in series: 1977.
[b] Excluding rent.
[c] Calculated as weighted averages of percentage changes using private consumption weights and exchange rates.

Source: OECD data.

regain control over prices. But one should also bear in mind that after 1974 the three countries experienced a wage explosion which followed the fall of dictatorships and the end of a long period of political oppression which had, among other things, kept wages down.

Let us now examine briefly the effects which this long period of growth had on the economic structure of the three countries. We have already seen from Tables 1.1 and 1.3 the shift in the relative importance of the manufacturing sector in terms of output and the changes in the composition of the labour force. Tables 1.5–7 provide information about changes in the sectoral composition of GDP in terms of value added as well as changes in the structure of the manufacturing sector between 1960 and 1975. The big drop in the share of the agricultural sector is matched in each country by a corresponding increase in the share of industry and services. However the differences among the Three are also remarkable. In 1975 the manufacturing sector accounted for 33·6% of GDP (a drop from 36·1% in 1970) in Portugal, 28·5% in Spain and only 19·9% in Greece. On the other hand construction, transport and communications, together with public administration and defence, occupy a much bigger place in Greek GDP.

Table 1.5   **Greece: Economic Structure**

Sectoral Composition of GDP
(Value added as a percentage of GDP; at factor cost)

		1960	1965	1970	1973	1975
1	Agriculture, forestry	24·6	24·9	18·9	20·4	18·7
2	Mining, quarrying	1·1	1·1	1·3	1·4	1·4
3	Manufacturing	17·0	16·5	19·5	20·1	19·9
4	Electricity, gas and waterworks	1·4	1·7	2·1	1·7	1·6
5	Construction	6·9	7·0	7·6	10·0	7·2
6	Transportation and communications	6·9	6·9	7·5	6·8	8·1
7	Wholesale and retail trade	11·2	10·8	10·7	13·0	13·9
8	Banking	2·2	2·3	2·4	2·2	2·8
9	Dwellings	10·4	8·8	8·6	6·7	6·5
10	Public administration and defence	7·9	8·0	9·1	7·5	8·8
11	Health and education	3·9	4·7	4·7	4·1	4·7
12	Other services	6·5	7·1	7·5	6·1	6·5

Structure of the Manufacturing Sector
(as a percentage of total manufacturing)

		1960	1965	1970	1973	1975
1	Food, beverages, tobacco	24·2	23·2	18·9	16·4	17·4
2	Textiles	16·4	15·9	14·5	16·3	17·3
3	Clothing and footwear	14·2	11·1	9·0	8·7	8·9
4	Wood and furniture	5·9	6·1	6·3	6·6	6·1
5	Paper, printing and publishing	4·6	5·0	5·2	4·1	4·5
6	Chemicals	8·8	9·5	11·2	12·5	13·2
7	Non-metallic minerals	5·8	7·8	8·5	6·4	6·7
8	Basic metal industries	1·8	1·5	7·2	6·9	5·9
9	Machinery, electrical machinery	12·3	12·8	12·7	14·0	11·0
10	Transport equipment	3·1	4·7	3·9	5·6	6·1
11	Other manufactures	2·9	2·5	2·6	2·7	2·9

Sources: National Statistical Service of Greece (NSSG), *Statistical Yearbook of Greece* (Athens, various issues); own calculations.

With respect to the changing structure of the three manufacturing sectors, one can immediately make the general observation that there has been a considerable decline in the share of traditional consumer goods industries, with very few exceptions, in favour of industries producing intermediate and capital goods. But it is not possible to make any further generalisations about the three countries since the differences are still quite remarkable. In Greece the most dynamic growth sectors have been basic metals and non-metallic minerals in the 1960s, textiles and transport equipment in the early 1970s and chemicals all through the period. Relative to the other two countries the Greek industrial structure still remains heavily concentrated on traditional, consumer goods sectors (1–5) which in 1975 accounted for 54·2% of total value added in the manufacturing sector. Basic metals (1960s) and chemicals also constitute important growth sectors in Portugal, but here the biggest increase is registered in the production of machinery and transport equipment which rises from 23·7% to 29·4% of value added between 1960 and 1975. Also interesting is the increase in production of food, beverages and tobacco after the 1974

Table 1.6 Portugal: Economic Structure

Sectoral Composition of GDP
(Value added as a percentage of GDP; at factor cost)

	1960	1965	1970	1973	1975
1 Agriculture, forestry, fisheries	25·1	21·3	17·3	16·3	15·5
2 Mining	0·6	0·5	0·6	0·5	0·6
3 Manufacturing	30·1	33·5	36·1	34·6	33·6
4 Electricity, gas and water	2·4	2·4	2·4	2·3	2·0
5 Construction	4·5	5·1	5·0	6·4	6·6
6 Transport and communications	5·4	5·4	6·1	6·2	6·9
7 Wholesale and retail trade	11·5	11·5	11·9	13·0	12·3
8 Banking	2·6	2·6	3·3	3·9	4·0
9 Dwellings	3·7	3·5	2·8	2·4	2·3
10 Public administration and defence	5·6	6·4	6·8	6·1	6·3
11 Health and education	2·6	2·4	3·0	3·4	5·6
12 Other services	5·9	5·3	4·7	5·0	4·2

Structure of the Manufacturing Sector
(as a percentage of total manufacturing)

	1960	1965	1970	1973	1975
1 Food, beverages and tobacco	13·5	11·5	10·9	10·6	12·5
2 Textiles / 3 Clothing and footwear	22·4	22·1	21·3	22·3	19·9
4 Wood and furniture	10·0	8·3	6·7	7·1	6·3
5 Paper, printing and publishing	5·4	5·4	5·8	4·2	4·4
6 Chemicals	10·8	10·5	12·6	12·1	13·6
7 Non-metallic minerals	7·1	7·1	7·1	7·9	7·7
8 Basic metals	1·7	4·4	3·2	2·0	1·8
9 Machinery / 10 Transport	23·7	24·5	27·5	28·7	29·4
11 Other manufactures	5·0	4·9	4·8	5·2	4·3

Sources: Instituto Nacional de Estatistica, *Estatísticas para o planeamento 1960–1970*; Instituto Nacional de Estatistica, *Contas nacionais* (July 1978).

revolution. Here traditional, consumer goods sectors accounted for 43·1% of total value added. The transformation of the Spanish manufacturing sector is by far the most dramatic. In the course of fifteen years the metallurgical sector (8–10 in the Greek and Portuguese tables) increases its share from 27·7% to 40·3%. With the main emphasis on the production of intermediate and capital goods, Spanish manufacturing industry now bears a much closer resemblance to that of Community countries than either of the other two applicants.

High rates of economic growth have also coincided with the gradual opening of the three economies to international trade (Table 1.8). With the odd exception in the representative years taken, there is an unmistakable trend for growing exports and imports of goods as a

Table 1.7 **Spain: Economic Structure**

Sectoral Composition of GDP
(Value added as a percentage of GDP; at factor cost)

	1960	1964	1969	1973	1975
1 Agriculture, fisheries	22·6	17·9	13·6	11·6	9·7
2 Mining	2·1	1·8	1·4	1·0	1·0
3 Manufacturing	26·7	28·5	27·9	28·5	28·5
4 Electricity, gas and water	2·7	2·5	2·5	2·3	2·3
5 Construction and public works	5·3	6·5	7·0	7·1	7·3
6 Transport and communications	6·5	6·0	6·4	6·4	6·2
7 Wholesale and retail trade	10·6	10·7	11·9	11·7	12·2
8 Banking	2·2	2·9	3·4	3·6	4·2
9 Dwellings	4·6	5·1	5·9	5·2	5·1
10 Public administration and defence	4·9	4·5	5·6	5·1	5·3
11 Other services	11·9	13·7	14·3	17·4	18·1

Structure of the Manufacturing Sector
(as a percentage of total manufacturing)

	1960	1964	1969	1973	1975
1 Food, beverages and tobacco	17·1	16·4	13·9	11·6	11·2
2 Textiles	15·0	11·8	9·0	7·3	5·9
3 Leather, footwear and clothing	9·1	10·5	9·8	9·7	9·6
4 Wood, cork and furniture	7·5	6·1	5·6	6·1	5·1
5 Paper, printing and publishing	4·4	4·5	4·5	6·2	6·9
6 Chemicals	15·0	14·4	15·3	14·4	15·4
7 Non-metallic minerals	4·2	5·4	5·8	6·0	5·6
8 Metal industries	27·7	31·0	36·1	38·7	40·3

Source: Banco de Bilbao, *Renta nacional 1977* (Bilbao, 1978).

percentage of GDP. The remarkable decline in Portuguese exports between 1973 and 1977 can be explained in terms of the exceptional combination of political and economic events after the revolution. It was actually reversed in the following year. In subsequent sections of this chapter we shall try to examine the contribution of export growth to economic development in the three countries. We shall also emphasise and explain the peculiar position of the Three, compared with other developing countries, in terms of their ability to overcome the balance of payments constraint, given the negative trade imbalance which can be deduced from Table 1.8. Compared with the corresponding figures for the Nine as a whole (X/GDP: 24·01%, M/GDP: 24·47% in 1977, OECD data) and given the size of the internal market, particularly in the case of Greece and Portugal, domestic production in the three countries is much less export-oriented than in the Community of the Nine. To a lesser extent a similar point can be made about the openness of the three economies to foreign produced goods.

We have so far used a small number of broad indicators, such as rates of growth, composition of the labour force and GDP, inflation rates and trade dependence, in order to draw a general picture of the kind of magnitude of economic transformation that Greece, Portugal and Spain have undergone since 1960. We now need a more qualitative analysis which also goes in greater depth into the characteristics and problems of each individual country. As we have already seen, economic development has been mainly characterised by a rapid process of industrialisation. It is therefore here that the main emphasis will lie, particularly on the manufacturing sector which will be most directly affected by accession to the Community. Agriculture will be examined separately in Chapter 5. We will focus our attention on the role of government policies and the external environment and particularly on institutional and trade relations with the Community. It should be obvious that in such an exercise economics is closely intertwined with politics.

Table 1.8 Trade Dependence: Greece, Portugal and Spain
Imports and exports of goods only[a] as a percentage of GDP (at current prices)

	1960 Imports	1960 Exports	1965 Imports	1965 Exports	1970 Imports	1970 Exports	1973 Imports	1973 Exports	1977 Imports	1977 Exports
Greece	20·0	5·8	18·9	5·5	19·7	6·4	21·5	8·9	24·9	10·0
Portugal	22·1	13·2	24·8	15·5	25·8	15·4	26·6	16·1	30·6	12·5
Spain[b]	9·3	6·0	14·0	4·5	12·8	6·5	13·4	7·3	15·2	8·8

[a] Goods includes Standard International Trade Classification categories 0–9.
[b] Data for 1961 for Spain.

Sources: OECD, *National Accounts of OECD Countries, 1952–1977*, Vol. 1 (Paris: OECD, 1979); OECD, *Trade by Commodities: Series B* (Paris: OECD, various issues).

Greece

The Athens Agreement of 1961

There were two main turning points in the external economic policy followed by successive Greek governments during the postwar period. One was in 1953 when the government announced a 100% devaluation of the drachma (the new exchange rate with the dollar remained stable until 1975), some liberalisation of imports by substituting moderate tariff rates for strict quantitative restrictions, and new legislation (Law 2687/1953) which was intended to encourage the inflow of foreign investment. These measures followed the early success of an internal stabilisation policy directed against rampant inflation which had destroyed any confidence in the national currency. The second turning point was in July 1961 when the Karamanlis government signed an association agreement with the EEC of the Six. According to Katsos this agreement marked a shift from an import substitution to an export promotion policy.[3]

It was in 1959, two years after the signing of the Treaty of Rome, that Greece asked for the opening of negotiations with the Six. This took place against the background of a domestic crisis which combined a worsening of the balance of payments and stagnation in industrial investment and production. The crisis had, in turn, led to the imposition of new import restrictions. The implementation of the association agreement coincided with a very favourable external economic environment – the economic boom of the 1960s – and it is therefore impossible to disentangle completely the effects of one from the other. Nor is it possible to draw a clear line of distinction between the effects of the association and internal policies.

Before we turn to the implementation of the agreement and its impact on Greek industrialisation let us first examine the motives and expectations on both sides, the main issues which arose during the negotiations and the actual contents of the Athens Agreement.[4] The creation of the EEC and the European Free Trade Association (EFTA) presented the remaining countries of Western Europe with a serious danger of political and economic isolation. For Greece the EEC choice was made for two basic reasons. One was the political aspects of the Rome Treaty which distinguished it clearly from the aim of establishing a simple free trade area. The other was the inclusion of agriculture. The forces of the right and centre in Greece saw an association with the EEC as strengthening ties with the West – the

EEC and NATO were seen as part and parcel of the same alliance – and consolidating the internal political status quo. It should also be borne in mind that the first application for association with the Six came from a country, a member of NATO, which had emerged in 1949 after a long and bloody civil war and where in 1958 the communist-controlled EDA (United Democratic Left) registered 25% of the popular vote. In addition Greece was witnessing an increasing dependence on Eastern European markets for its exports (22·1% in 1960; see Table 1.9) and this was occurring in the peak of the Cold War era.

The above arguments help to explain the attitude of the forces on the right and centre of the political spectrum in Greece as well as the positive reaction of the EEC countries and the United States. For the Six, except for security reasons, the Greek application came at the time when they were faced with the British challenge and the formation of EFTA and constituted the first sign of a growing appeal in the Mediterranean region which was soon to become almost embarrassing.[5] As for the United States, Joseph Loeff writes about 'la belle époque de la politique européenne de la Maison Blanche' and refers to Greece as the 'enfant chéri' of the Americans.[6] Given this background it is not difficult to guess the reaction of the Greek left – at a time when Eurocommunism was still completely unimaginable. The EEC was denounced as a plot of revanchist Germany and the imperialists, while the signing of the association agreement was seen as putting an end to the last vestiges of national sovereignty and all hopes for economic development.[7] It is interesting that the leader of EDA has now voted in favour of the Treaty of Accession.

On the economic side the Karamanlis government seemed to have various expectations in relation to the agreement such as the provision of free access to Greek agricultural exports (farm products and raw materials accounted for 94·6% of total Greek exports to the Six in 1960; see Table 1.11), the financing of domestic economic development and the attraction of foreign investment. It was therefore natural that the main issues in the negotiations would centre around agriculture, and tobacco in particular (40·7% of total Greek exports to the EEC in 1960), financial aid and, last but not least, the degree of reciprocity in the elimination of trade restrictions between the two sides. The latter point was the cause of a great deal of worry and scepticism even among people who on political grounds would be in favour of the association agreement.[8] The fundamental question was whether the creation of a customs union between the Six and an underdeveloped country like Greece made any sense and whether the latter would sacrifice its chances of industrialisation by abandoning the right to protect its infant industries. The second related question was about the balance of payments implications of the gradual liberalisation of imports.

The agreement signed in Athens in July 1961 established a two-tier transitional period leading gradually towards a full customs union for industrial products. Tariffs and quotas were to be abolished within twelve years (by 1974) by both sides, but for a list of products being manufactured in Greece at the time – amounting then to 40% of Greek imports – trade restrictions imposed by Greece would be eliminated over twenty-two years (by 1984). This was a *de facto* acceptance of the infant industry argument. The agreement also envisaged the eventual harmonisation of agricultural policies on a product-by-product basis, although this would have to wait the translation of the general points of agreement referring to agriculture in the Rome Treaty to concrete policies within the EEC. Moreover Greece's approval would be required for changes to the Common External Tariff (CET) applicable to certain products such as tobacco, raisins and olives. Wishes were also expressed for the liberalisation of the movement of persons, services and capital, and the harmonisation of competition rules and taxation. Finally, an agreement was reached about the provision of EEC financial aid and the setting up of common institutions.

The association agreement with Greece has been the most encompassing and complex agreement ever signed by the Community with a third country. A cynic might say that member countries had to learn from their own mistakes. It is certainly true that the problems – both political and economic – which arose later in its implementation, together with the difficulties in EEC relations with Turkey and the growing number of applications from other third countries, made Community members increasingly cautious in their response.

The agreement was approved by the opposition parties with the exception of the communist-led left. There was certainly the inevitable general criticism of the terms negotiated, while others thought that Greece should have applied for full membership.[9] Nevertheless there seemed to be genuine fear combined with widespread confusion about the implications for future economic development. The agreement was not preceded or followed by any real economic analysis. Triantis argued that certain economic observers believed that the association was necessary for political reasons while political observers thought that the main benefits were supposed to be economic.[10] The initiative taken by the Greek government was a necessary response to the first moves towards economic integration in Western Europe. It was also encouraged by domestic and international political considerations. But in economic terms it was an extremely risky bet. It is not accidental that the Greek negotiator, John Pesmazoglou, did not exclude the possibility of Greece's seeking a revision of the agreement or even completely withdrawing.[11] The idea of revision was later

(1967) taken up by Andreas Papandreou and was linked with the need for nationalisations and economic planning.

Implementation and 'Freezing'

The association agreement was put into effect in November 1962. The major problem which soon arose with respect to its implementation was over the harmonisation of agricultural policies between the two sides. For Greece harmonisation meant participation in the institutions of the common agricultural policy (CAP) – including the price support system and the Agricultural Fund (FEOGA). For the Six harmonisation meant something more simple and certainly less costly, namely, trade liberalisation. Negotiations dragged on while the Six were involved in long internal discussions for the adoption of market organisations and price support systems to apply to intra-EEC trade.

While no agreement was as yet in clear sight, the *coup d'état* of 21 April 1967 cut short the deliberations. The following month the Commission decided to limit the application of the agreement to its 'current administration'. This led to the so-called freezing of the association. However the use of the term needs some further clarification. Both sides continued to adhere to the timetable for the elimination of tariffs. Thus Greek industrial exports have enjoyed free access since 1968, earlier than originally envisaged, while by 1974 two-thirds of Community exports entered Greece duty-free. The freezing applied to negotiations about the harmonisation of policies, with agriculture holding a prominent place, and financial aid. Calls from the European Parliament for a unilateral abrogation of the agreement were not followed, while the Community was finally forced to enter into direct negotiations with the Greek colonels, following the adoption of the market organisation for wine and the first round of enlargement. In the end the freezing of the association was not at a particularly low temperature. Yannopoulos concludes that 'both the cautious responses of the Greek colonels and the reluctance of the Commission to follow the logic of its unilateral action in 1967 in moving towards the suspension of the treaty illustrates one vital point, namely that once the degree of market interdependence among nations reaches a critical point it makes their relationship one that often transcends and bypasses political preferences'.[12] Others would argue that the Community's policy could not be based on pure idealism since the political change in Greece provided a *deus ex machina* for the elimination of agriculture from the agenda.[13] The fact that no real progress was achieved on this subject after the restoration of democracy in Greece adds another weapon to the armoury of cynics. Agriculture has been a sore point in relations between Greece and the

Community prior to membership. We think that the experience suggests how unrealistic was the objective set in the Athens Agreement to harmonise agricultural policies with a country which did not have the right to participate fully in the Community decision-making system. It was already a miracle that some agreement was reached – whatever its intrinsic merits – at the level of Six and later Nine about an economic sector where there is a long history of heavy government intervention and where 'world market prices' do not usually have much meaning in terms of 'economic efficiency'. After the fall of the dictatorship in 1974 some Greeks were quick to understand the objective constraints to Greece's participation in the CAP without the country being a full member. It is however only fair to add that while Greece was complaining about the lack of progress in the agricultural field the Commission could easily point to the battery of non-tariff barriers and state aids still existing in Greece.[14]

Despite the damaging statements made by the Commission and the constant denunciations of the Greek political regime made by members of the European Parliament, the colonels never thought of questioning the principle of the association. On the contrary, they always played up any aspects of the agreement which remained unfrozen. It is characteristic that in 1973 the Markezinis government thought that Greece was then ready to apply for full membership. This view was also shared by the Federation of Greek Industrialists (SEV).[15] Thus the degree of economic integration already achieved and fears of further international isolation made the Greek colonels very sensitive to the state of their relations with the Community. One serious problem at that time was the fear entertained in Greece that the global Mediterranean policy of the Community would lead to a further erosion of the preferential treatment which Greek exporters used to enjoy *vis-à-vis* their competitors in the area in obtaining access to Community markets. In addition, relations with Europe served as the main weapon with which the democratic opposition attacked the regime. As with the Spanish case, both opponents of the colonels and Community representatives stressed that the only real obstacle in Greece's relations with the Community was the existence of the dictatorship.

It is also worth pointing to the apparent contradiction between the attitude of Western European governments – at least the majority of them – as members of the Community or even the Council of Europe, and their attitude as members of NATO or in bilateral relations with the colonels. A member of the European Parliament, for example, questioned how it was possible that EC countries could furnish the junta with the arms by which it imposed its rule on the Greek people. He referred to it as an illustration of 'la politique du contrepied.'[16] This may provide an interesting case-study of contradictory behaviour of nation-states within different international organisations. Furthermore it also helps to explain at least partly the different attitudes adopted subsequently within Greece itself on the subject of full membership. There were enough arguments to be found for both supporters and opponents. While one would point to the ostracism of the colonels' regime by democratic Europe and the need to consolidate democracy by becoming a member of the Community, the other would prefer to emphasise the NATO dimension of member countries and the tolerance/support of the dictatorial regime. Therefore the long discussions within Greece about the links between the Community and NATO do not appear to be totally irrelevant.

The Athens Agreement of 1961 was a highly ambitious one signed in a period of euphoria. It is now idle to speculate as to whether it would have been implemented successfully if the *coup d'état* in Greece had not intervened. One can only say that there would have been many serious difficulties. In the end it was only the customs union part of the agreement where real progress was made. However, its political and economic effects on Greece were more than sizeable. One can never understand Greek reactions on the subject of membership unless the experience of the association agreement is taken into account.

Government Policies

Since the end of the civil war all Greek governments have emphasised their strong attachment to liberal economic ideas and the free working of the market mechanism. This was a necessary ideological weapon against the left but also the direct result of American influence. But, fortunately or unfortunately, real practice is not always consistent with ideology. Since independence in 1828 the Greek state has always played a pervasive role in every sphere of economic life. If the market mechanism does not provide the 'right' incentives, then the state has to offer a helping hand. In this respect Greece is certainly not a unique case. On the purely negative side it can be argued that the overwhelming size of the state bureaucracy – not only the result of political patronage but also another form of social security system – and the high degree of inefficiency constitute a major obstacle to economic development.

The association agreement led to a considerable reduction of external protection and put an end to the strong anti-export bias of the pre-1962 tariff system. It did not however change the tariff structure itself which is most favourable to domestic producers of consumer goods and least favourable as far as capital goods are concerned. But this should be expected, given the need for a country in the first stage of its industrialisation to import capital equipment at low prices and the comparative advantage it is likely to have in light, labour-intensive industries.

Although adherence to the timetable set in the Athens Agreement has led to a considerable reduction in tariff rates both nominal and effective protection is still high relative to Community levels for a number of important Greek industries.[17] Moreover non-tariff protection is certainly more effective. Quantitative restrictions apply to luxury goods and some other goods for which a sufficient domestic production exists; indirect taxes imposed on imported goods are only in theory equivalent to the ones imposed on domestic production. One should also add the advance deposit requirements for importers, the invoice control effected by the chambers of commerce as well as the system of government procurement.[18] On the other hand export subsidies take the form of interest rate subsidisation and the partial exemption from indirect taxation. Since 1953 Greek governments have also offered a favourable regime to foreign investment in terms of tariff and tax exemption but also by guaranteeing, in some instances, the preservation of a monopolistic or oligopolistic market structure. As far as existing restrictions on the repatriation of profits, capital and capital gains are concerned, there is real doubt as to their effectiveness with transnational corporations.[19]

On the domestic front the role of the state in economic development has taken the following main forms: (i) continuous investment in infrastructure; (ii) a long series of incentives and state aids to private industry; and (iii) provision of ample finance through the banking system. We are not talking here about the agricultural sector where, as should be expected, government intervention is much more direct.

Between 1964 and 1975 the state share in the accumulation of fixed capital in the manufacturing sector was only 1·4%. Two-thirds of state investment (or 30·4% of total investment) were concentrated in energy, transport and telecommunications.[20] Apart from increasing the 'external economies' for private entrepreneurs the state also provided a series of incentives and aids which included tax exemptions of various kinds, investment grants, exemption from customs duties, interest rate subsidisation and preferential purchases by government departments. Special incentives also existed for tourist development which became the number one priority of the colonels. It has been estimated that the total cost of incentives for the state during the period 1961–75 represented about 35% of the total private investment undertaken.[21]. We should however add that 40·5% of this figure accounted for the loss of customs duties, which is simply the result of the high level of tariffs in the country.

The underdevelopment of the stock market in Greece meant that investible funds could come either from internal funds or the banking system. The latter is characterised by a duopoly since the two biggest banks control about 85% of all deposits. The larger of the two has been under government control and later in 1975 this was also extended to the second. Thus although the state refused to play the role of entrepreneur it did so, at least indirectly, through the National Bank of Greece and now the Commercial Bank which have been major shareholders in many Greek companies. All commercial banks have also been required to use a minimum percentage of their deposits for medium- and long-term lending to manufacturing. But the policy has not been entirely successful, not because of a lack of funds available but because of insufficient demand for productive investment.[22] In fact Greece experienced high rates of capital accumulation but with a relatively large share of investment expenditure going to construction. The share of the latter has been higher than in either of the two Iberian countries.

Last but not least, one does not have to be a Marxist in order to notice the role played by governments in industrial relations. This applies particularly to the case of Greece, where there has been traditionally a close government involvement in the trade union movement, an involvement which obviously became even more pronounced during the dictatorship. During the period 1960–73 increases in real wages consistently lagged behind the rates of growth of GDP.[23] But the existence of surplus labour is also an important factor to bear in mind. Massive emigration during the 1960s did not only bring about a sizeable contribution to the balance of payments and the economy in general, but also constituted a veritable safety valve for the system.[24]

The fall of the dictatorship in July 1974 and the return of parliamentary democracy have coincided, in exactly the same way as in both Spain and Portugal, with a prolonged world economic recession. The old conservative leader, Constantine Karamanlis, who led all Greek governments after 1974 until he moved to the presidency in May 1980, followed economic policies which marked a fairly clear departure from past trends. The role of the public sector has expanded while at the same time governments seem to have accepted some modifications in the so far prevalent economic philosophy. The nationalisation of the Commercial Bank of Greece has given the state virtually complete control of the banking sector. Through the nationalisation of this bank the state has also assumed direct control of other companies, including the Hellenic Shipyards. Some nationalisation has also taken place in the transport sector. During the same period a consortium of four domestic banks (ELEVME) was created with the aim of complementing private initiative in the industrial sector, particularly mining and chemicals. The post-1974 governments have also tried to increase the progressivity of taxation and cut widespread tax evasion, which is extremely difficult to control in a country where the self-employed account for 65% of non-agricultural employment (OECD surveys). However, government expenditure as a percentage of GDP still remains much lower in Greece when compared with the OECD average. Moreover, despite extensive government intervention in economic affairs, state ownership is limited to public utilities and is almost nil in the manufacturing sector. This is very much different from both Spain and post-1974 Portugal. The five-year plans still remain theoretical exercises rather than a serious attempt to shape long-term economic trends. One recent development however is the growing realisation that industrial concentration in the Athens area has to come to an end and that an active regional policy is needed.

First Stage of Industrialisation

During the 1960s and early 1970s Greek industrialists were faced with ample finance, low wages and an abundant labour supply, although this last was progressively reduced as a result of massive emigration to Western Europe and especially Germany. The 1961 Agreement put an end to the anti-export bias of the tariff structure and gradually offered Greek industrial exporters free access to Community markets, which in turn meant positive discrimination *vis-à-vis* exporters from other developing countries. During this period reciprocal concessions offered by Greece led to various reductions in the effective protection of Greek industry. But this was much smaller in the case of already existing industry, while non-tariff protection also remained.

As we have already seen, the manufacturing sector enjoyed very high rates of growth while also going through some important changes in its internal structure. However, despite the rapid rates of growth the manufacturing sector and industry in general were unable to absorb the surplus labour which voted with its feet and left the country. Katsos concluded that capital played a much more important role than labour as a source of growth. In the early 1970s shortages of skilled labour appeared and the low rates of unemployment combined with the economic crisis in Western Europe led to net inflows of workers after 1975.

Table 1.9 shows that there has been a big shift in Greece's trade towards the Community. The association agreement must have played an important part, although given the remarkable change in Greece's economic and trade structure during this period it is virtually impossible to isolate the effect which the agreement has had on trade between the two sides. The shift is even more pronounced in the case of Greek exports to the EC, particularly when compared with exports to EFTA (before 1973) and centrally planned economies, where there is a clear downward trend. The reversal of the trend with the EC after 1973 can be attributed to the big rise in oil prices and the growing importance of Middle Eastern markets for Greek exports. Still, in 1977 the Community of Nine accounted for 47·7% of Greek exports and 42·5% of imports, which was not substantially different from the Community average (50·7% for exports and 49·3% for imports). West Germany together with Japan were the most important suppliers, while the German market provided by far the most important outlet for Greek exports.

Table 1.9 **Greece: Geographical Distribution of Foreign Trade as a Percentage of Total Trade (goods only)**

	Imports					Exports				
	1960	1965	1970	1973	1977	1960	1965	1970	1973	1977
EC–6	33·6	44·4	40·4	—	—	32·8	37·2	45·9	—	—
EC–9	—	—	—	50·1	42·5	—	—	—	55·0	47·7
*EFTA	16·9	18·3	18·8	6·1	7·6	15·3	12·5	11·0	5·7	2·8
Centrally Planned Economies	7·9	9·0	5·2	5·5	5·7	22·1	22·8	16·8	11·6	12·6
USSR	n.a.	n.a.	1·8	1·3	1·7	n.a.	n.a.	5·4	3·1	3·7
Middle East	n.a.	4·0	3·8	6·8	9·7	n.a.	4·3	2·9	5·3	11·6
USA	13·5	9·9	5·9	8·3	5·1	13·4	9·5	7·5	6·4	4·6
Japan	n.a.	3·4	12·8	7·0	15·1	n.a.	2·4	1·3	1·2	0·8
UK	10·2	n.a.	8·6	5·6	5·5	9·5	n.a.	5·9	7·0	5·0
Germany	15·9	n.a.	18·5	19·5	15·1	18·5	n.a.	20·2	21·6	21·3
France	4·6	n.a.	7·3	7·6	6·1	4·8	n.a.	5·6	6·6	6·9
Italy	5·8	n.a.	8·4	9·1	9·0	6·2	n.a.	10·0	9·5	7·0

*From 1973 the UK and Denmark are no longer members of EFTA.

Sources: OECD, *Trade by Commodities: Series B* (Paris: OECD, various issues); own calculations.

The figures in Table 1.10 indicate that despite the impressive rates of growth of Greek exports between 1960 and 1977 the coverage of imports by exports has not improved at all. But unlike other developing countries in their first stage of industrialisation Greece has not been faced as yet with a serious balance of payments constraint.

Table 1.10   **Greece: Balance of Payments Profile (in percentage terms)**

	1960	1965	1970	1973	1977
Exports[a]/Imports[a]	44·9	35·6	39·9	33·8	43·6
Tourism/Exports[a]	22·3	32·6	31·7	41·8	38·9
Migrant Remittances/Exports[a]	42·9	62·5	56·0	59·7	36·6
Transportation/Exports[a]	36·6	49·5	44·1	48·7	44·7

[a] Goods only.

Source: OECD, *Balance of Payments of OECD Countries 1960–1977* (Paris; OECD, 1979).

The large trade deficits (14·5% of GDP in 1977) have been covered in their biggest part by growing invisible earnings and autonomous capital movements. Earnings from tourism and remittances from migrant workers constitute a very large percentage of total exports of goods for all three Mediterranean countries (75·5% for Greece in 1977). Greece has an additional important source of invisible earnings, namely, shipping. As far as the capital account is concerned, deposits in foreign currency with Greek banks and purchases of real estate have provided the big bulk of capital inflows in recent years. Greece, unlike the two Iberian countries, has run persistent deficits in its current account and basic balance, which were financed through international borrowing. Thus Greece has a higher debt ratio than the other two applicants, but it is still much smaller than that of other NICs, such as Brazil, Mexico or Yugoslavia.[25]

The worsening of Greece's terms of trade since 1973, as a result of a series of increases in oil prices, coupled with the structure of the Greek economy and its high import dependence have led to a continuous deterioration of the balance of payments which could re-emerge as a serious constraint on economic growth in the future. In December 1979 Greece was forced to introduce emergency measures in order to curtail imports. Meanwhile in March 1975 the drachma was floated after twenty-two years of stability *vis-à-vis* the dollar. Floating was actually a euphemism since the exchange rate was effectively managed by the Central Bank. Whether we take 1970 or 1975 as an index, the data in Table 1.11 show that the drachma has depreciated considerably *vis-à-vis* all Community currencies, with the exception of the Italian lira. The depreciation of the currency has certainly contributed to the continuation of the inflationary spiral.[26]

Table 1.11 **Indices of Exchange Rates – Weighted average exchange rates *vis-à-vis* currencies of twenty-seven selected trading partners**

	Dollar rates		Export-weighted[1]		Import-weighted[2]		Overall[3]	
	1970=100 annual 1978	1975=100 annual 1979	1970=100 annual 1978	1975=100 annual 1979	1970=100 annual 1978	1975=100 annual 1979	1970=100 annual 1978	1975=100 annual 1979
Belgium	159·05	125·15	129·35	116·59	88·86	90·79	120·81	113·32
Denmark	136·21	109·02	128·31	108·58	99·97	102·08	113·21	102·91
France	123·30	100·67	108·08	95·91	113·97	113·35	97·86	92·05
Germany	182·59	134·02	169·72	134·57	70·81	80·27	157·02	130·11
Ireland	79·98	92·17	87·45	93·25	127·62	109·97	82·77	92·06
Italy	73·69	78·49	62·91	74·39	192·59	145·32	57·55	71·67
Netherlands	167·64	125·83	137·84	115·94	83·78	91·14	128·94	112·94
UK	79·98	95·49	78·48	100·48	162·40	112·50	69·37	94·23
Greece	81·87	85·62	70·51	81·66	164·70	128·01	63·71	79·20
Portugal	65·63	52·14	63·08	51·82	192·17	205·49	56·29	49·88
Spain	91·59	85·66	84·05	85·51	138·99	126·23	76·40	81·53

[1] The export-weighted index can be considered as an indicator of the direct impact of exchange rate changes on the foreign currency prices of exports of the currency concerned, i.e. their impact prior to any adjustment in the domestic price level of the exporting country. The weights are derived from bilateral export shares in 1975 and all cross rates are expressed in terms of the foreign currency price of a unit of domestic currency.

[2] The import-weighted index can be considered as an indicator of the direct impact of exchange rate changes on the domestic currency prices of the country concerned. The weights are derived from bilateral import shares in 1975 and all cross rates are expressed in terms of the domestic currency price of a unit of foreign currency.

[3] The overall (effective exchange rate) index is a composite measure of the external value of each currency in terms of the other twenty-seven currencies and is computed by averaging the export- and import-weighted indices. The average is weighted in accordance with the relative importance of exports and imports in the total trade of the country concerned. It should be noted that in deriving the average the import-weighted index is inverted.

Source: IMF data.

Table 1.12 **Greece: Structure of Trade with the EC (in percentage terms)**

Product classification	SITC No.	1960 Imports	1960 Exports	1965 Imports	1965 Exports	1970 Imports	1970 Exports	1973 Imports	1973 Exports	1977 Imports	1977 Exports
Food and live animals	(0)	4·5	20·8	5·5	29·9	5·3	23·8	7·0	25·2	4·9	28·2
Beverages and tobacco	(1)	—	42·3	0·1	41·9	—	21·4	0·3	5·5	0·4	4·0
Beverages	(11)	—	1·6	0·1	3·7	—	5·5	0·3	3·4	0·3	1·7
Tobacco	(12)	—	40·7	—	38·2	—	15·9	—	2·1	0·1	2·3
Crude materials, inedible except fuels	(2)	3·7	27·6	2·8	17·5	2·9	12·4	4·6	8·0	3·5	6·3
Wood, lumber and cork	(24)	0·1	—	—	—	0·2	—	0·3	—	—	—
Pulp and paper	(25)	—	—	—	0·1	0·2	—	0·2	—	—	—
Textile fibres (not yarns)	(26)	1·9	7·8	1·4	1·6	1·1	4·1	2·7	1·2	2·0	0·5
Mineral fuels, lubricants and related materials	(3)	1·7	n.a.	3·3	—	4·2	0·4	2·8	15·4	2·9	4·1
Petroleum and petroleum products	(33)	—	n.a.	1·9	—	2·6	0·4	2·7	15·4	2·7	4·1
Animal and vegetable oils and fats	(4)	0·1	4·3	0·1	0·7	0·3	0·8	0·2	1·9	0·4	0·2
Aggregate SITC sections 0–4		10·1	94·6	11·8	88·6	12·8	56·7	14·9	56·0	12·1	42·8
Chemicals	(5)	12·8	2·5	13·9	2·1	12·6	7·9	14·2	5·0	14·5	5·6
Manufactured goods, classified by material	(6)	30·2	2·4	25·4	9·0	21·3	30·2	22·1	29·2	18·0	32·4
Leather, leather manufactures, NES	(61)	0·3	2·0	0·4	3·3	n.a.	3·0	1·3	2·8	1·3	3·7
Wood and cork manufactures	(63)	0·3	—	0·3	—	0·1	—	0·1	0·5	0·1	0·5
Paper, paperboard	(64)	0·5	—	0·6	0·3	1·1	—	1·4	—	1·3	0·1

Textile yarn, fabrics, made-up articles	(65)	7·5	0·1	4·8	3·1	4·0	8·5	3·9	13·3	3·6	17·2
Non-metallic mineral manufactures	(66)	1·2	—	1·9	0·1	2·1	0·2	1·7	0·3	1·8	0·4
Iron and steel	(67)	n.a.	—	10·3	0·2	6·9	5·5	7·3	3·7	5·2	2·9
Non-ferrous metals	(68)*	15·4	—	1·2	0·6	1·7	11·8	2·1	8·1	1·7	6·4
Manufactures of metal, NES	(69)	3·6	—	4·7	0·5	3·4	0·1	3·4	0·4	2·1	1·0
Machinery and transport	(7)	42·4	—	44·6	0·6	49·1	1·7	44·6	1·7	50·7	1·5
Machinery, not electric	(71)	13·0	—	21·5	—	23·0	—	23·4	0·2	17·9	0·2
Electrical machinery	(72)	7·8	—	8·8	0·2	10·4	1·4	9·0	1·1	6·7	1·0
Transport equipment	(73)	21·5	—	14·3	0·3	15·8	—	12·2	0·3	26·3	0·3
Miscellaneous manufactured articles	(8)	4·4	0·1	4·2	0·4	4·2	3·4	4·1	8·1	4·5	17·6
Furniture	(82)**	—	—	0·1	—	—	—	0·2	—	0·2	—
Clothing	(84)	0·2	—	0·2	0·1	—	2·3	0·5	5·5	0·4	14·6
Footwear	(85)	—	—	0·1	—	—	0·6	—	1·2	—	2·0
Aggregate SITC sections 5–8		89·8	5·2	88·1	11·4	87·2	43·3	85·0	44·0	87·7	57·1

* In 1960 SITC 67 is included in SITC 68.
** SITC 82 includes only SITC 821 from 1973.

Sources: OECD, *Trade by Commodities: Series B* (Paris: OECD, various issues); own calculations.

Table 1.13   Greece: Structure of Trade with the Rest of the World (in percentage terms)

Product classification	SITC No.	1960 Imports	1960 Exports	1965 Imports	1965 Exports	1970 Imports	1970 Exports	1973 Imports	1973 Exports	1977 Imports	1977 Exports
Food and live animals	(0)	13·7	28·1	20·1	2·0	12·7	22·2	15·7	16·4	9·8	22·5
Beverages and tobacco	(1)	—	34·6	0·1	33·3	0·1	16·0	0·4	11·3	0·6	9·6
Beverages	(11)	—	1·0	0·1	0·9	n.a.	1·0	0·3	1·9	0·1	1·1
Tobacco	(12)	—	33·6	—	32·3	n.a.	13·1	0·1	9·4	0·5	8·5
Crude materials, inedible except fuels	(2)	12·2	24·0	15·2	21·9	12·2	20·7	14·3	20·2	9·8	9·5
Wood, lumber and cork	(24)	3·0	—	4·4	—	3·6	n.a.	4·6	—	2·5	0·1
Pulp and paper	(25)	1·6	n.a.	1·8	—	1·7	n.a.	1·3	—	0·7	—
Textile fibres (not yarns)	(26)	4·5	10·9	5·4	9·8	3·1	8·6	3·4	11·2	3·7	2·3
Mineral fuels, lubricants and related materials	(3)	10·4	—	12·0	0·1	8·7	1·5	21·8	12·3	24·3	5·5
Petroleum and petroleum products	(33)	n.a.	n.a.	11·4	0·1	7·9	0·9	20·7	12·2	23·6	0·6
Animal and vegetable oils and fats	(4)	0·1	1·0	1·5	1·6	0·9	0·7	0·4	0·2	0·6	0·6
Aggregate SITC sections 0–4		36·5	87·7	48·9	84·9	34·6	61·1	52·2	60·4	43·9	47·7
Chemicals	(5)	5·1	4·9	5·6	4·5	5·1	6·5	4·2	6·1	3·2	6·0
Manufactured goods; classified by material	(6)	11·4	4·9	14·6	8·3	11·8	27·2	13·0	24·5	9·2	31·1
Leather, leather manufactures, NES	(61)	0·4	0·8	0·3	1·3	n.a.	2·0	0·7	1·8	0·5	1·8
Wood and cork manufactures	(63)	0·8	0·2	0·7	0·1	0·3	n.a.	0·5	0·6	0·3	0·7
Paper, paperboard	(64)	1·6	0·1	2·5	0·4	1·5	n.a.	2·0	0·4	2·1	0·7
Textile yarn, fabrics, made-up articles	(65)	2·5	1·9	3·3	2·4	1·8	3·4	1·4	4·0	1·3	3·9

Non-metallic mineral manufactures	(66)	0·9	0·8	0·8	0·9	0·1	1·9	0·5	2·1	0·3	10·5
Iron and steel	(67)	n.a.	n.a.	2·3	1·3	33·4	16·2	4·7	12·5	2·6	6·0
Non-ferrous metals	(68)*	3·1	0·7	1·8	0·5	1·6	1·8	1·9	1·4	1·0	3·4
Manufactures of metal, NES	(69)	0·7	0·2	1·7	1·2	1·2	1·1	0·9	1·6	0·7	3·8
Machinery and transport	(7)	45·3	1·3	28·5	2·8	46·5	1·3	28·4	2·8	41·9	8·6
Machinery, not electric	(71)	6·3	1·0	11·5	1·2	8·5	n.a.	7·9	0·5	5·2	1·0
Electrical machinery	(72)	2·0	—	3·8	0·3	2·6	0·3	3·1	1·4	2·3	3·3
Transport equipment	(73)	37·1	0·3	13·1	1·3	35·4	n.a.	17·4	0·8	34·4	4·4
Miscellaneous manufactured articles	(8)	1·5	1·3	2·4	2·1	1·9	3·9	1·8	6·2	1·7	6·5
Furniture	(82)**	—	0·1	0·1	0·1	n.a.	n.a.	—	0·1	—	0·3
Clothing	(84)	0·1	0·3	0·1	0·2	n.a.	0·9	—	1·5	0·1	1·7
Footwear	(85)	—	—	—	0·3	n.a.	1·1	—	2·3	—	1·9
Aggregate SITC sections 5–8		63·3	12·4	51·1	17·7	65·3	38·9	47·4	40·0	56·0	52·3

* In 1960 SITC 67 is included in SITC 68.
** SITC 82 includes only SITC 821 from 1973.

Sources: OECD, *Trade by Commodities: Series B* (Paris: OECD, various issues); own calculations.

Tables 1.12 and 1.13 on the structure of Greece's trade with the Community and the rest of the world are an illustration of a real success story. As regards trade with the Six and later the Nine, Greek industrial exports jumped from 5·2% of total exports in 1960 to 57·1% in 1977. This is very remarkable indeed. But within the industrial sector there is a strong concentration on a small number of products, which is a sign of a clear intersectoral division of labour and a thin industrial structure. The most dynamic exporting sectors have been textile yarns through the whole period, basic metals in the 1960s and clothing in the 1970s. In 1977 those three sectors accounted for 38·2% of total Greek exports and 66·9% of industrial exports. Thus Greek industrial competitiveness is based mainly on traditional labour-intensive goods and processed resource-based materials. Various studies undertaken show that export expansion has been the main source of growth in all these sectors.[27] Chemicals have also been an important exporting sector particularly in the late 1960s. All the above-mentioned have also been the fastest growing sectors of Greek industry. Given the limited size of the domestic market, export expansion has therefore been a determining factor. One should however add that in the case of basic metals and chemicals some import substitution has also taken place.

On the export side two further points could be made. The first refers to the virtual non-existence of machinery and transport equipment goods among Greek exports. This makes Greece very different from either Spain or Portugal. The second point is about the relative disappearance of tobacco among Greek exports. With tobacco accounting for 40·7% of total exports in 1960, Greece could be considered then as a mono-product country.

The structure of imports from the EC has not changed substantially during the period examined. Industrial imports still account for 87·7% of the total, with the main bulk in machinery and transport equipment goods. The only important change which appeared in 1977 is the rapid growth of transport equipment, consisting mainly of private cars. This is certainly an indication of the changing standard of living in the country, coupled with foreign-imported consumption habits and the lack of any big car-assembly plant in Greece. But the relative increase in imports of transport equipment was matched by a decline in the share of imports of machinery. This was a more alarming sign of the state of health of the Greek economy because it showed that industrial investment had fallen.

Table 1.13 suggests that Greece's trade with the rest of the world does not follow the same pattern as that with the EC. Both textile yarns and clothing have fallen substantially as a percentage of total exports, while machinery and transport equipment, iron, steel and non-metallic minerals have gone up. If we could look at Greece's exports to non-OECD countries the difference would be even more pronounced. This relatively small importance of textile yarns and clothing, which dominate Greece's exports to the Community, can be explained both in terms of the high degree of protection of foreign markets, which in turn suggests that the association agreement has offered Greek exporters a tremendous opportunity to make an inroad into EC markets, and the much lower labour costs in developing countries. The main success story of the 1970s has been the export of non-metallic minerals, which mainly consists of cement exports to the Middle East. On the import side, oil accounts for 23·6% of total imports, while transport equipment (mainly cars from Japan) for 34·4%.

The two tables on Greece's structure of trade suggest that although Greece has been highly successful in switching to industrial exports there is still a clear vertical division of labour between Greece and industrialised countries. As regards the international competitiveness of the main exporting industries one may point out that consumer goods industries are those which are the most highly protected in Greece. One possible explanation would be that exports are the result either of dumping or big export subsidies or both. We think that a more plausible explanation would be in terms of the dualistic nature of most sectors – a small number of internationally competitive firms and a majority of small and inefficient ones catering for the domestic market – and also in terms of the relative power of industrial pressure groups.

Let us now examine the role of foreign investment in Greek exports and the process of industrialisation in general. Throughout the period 1961–77 the total inflow of capital which came under Law 2687/1953 was 613 million dollars (Bank of Greece data). According to a study made by Giannitsis,[28] the assets of industrial firms in Greece with more than 50% foreign participation accounted for 28·6% of the assets of all companies (Table 1.14). But we can see that there were very clear variations among different sectors. Oil refinery, transport equipment, basic metals and chemicals were the sectors with the highest foreign participation, while clothing, footwear and textile yarns registered very low percentages.

Back in 1961 when the association agreement was signed Greek policy-makers had great hopes of the positive effect which the agreement would have on the inflow of foreign investment. Free access to Community markets was seen as a major incentive. On the other hand it was thought that Greece could play the role of an intermediary for foreign companies which would like to increase their sales to the Middle East and North Africa. Experience to date suggests that those hopes have not been realised. It is true that foreign investment in Greece has played a much more important role both in terms of its share of capital accumulation and industrial value added than in either Spain or Portugal. But in most cases the existence of a protected home market seems to have been a determining factor. A disaggregated analysis by Roumeliotis has actually established some correlation between foreign investment in Greece and import substitution.[29] As

Table 1.14   **Assets of Foreign-controlled Companies* in Greece's Manufacturing Sector as a Percentage of Total Assets of all Companies (1975)**

Sectors	Assets of foreign-controlled companies	Assets of foreign-controlled companies by country of origin			
		USA	*EC-6*	*Greece*	*Others*
Food	16·3	1·2	2·4	9·5	3·2
Beverages	13·9	7·2	5·8	—	0·9
Tobacco	9·8	—	0·1	—	9·7
Textile yarns	5·3	0·2	1·8	0·3	3·0
Clothing, footwear	13·5	—	7·6	—	5·9
Wood	32·8	7·4	3·7	10·8	7·9
Furniture	—	—	—	—	—
Paper	16·7	14·3	1·7	—	0·7
Printing	0·4	—	0·4	—	—
Leather	12·5	—	—	—	12·5
Plastics, rubber	30·4	16·1	11·7	1·9	0·7
Chemicals	45·7	23·0	9·5	9·8	3·4
Petroleum products	97·0	20·7	0·7	75·0	0·6
Non-metallic minerals	6·8	1·6	1·7	0·1	3·4
Basic metals	47·0	0·8	34·1	—	12·1
Metal products	11·2	6·5	0·6	—	3·1
Machinery	6·5	0·5	6·0	—	—
Electrical machinery	40·0	7·1	25·0	—	7·9
Transport equipment	62·3	1·3	3·6	47·6	9·8
Others	32·5	1·3	8·0	0·4	22·8
Total	28·6	6·0	7·0	11·0	4·6

* Companies with foreign participation > 50%.

Source: Giannitsis, op. cit., table 4, p. 156.

regards basic metals, where the main investment is the aluminium factory of Pechiney, the chief attraction for foreign companies has been the availability of minerals in the country. Giannitsis has drawn the conclusion that the association agreement has had very little effect on foreign investment since this has been directed either towards resource-based materials or the home market. He goes on to argue that the lowering of tariff protection had a negative effect by considerably reducing the scope of an infant industry policy and restricting the chances of developing Greek-owned industries in the modern sectors. This in turn meant that the development of those sectors had to rely mainly on investment by transnational enterprises.

More recent data collected by Giannitsis in fact show that the share of exports in the total sales of foreign-owned companies in Greece is about twice as high as that of Greek companies. The highest figures in percentage terms are registered with respect to textiles, clothing, leather and metal products. Until recently exports of textiles and clothing were almost the exclusive domain of Greek companies. But after 1970 a few foreign firms, mainly German, started production in Greece which has been mostly geared towards export to Community markets. Another interesting fact which emerges from those data is that foreign firms in Greece have shown little interest in the fast-expanding markets of the Middle East. It was Greek entrepreneurs who stepped in and helped to recycle some of the petrodollars back home! Down, therefore, goes the so-called bridge theory which will be discussed at greater length in Chapter 2. Giannitsis' recent data do not really invalidate the previous arguments about the role of the home market and the availability of raw materials as the main determining factors for foreign investment in the country. In this respect the Greek experience has been very different from that of many South-East Asian countries or even Portugal, as we shall see below. They do however suggest that transnational enterprises in Greece play an important role in industrial exports.

When we look at the data concerning the country of origin of foreign investment the share of the Six is higher than that of the United States, with French capital being the most important. Another interesting point is that most of the US share of capital inflow has come in the form of direct fixed investment under Law 2687/1953, while European companies have shown a preference for commercial credit which does not appear in Table 1.14. Since 1968 the share of European investment flow has been substantially higher than the corresponding share of the total foreign investment stock. The same applies to investment by all foreign-controlled firms as a percentage of total investment in Greek industry. On the other hand one peculiarity of foreign investment in Greece is that 38·4% of the assets held by foreign-controlled companies (Table 1.14) are actually held by Greeks who made the investment concerned in foreign currency.

The association agreement with the EEC was an important turning point for Greek commercial policy. Its application also coincided with the boom years of the 1960s. Free access to the growing markets of Western Europe, coupled with the small size of the domestic market, has been a determining factor for the fast expansion of the manufacturing sector in Greece. For some products, exports actually constitute a very high percentage of total value added.[30] At the same time the different timetables involved in the establishment of the customs union and the existence of important non-tariff barriers preserved prior to accession a relatively high rate of protection for sensitive domestic industries. It is here that the counter-argument could be presented, namely, that the lowering of tariff protection and the tariff structure itself have led Greek industry to concentrate more on traditional consumer goods sectors. But could we expect a small country in its first phase of industrialisation to specialise in modern high-technology goods? Moreover is tariff protection the most important factor in encouraging the creation of infant industries?

Greek industry seems to suffer from very limited vertical integration, a high degree of dualism, which seems to be the main factor explaining the apparently peculiar combination of international competitiveness and high domestic protection, and very serious regional problems. Moreover, given the structure of Greek industry, there is a very high dependence on imported technology while exports and economic growth in general have a high import content. Until 1979 the world's economic crisis seemed to have left the Greek economy almost unaffected. With the exception of the year 1974, when there was a decline in real output, Greek GDP continued to grow at about 6% per annum. But this rate of growth was the result of domestic expansionary policies which in turn contributed to the high rates of inflation experienced in recent years.

With the above qualifications, one can conclude that the fears entertained at the time of the signing of the 1961 Agreement proved to be largely unsubstantiated. This was actually recognised by some political leaders of the left who now support full membership. The importance of Community markets for Greek exports, especially for the leading dynamic sectors of the economy, coupled with the obligations emanating from the association agreement under which Greece would have to liberalise all imports from Community countries by 1984, and the expected gains from its incorporation into the CAP seemed to leave post-1974 Greece with no real option but to apply for membership. The latter will at least couple economic dependence with full participation in Community decision-making. The continuation of the association agreement was not a real alternative. However the question remains as to whether the Greek economy, and the manufacturing sector in particular, will continue to develop and climb the ladder of the international division of labour with much lower protection (at least in its tariff form), a less favourable external environment and a different domestic political climate, which may actually lead to a different role played by the state within an enlarged Community context.

Portugal

From Africa to Europe

The authoritarian regime of António Salazar (1932–68) and his successor, Marcello Caetano (1968–74), kept Portugal isolated from the political and economic developments which took place during this period in the rest of Western Europe. The 'estado novo' of Salazar combined strong nationalism – parochialism may be a more appropriate term – with the belief, widely held among the public until the early 1960s, that the loss of the colonial empire would be tantamount to a national disaster. However the isolation of Portugal did not mean that the regime was not dependent to a large extent on the acquiescence or tolerance of foreign powers. Nor did it mean that the Portuguese economy remained unaffected by the external economic environment. What Salazar and Caetano attempted to do while Portugal was becoming increasingly dependent on Western countries was to preserve a political and economic structure which was of archaeological rather than current interest.

The beginning of the Cold War and Portugal's entry into NATO marked the end of all hopes entertained by the democratic opposition after the defeat of the Axis powers. This was followed by membership of the Organisation for European Economic Co-operation (OEEC), the European Payments Union (EPU) and the European Monetary Agreement (EMA). The Salazar regime was reinforced once again and international recognition, or at least tolerance, was not lacking. The disruption of foreign supplies during the war had forced Portugal to undertake a certain amount of import-substituting industrialisation. With the postwar renewal of confidence the regime decided to give a new impulse to policies leading to the settlement of Portuguese farmers and artisans in the colonies and the launching of a sustained industrialisation effort under a protective tariff umbrella. The colonies could provide both the raw materials and the market, which would be reserved for home industries. One characteristic example is that the metropolis was importing cotton from Angola and Mozambique and sending it back in the form of textiles and clothing. Therefore economic growth in the 1950s was based on import substitution and heavy protection.[31]

The economic philosophy changed gradually during the 1960s as a result of the integration movement in Western Europe, internal economic changes and developments in Africa. Portugal became a signatory to the Stockholm Convention of 1960 which led to the establishment of EFTA. The creation of a free trade area association was the result of an initiative taken by the UK which looked upon EFTA as a rival organisation to the EEC and a useful bargaining card in any further negotiations with the latter.[32] Portugal could not join the EEC because of its supranationalist character and also because the Treaty of Rome was interpreted to imply the 'common exploitation' of the African colonies.[33] This is not to mention the simple fact that the political regime in Portugal immediately disqualified it from membership. On the other hand the price of economic isolation from Europe would be too high. EFTA provided a suitable alternative not only because Britain was Portugal's main trading partner at the time but also because the country was offered special treatment under Annex G of the Convention.[34] While member countries of EFTA agreed to eliminate tariff restrictions and quotas in industrial trade by 1967, Portugal was allowed a much longer timetable, which would lead to free imports by 1980. Annex G applied to about two-thirds of imports from the EFTA countries. Portugal was also given the possibility to introduce new import duties or increase existing ones by July 1972, the objective being the protection of infant industries. This allayed the fears of many industrialists in Portugal. At the same time concessions were made for the most significant Portuguese non-industrial exports such as canned fish and tomato paste.

The signing of the Stockholm Convention marked an important step towards the progressive integration of Portugal into the Western economy. However this was not necessarily the intention of the political leadership. Cravinho argues that participation in EFTA was a form of political window-dressing and a choice for non-commitment in European affairs.[35] By 1961 guerrilla warfare had broken out in Angola, followed shortly after by Guinea–Bissau in 1963 and Mozambique in 1964. Developments in the African colonies had a much greater effect on the foreign and domestic policies pursued by the Salazar regime. The creation of a Portuguese Common Market, 'an integrated multicontinental state and a common escudo currency' was set as the main priority.[36] Trade barriers were eliminated between the metropolis and the colonies but persistent payments deficits in the colonies made monetary union totally unfeasible. The increasing cost of war in Africa, together with the gradual opening of the economy to imports from EFTA and the fact that the old development policy based on import substitution seemed to have exhausted itself, forced the regime to adopt liberalisation measures. A more flexible policy towards foreign investment was also adopted, with the promulgation of a new decree-law in 1965. In the meantime the regime was forced to abandon its old introverted posture and raise loans in European capital markets and with international organisations.

The growing realisation of the difficulties involved in suppressing guerrilla warfare in Africa was linked with the declining economic importance of the colonies following a shift of Portuguese exports towards the EFTA countries (Table 1.16). But although the increasing importance of EFTA for Portuguese exports (from 20·6% in 1960 to 35·4% in 1970) was a continuous trend until Britain and Denmark became members of the Community in 1973, the decline of the escudo area as an outlet for exports was only felt – although in a dramatic way – in the 1970s. The continuing war, the narrowness of colonial markets and the growing need for capital goods which the Portuguese industry was unable to provide, as well as the long delays involved in the payment of imported goods to the colonies, all contributed to the reduced economic importance of the Portuguese Common Market. However the economic interests of some big Portuguese families in the colonies and their strong influence on the government in Lisbon help to explain why the Salazar regime adopted this particular interpretation of 'national interest', which meant the continuation of the colonial wars.

The succession of Salazar by Caetano in 1968 led to further attempts to liberalise the economy. It was also marked by the entry of some young technocrats in the government who favoured a negotiated solution for the colonies and further integration into Europe. But their influence on decisions was only marginal compared with the impact which Opus Dei technocrats have had on Spanish policies. They all had to resign by 1972. One factor which clearly distinguishes Portugal from both Greece and Spain is the degree of its isolation and the apparent insensitivity to political developments in Europe. Signs of such isolation can be discerned even in post-1974 Portugal. The length of the dictatorship and the geographical position of the country are at least two explanatory factors. But the colonial wars in Africa seemed to play the most decisive role in this respect. It is true however that some leading members of the Portuguese industrial class gradually came to see the necessity of becoming more closely associated with the integration process in Western Europe. The growing importance of European markets for Portuguese exports and the inflow of foreign investment, mainly European, contributed to this change of attitude. This change is most aptly described by a chapter heading 'The long discovery of the maritime route to Europe', contained in a book by João Martins Pereira.[37] But the process was very slow and the opening to Europe was not seen as a substitute for the African colonies.

The tragic irony was that while the political and economic élite seemed prepared to pay any price in order to keep the overseas territories under Portuguese rule, hundreds of thousands of Portuguese had to migrate to Europe in order to earn a living. Unlike Greece and Spain, Portugal's isolation from Europe did not become an embarrassment for the regime or an important weapon in the hands of the democratic opposition. For one thing, this isolation was not so apparent, at least in political terms. Portugal remained a member of both NATO and EFTA. If there was an element of 'la politique du contrepied' in the attitude of Western European governments towards the Greek colonels at least there were concrete signs of disapproval from democratic Europe. In the case of Portugal there were no signs at all, at least at the official level, except for the noises coming from the Scandinavian countries and the Netherlands. In sharp contrast there was growing disapproval of the regime and its colonial wars within the United Nations and by world public opinion in general.

Portuguese official attitudes towards the Community were until 1973 entirely determined by the UK position. Following the first UK application of 1961, Portugal asked for the opening of negotiations with the Six. The new British application led to two Portuguese memoranda which were addressed to the Commission in February 1969 and May 1970 respectively. The first priority for the Portuguese negotiators was to retain their free access to the British and Danish markets and obtain the same rights for the Community as a whole. With the entry of the UK and Denmark, the Community accounted for 48·6% of Portuguese exports and 44·9% of imports (Table 1.16, 1973). At the same time, Portugal was interested in obtaining access for its agricultural products. Given the low level of its economic development and the EFTA precedent with Annex G of the Stockholm Convention, Portugal hoped to achieve some degree of non-reciprocity in trade concessions with the enlarged Community.[38]

The free trade area agreement was signed in July 1972. It made provisions for the elimination of all tariff barriers applicable to exports from Portugal by July 1977, with the exception of some 'sensitive' products – textiles, clothing and cork manufactures – for which quantitative restrictions would apply until 1983. However those sensitive products accounted for a considerable part of Portuguese exports (33% of total exports in 1973). On the Portuguese side, imports from the Community were divided into three categories for which trade liberalisation was to be achieved by 1977, 1980 and 1985 respectively. Although the free trade area agreements signed with all remaining EFTA countries were limited to industrial trade some concessions were also given for specific Portuguese exports of agricultural products. While Ferreira argues that the agreement to a large extent satisfied the objectives set by the Portuguese themselves, Cravinho thinks that it conveyed the usual message, that is, 'that the rich and strong must be defended from the poor and weak'.[39] Cravinho also draws attention to the 'evolution clause' (Article 35 of the EEC Agreement and Article 29 of the ECSC one) which left the possibility open for further co-operation between the two sides. He seems to think that this was a clear indication of the conscious decision made by the Caetano regime and its main followers to integrate the Portuguese economy in Western Europe. Similar indications were given in the Fourth Development Plan (1974–9). But the uncompromising attitude with respect to the African wars and the sacking of liberals from the government after the signing of the 1972 Agreement leave some doubts as to whether European orientation was accepted by many people outside certain business circles and a few enlightened technocrats.

The revolution of 25 April 1974 completely changed the picture. The granting of independence to the colonies marked the end of the African wars and led to a further decline in trade with the escudo area and an inflow of more than half a million *retornados* to the old metropolis. However, as we shall see in Chapter 2, even then the European option did not appear as the only alternative. The provisional government referred to the evolution clause and asked for revision and extension of the 1972 Agreement. Amidst fears of a complete takeover by the radical left and the communist party, the Council of Ministers agreed to emergency aid amounting to 150 million units of account in October 1975. Portugal was also allowed to introduce a 30% import surcharge – cut down to 10% by 1979 – and quantitative restrictions for imports because of balance of payments difficulties. In September of the following year an additional protocol was signed with the Nine, together with a financial protocol. Further concessions were made for Portuguese exports of textiles, paper and wine, the timetable for the elimination of tariffs on all Portuguese exports was brought forward one year and Portugal was allowed to raise customs duties for specific products up to a maximum of 20%. A Portuguese request for further revision of the 1972 Agreement is still pending. At the same time the remaining EFTA countries allowed Portugal to extend the timetable for import liberalisation by 1985.

Despite the measures taken after the 1974 revolution Portugal appears to have the least protected industry when compared with Spain and Greece. The terms offered by the Community in the 1972 Agreement were certainly less generous than those offered to Greece in 1961 and even Spain in 1970. This must be a reflection of the different times at which negotiations took place as well as the limited bargaining power of the Portuguese under Caetano. In 1980 about 80% of all imports from the Nine and EFTA entered Portugal duty-free, while for most of the remaining 20% tariff duties were very low.[40] The low level of tariff protection in Portugal is the result not only of deliberate liberalisation measures but also to the fact that most tariff rates are specific and have therefore been eroded by inflation. On the surface it also appears that the Portuguese have been relatively less inventive with non-tariff protection, probably because of the inefficiency of the state machine. But this is a very difficult subject to investigate in any country.

We have tried to focus on the African/Third World legacy in Portugal and the relative isolation from Europe. We believe that these factors will continue to play an important role even after Portugal's accession to the Community. Although national interest was defined in the 1960s very much in terms of the preservation of the colonial empire, basic economic trends and the changing pattern of Portuguese trade led to a gradual integration of Portugal in the Western European economy. This was bound to have an effect on perceptions and attitudes within the country. The revolution opened the way for such economic changes to be translated into policies on the political level.

From Corporatist State to the 'Construction of Socialism'

The economic philosophy of the 'corporatist state', which proved to be much more resistant to change in the Portugal of Salazar and Caetano than in Franco's Spain, was manifest in the form of extensive state intervention in the economy coupled with totally private ownership of the means of production, excessive centralisation of private economic power and absolute control of workers through the guilds and syndicates. If this was not entirely consistent with Roman Catholic social theory which was supposed to provide the foundation of the 'estado novo', so much worse for the theory.

A system of industrial licensing (*condicionamento industrial*) required prior authorisation by the state for any new industrial investment. The state also had extensive control over both prices and wages. This led to a high concentration in industry where most sectors were characterised by monopolistic or oligopolistic structures. Under the old regime Portuguese industry was dominated by a small number of families, some of which were allied by marriage to the large landowning families of the south. The economic oligarchy naturally played a dominant role in the production of raw materials in the colonies and also controlled trade between the latter and the metropolis. The situation was further exacerbated by the fact that all important commercial banks were controlled by the top ten families which, because of the lack of a capital market, had direct control over Portuguese industry. This also had a further consequence, namely, the highly dualistic structure of the economy with small- and medium-sized firms being short of capital, highly inefficient and in need of external protection. The role of the state was to provide investment in economic and social infrastructure and the institutional framework for the preservation of the status quo.

Until 1960 direct control of the economy was also coupled with a policy based on self-sufficiency for the Portuguese empire as a whole. Therefore the creation of new industries in the metropolis relied a great deal on import substitution and the existence of protected markets in the colonies. The signing of the Stockholm Convention marked the beginning of a new era, although it took some time before this led to a set of measures which meant a conscious acceptance of the opening of the economy and its wide ramifications. In the meantime internal social and economic factors pushed the regime towards the same direction.

One important turning point was the introduction of a new foreign investment code in 1965 which allowed the repatriation of capital and the transfer of profits as well as access to domestic finance. This was also accompanied by some liberalisation of the licensing system and measures for the promotion of exports. After 1968, with the entry of some liberals in the Caetano government, there was a further attempt to allow more competition in the Portuguese economy which was suffering under the stranglehold of the state bureaucracy. This led to the industrial development bill of 1972. Moreover, in both the Interim Plan (1965–7) and the Third Plan (1968–73) it became very clear that European integration and the prospect of Portugal's association with the Community, linked to the UK application for membership, had become a major consideration in official policy-making.

Given the legacy of the Salazar–Caetano regime and the excessive concentration of political and economic power – accompanied by an extremely unequal distribution of income (before 1974 the bottom 50% of all Portuguese households were receiving only 14% of total income while the top 5% received 40%)[41] – any attempt to change the political and social status quo was bound to have very important repercussions on the economy itself. This is what happened after the 1974 revolution. Since then the Portuguese economy has had to digest the effects of a drastic change in the internal rules of the economic game, decolonisation, as well as the international economic crisis and the big increase in oil prices.

The nationalisation of banks and insurance companies in 1975 brought a large part of industry under state control. The public sector was extended further by nationalisation in other basic industries such as iron and steel, shipbuilding and petroleum as well as the transport sector. Thus after the revolution the public sector accounted for 24·4% of total value added, as opposed to 8·9% in 1973.[42] As shown in Table 1.15 the state could now play, for the first time, a significant role within the manufacturing sector, with a high degree of direct control in basic metals, paper and printing, chemicals and non-metallic minerals.

Table 1.15   **State Participation in the Portuguese Economy, 1976* (as a percentage of total value added)**

Sectors	Public enterprises	Controlled enterprises	Enterprises with 20–50% state participation
Agriculture, fisheries	—	—	—
Mining	—	4·5	2·4
Manufacturing industry	8·4	3·6	3·7
Food, beverages, tobacco	13·5	3·4	1·0
Textile, clothing, footwear	—	—	—
Wood, cork, furniture	—	4·5	1·5
Paper, printing, publishing	25·4	—	17·4
Chemicals	25·1	1·8	3·4
Non-metallic minerals	10·9	7·3	0·9
Basic metals	37·5	1·6	—
Machinery, transport equipment	3·4	5·7	6·8
Other manufactures	—	4·1	0·1
Construction, public works	—	1·3	—
Electricity, gas, water	78·2	—	—
Trade	0·3	0·7	0·9
Banks, insurance, real estate	47·5	0·6	—
Transport, communications	34·6	8·7	0·7
Public administration, defence	—	—	—
Education, health	—	—	—
Other services	1·7	2·6	1·3
Total	10·4	2·2	1·5

* It only includes enterprises taken over by the state after the revolution of 25 April 1974. The calculations are based on provisional figures for Portuguese GDP.

Sources: Instituto das Participações do Estado, *Relatório e contas-exercício 1977* (Lisbon, July 1978); Instituto Nacional de Estatística, *Contas nacionais*, op. cit.; own calculations.

Public enterprises in industry and other sectors were put under the direct supervision of government ministries, while the so-called controlled enterprises became the responsibility of the Institute of State Participation, formed in November 1976. Although the public sector accounted for 24·4% of value added its share in gross capital formation was 45·4%. This was the result of big investment projects – the Sines complex being by far the most important – undertaken by the state and the lack of confidence by private investors.

Foreign companies were excluded from nationalisation. Moreover the new foreign investment code of August 1977, which amended the previous one of April 1976 and also reflected the significant political shift that had taken place in the meantime, showed an open-door policy towards transnational corporations, with some qualifications. Apart from the obvious exception of public utilities and defence, foreign entry into banking and insurance would also be restricted.[43] In addition the Portuguese government expressed a preference for joint ventures, with only minority participation by foreigners in the case of all basic industries.

Nationalisations in industry were accompanied by a large scale agricultural reform, with the expropriation of many latifundia in the south. Moreover big changes also took place in labour legislation, taxation policy and government expenditure on social services. In the first years after the revolution there was also a large number of takeovers of firms and the creation of workers' co-operatives. This took on a much bigger dimension with the seizure of lands in Alentejo, a serious political problem which still remained unsolved in 1980, since the *de facto* situation clearly contravened government policy.

Decolonisation has meant the loss of protected markets and an end to guaranteed supplies of raw materials. It has also brought about an influx of more than half a million people from the colonies, close to 7% of the population, whose rehabilitation has presented an enormous task in terms of unemployment and housing. The efforts to cope with a problem of this size were not facilitated by the return of immigrant workers from Western Europe, the stagnation of export markets and the rapid deterioration in the terms of trade.

Every transition from one regime to another implies a certain economic cost. This cost was exacerbated in post-1974 Portugal by the uncertainty created over the boundaries between the private and the public sector and the general rules of the economic game. This uncertainty continued until the second half of 1976 when the election of General Eanes to the presidency and the formation of the first constitutional government seemed to clarify the political situation in the country. However the economic status quo was still clearly challenged by the parties to the right of the socialists, while the country did not have any clear majority in the parliament or a real government. Between April 1974 and the elections of December 1979 Portugal had six provisional and five constitutional governments. The country needed to absorb the economic changes brought about by the revolution. At the same time it was faced with a world recession and the urgent need to restructure the economy in order to meet the challenge of Community membership. With the control of the banking sector and a major share in basic industries, the state was expected to play a central role in economic development. There were at least two attempts to produce comprehensive development plans, the Melo Antunes (1975) and the Medium-Term Plan (1977–80) but both finally remained simple exercises on paper. The succession of short-lived governments and the lack of any clear majority in the parliament was the main explanation. The elections of December 1979 gave the Democratic Alliance, a grouping of centre and right-wing parties, an overall majority in parliament. There is a certain contradiction between the economic philosophy of the government, based on private initiative, and the explicit aim of the country's constitution, namely, the construction of socialism. It remains to be seen how this contradiction will be solved in the future. At least part of the answer will be given by the Portuguese electorate in the presidential and parliamentary elections both planned for 1980 (see also Chapter 2).

Structural Changes in the Portuguese Economy

The period between 1960 and 1974 was characterised by rapid rates of growth, changes in the structure of the overall economy and within the manufacturing sector itself, as well as a changing pattern of foreign trade. At the macro level, the two obvious failures of economic policy were in the agricultural sector and in employment in general. Agricultural output barely increased during this period, with produc-tivity increases compensating for big losses in employment. Since the revolution there has been a real decline in output and Portugal, with 32·5% of its labour force engaged in agriculture, is now even more heavily dependent on imports of food. On the other hand between 1961 and 1970 an estimated number of 785,600 people left the country in search of work abroad. The number of emigrants represented 9·5% of the 1960 population.[44]

In terms of the foreign economic policy followed by the Salazar–Caetano regime the data in Table 1.16 indicate that while membership of EFTA had a strong effect on the geographical orientation of Portugal's trade, especially with respect to exports, the creation of the escudo zone only succeeded in stabilising the relative trade importance of the colonies, with a big decline occurring after 1970. A striking feature during the 1960–77 period is the continuously growing importance of Western European markets (EC and EFTA) for Portuguese exports (66·8% of total exports in 1977) at the expense of the American and Third World markets. Until the 1973 enlarge-ment Portuguese foreign trade was characterised by big deficits with the Six and surpluses with EFTA and the colonies. A study undertaken by the EFTA secretariat confirms that the export effects of membership were much stronger than the import effects.[45]

Table 1.16   **Portugal: Geographical Distribution of Foreign Trade as a Percentage of Total Trade (goods only)**

| | Imports | | | | | Exports | | | | |
	1960	1965	1970	1973	1977	1960	1965	1970	1973	1977
EC–6	38·3	34·9	33·0	—	—	21·6	20·7	18·3	—	—
EC–9	—	—	—	44·9	43·6	—	—	—	48·6	51·7
EFTA	20·0	21·5	24·5	11·6	8·4	20·6	26·9	35·4	13·8	15·1
Escudo zone	14·0	17·3	14·7	10·1	4·1	25·0	26·6	24·5	14·8	9·0
USA	7·3	8·1	7·1	8·2	10·2	11·2	10·6	8·7	9·7	6·7
Middle East	n.a.	4·3	6·0	4·0	10·8	n.a.	1·7	—	0·6	2·1
Spain	0·9	4·8	4·3	5·4	4·8	1·0	3·7	1·6	2·2	2·1
UK	11·9	n.a.	14·0	11·4	10·5	13·6	n.a.	20·4	23·8	18·2
Germany	17·1	n.a.	15·5	14·4	12·4	9·1	n.a.	6·3	7·5	11·8
France	8·3	n.a.	7·0	6·9	8·1	3·4	n.a.	4·6	5·2	7·9
Italy	3·6	n.a.	5·3	5·2	5·4	3·5	n.a.	3·1	3·2	3·7
Japan	n.a.	0·2	n.a.	4·2	3·8	n.a.	0·7	n.a.	1·8	0·9
Centrally Planned Economies	1·4	1·3	n.a.	0·9	3·3	2·2	1·1	n.a.	0·6	4·0
USSR	n.a.	n.a.	n.a.	n.a.	2·5	n.a.	n.a.	n.a.	n.a.	2·1

Sources: OECD, *Trade by Commodities: Series B* (Paris: OECD, various issues); own calculations.

The coverage of total imports by exports increased in 1965 and then declined in the 1970s, with 1977 being an exceptionally bad year (Table 1.17). The deficits in the trade balance were overcompensated (with the exception of 1960–3 and 1974–7) by surpluses in the invisible balance. The relative importance for the Portuguese balance of payments of remittances from migrant workers and tourism has been smaller than in the case of Greece, where exports have persistently covered only a small proportion of imports. Between 1960 and 1972, with surpluses in the basic balance and growing foreign reserves, the exchange rate of the escudo remained stable *vis-à-vis* the dollar. Then there were a series of devaluations with a fast acceleration of the trend after 1975. In September 1977 the authorities introduced a crawling-peg system in order to limit the devaluation of the escudo which was getting almost out of hand (see Table 1.11). In 1979, after the big recovery on the balance of payments front, there were clear signs that the Portuguese authorities had decided to limit the rapid downward trend in the exchange rate.

Table 1.17 **Portugal: Balance of Payments Profile (in percentage terms)**

	1960	*1965*	*1970*	*1973*	*1977*
Exports[a]/Imports[a]	71·2	75·4	67·2	67·2	44·5
Tourism/Exports[a]	7·6	30·0	25·9	29·8	20·0
Migrant Remittances/Exports[a]	14·1	16·5	35·0	39·6	n.a.
Transportation/Exports[a]	7·0	4·0	7·2	8·6	11·8

[a] Goods only.

Source: OECD, *Balance of Payments of OECD Countries 1960–1977* (Paris, OECD, 1979).

Let us now examine the changes in Portugal's structure of trade and their effects on the domestic economy. We will first of all concentrate on trade with EFTA countries between 1959 and 1972 (Table 1.18), which coincided with the application of the Stockholm Convention prior to the shifting of alliances by the UK and Denmark. During this period Portugal was offered special treatment based on limited reciprocity in trade concessions. In this respect it was very similar to the first twelve years of Greece's Association with the Six. In 1959 40·6% of Portuguese exports to the Seven were composed of industrial goods, but 60·3% of these were wood and cork manufactures as well as textile yarns. The only other important item in the industrial goods category was chemicals. If we also have a look at the import side with EFTA in 1959 we realise that the division of labour between Portugal and the Seven was not so different from that between Greece and the Six as might at first appear. Between 1959 and 1972 Portugal witnessed a big increase in industrial exports while the structure of imports remained virtually unchanged. The two main items on the export side were textile yarns and clothing (34·9% of total exports in 1972) – very similar to the Greek experience. At the same time the relative importance of wood and cork manufactures and chemicals dropped considerably. There was also a noticeable increase in exports of electrical machinery and non-metallic minerals (the latter having had an outburst of exports in 1965). It therefore becomes clear that Portuguese industry took advantage of its free access to EFTA markets in order to increase and also diversify its exports. It is also noticeable, but not very surprising, that most of the main export sectors are exactly the same as those in Greece.

Table 1.18 Portugal: Structure of Trade with EFTA (in percentage terms)

Product classification	(SITC No.)	1959 Imports	1959 Exports	1965 Imports	1965 Exports	1970 Imports	1970 Exports	1972 Imports	1972 Exports
Food and live animals	(0)	3·5	19·3	4·7	15·0	5·1	8·4	9·4	6·1
Beverages and tobacco	(1)	0·2	13·5	0·2	6·7	0·3	4·0	0·4	4·4
Beverages	(11)	0·2	13·5	0·2	6·7	n.a.	4·0	0·3	4·4
Tobacco	(12)	—	—	0·1	—	0·1	—	—	—
Crude materials, inedible except fuels	(2)	6·3	23·2	6·7	12·3	4·5	13·0	4·1	8·9
Wood, lumber and cork	(24)	0·3	7·9	0·2	4·5	0·2	4·4	0·2	3·1
Pulp and paper	(25)	2·6	6·8	1·5	5·9	1·1	5·4	0·6	4·4
Textile fibres (not yarns)	(26)	2·5	0·1	4·1	0·1	2·6	n.a.	2·6	0·1
Mineral fuels, lubricants and related materials	(3)	2·5	2·4	2·7	1·2	2·1	2·1	1·0	1·2
Petroleum and petroleum products	(33)	n.a.	n.a.	•1·3	1·2	1·4	2·1	0·6	1·2
Animal and vegetable oils and fats	(4)	0·1	0·9	0·1	0·7	0·1	0·2	0·1	0·1
Aggregate SITC sections 0–4		12·6	59·3	14·4	35·9	12·1	27·7	15·0	20·7
Chemicals	(5)	16·1	12·9	13·4	3·7	14·9	2·6	12·9	2·6
Manufactured goods, classified by material	(6)	22·5	26·4	26·8	53·1	27·4	44·3	24·4	43·6
Leather, leather manufactures, NES	(61)	0·5	—	0·2	0·2	n.a.	n.a.	0·3	0·1
Wood and cork manufactures	(63)	0·1	16·0	0·1	9·2	n.a.	3·9	0·1	3·7
Paper, paperboard	(64)	2·1	0·5	2·1	0·3	3·6	0·3	2·9	0·4
Textile yarn, fabrics, made-up articles	(65)	5·7	8·5	9·2	20·2	9·1	22·5	9·2	25·5
Non-metallic mineral manufactures	(66)	0·7	0·6	1·1	22·1	1·0	14·9	1·3	12·0
Iron and steel	(67)	n.a.	n.a.	6·3	0·3	5·1	0·5	3·5	0·3
Non-ferrous metals	(68)*	7·2	0·5	3·9	0·1	4·4	n.a.	3·2	0·1

Manufactures of metal, NES (69)	4·9	0·2	2·9	0·5	11·0	1·0	2·8	0·9
Machinery and transport (7)	41·8	0·5	40·2	0·7	39·9	5·4	40·8	9·4
Machinery, not electric (71)	21·3	0·4	18·2	0·5	18·5	0·7	20·2	1·2
Electrical machinery (72)	7·5	—	7·5	0·2	9·7	3·9	8·7	6·0
Transport equipment (73)	13·0	0·1	14·6	—	11·6	0·8	11·9	2·2
Miscellaneous manufactured articles (8)	6·9	0·8	5·0	6·4	5·7	19·6	7·1	23·3
Furniture (82)**	—	—	0·1	—	n.a.	n.a.	0·2	—
Clothing (84)	0·7	0·4	0·8	—	1·1	17·3	1·5	19·4
Footwear (85)	0·1	—	—	5·5	n.a.	1·7	0·1	2·2
Aggregate SITC sections 5–8	87·3	40·6	85·4	63·9	87·9	71·9	85·2	78·9

* 1959 SITC 67 is included in SITC 68.
** SITC 82 includes only SITC 821 from 1973.

Sources: OECD, *Trade by Commodities: Series B* (Paris: OECD, various issues); own calculations.

Table 1.19 Portugal: Structure of Trade with the EC (in percentage terms)

Product classification	(SITC No.)	1960 Imports	1960 Exports	1965 Imports	1965 Exports	1970 Imports	1970 Exports	1973 Imports	1973 Exports	1977 Imports	1977 Exports
Food and live animals	(0)	2·4	28·2	4·0	29·8	3·4	16·0	2·7	9·8	3·9	7·1
Beverages and tobacco	(1)	0·4	8·3	0·2	10·6	0·1	8·7	0·4	7·2	0·2	7·2
Beverages	(11)	0·1	8·3	0·1	10·6	—	8·7	0·3	7·2	0·2	7·2
Tobacco	(12)	0·3	—	0·1	—	0·1	—	0·1	—	—	—
Crude materials, inedible except fuels	(2)	3·0	20·3	4·7	18·4	4·2	28·5	4·6	14·8	3·7	12·0
Wood, lumber and cork	(24)	0·1	9·3	0·1	4·7	0·1	5·6	0·1	4·4	0·1	5·3
Pulp and paper	(25)	—	0·3	—	2·8	—	13·1	—	7·3	—	7·4
Textile fibres (not yarns)	(26)	1·7	0·4	2·8	0·1	2·2	—	2·8	0·1	1·6	0·1
Mineral fuels, lubricants and related materials	(3)	2·0	1·1	4·0	2·0	4·1	2·9	2·6	0·9	3·9	0·2
Petroleum and petroleum products	(33)	n.a.	n.a.	1·6	2·0	1·6	2·9	1·5	0·9	1·7	0·2
Animal and vegetable oils and fats	(4)	0·8	2·5	0·5	1·0	0·2	1·8	0·2	0·4	0·2	0·2
Aggregate SITC sections 0–4		8·5	60·6	13·3	61·9	12·1	58·0	10·4	33·1	11·9	31·0
Chemicals	(5)	14·1	12·4	13·8	8·1	15·0	11·3	16·8	5·4	17·5	5·1
Manufactured goods, classified by material	(6)	32·7	25·7	25·4	24·4	20·9	21·3	20·5	38·3	22·6	24·7
Leather, leather manufactures	(61)	—	—	0·1	0·5	n.a.	n.a.	0·3	—	0·3	—
Wood and cork manufactures	(63)	—	16·2	0·1	14·4	—	9·1	0·1	5·6	—	7·8
Paper, paperboard	(64)	0·6	1·0	0·9	0·7	0·7	0·8	0·7	0·7	0·7	2·2
Textile yarn, fabrics, made-up articles	(65)	2·9	5·4	3·6	4·7	3·2	5·7	4·6	16·5	3·9	16·2

Non-metallic mineral manufactures (66)	1·2	0·6	1·2	2·2	1·3	2·1	1·5	13·1	1·8	4·1
Iron and steel (67)	n.a.	2·0	12·6	1·2	8·7	1·2	6·2	0·7	7·9	1·2
Non-ferrous metals (68)*	24·0	0·2	3·8	0·5	3·3	—	3·6	0·2	4·2	0·1
Manufactures of metal, NES (69)	2·4	0·8	2·3	0·8	2·9	1·8	2·7	1·1	2·4	1·2
Machinery and transport (7)	36·9	0·6	42·8	1·4	46·1	6·1	44·9	9·8	43·0	11·2
Machinery, not electric (71)	17·0	—	22·4	0·9	22·9	1·6	22·9	2·4	21·3	3·5
Electrical machinery (72)	8·5	—	8·8	0·3	10·5	4·3	9·4	6·9	8·8	10·6
Transport equipment (73)	11·4	—	11·6	0·1	12·8	—	12·6	0·5	12·9	0·7
Miscellaneous manufactured articles (8)	4·9	0·4	4·7	3·9	5·7	3·0	7·4	13·1	4·9	11·0
Furniture (82)**	0·1	—	0·1	0·1	—	—	0·4	—	0·2	—
Clothing (84)	0·1	—	0·4	3·4	0·5	2·0	1·1	10·9	0·3	10·7
Footwear (85)	—	—	—	0·2	—	0·1	—	0·8	—	1·8
Aggregate SITC sections 5–8	88·7	39·4	86·7	37·8	87·8	41·8	89·6	66·6	88·0	68·2

* In 1960 SITC 67 is included in SITC 68.
** SITC 82 includes only SITC 821 from 1973.

Sources: OECD, *Trade by Commodities: Series B* (Paris: OECD, various issues); own calculations.

If we now compare Portugal's changing structure of trade with EFTA and the EC (Tables 1.18 and 1.19) we find that the main difference is in terms of Portuguese textiles and clothing exports, which were not offered the same preferential treatment by EC countries. As a consequence they reach a much higher share of total exports to the Seven in relation to exports to the Six. After 1973 trade with the Community changed substantially because of the British and Danish accession and the signing of the 1972 Agreement. The fact that the application of the Agreement coincided with the enlargement of the Community, the economic recession and the revolution in Portugal makes it difficult to isolate its effects on trade between the two sides. However Silva Lopes has found enough evidence to suggest that the 1972 Agreement had a big beneficial effect on Portuguese exports to the six original members of the Community, which according to his calculations were in 1978 almost the double of what they would otherwise have been.[46] As shown in Table 1.19, Portuguese industrial exports to the Community have increased very fast with a growth in importance of textiles, clothing, electrical and non-electrical machinery and non-metallic minerals (1973 must have been an exceptional year for these last).

In all the cases examined so far there is a sharp decline in the relative importance of chemicals and wood and cork manufactures. Imports continue to be dominated by industrial goods, especially machinery and transport equipment. The conclusions drawn about Greece's present pattern of trade with the enlarged Community also apply to the Portuguese case, with one qualification. Portugal's exports are certainly more diversified and the most noticeable difference is in number 7 of the SITC classification (electrical and non-electrical machinery).

The pattern of trade with the rest of the world is substantially different (Table 1.20). This table includes imports and exports with member countries of EFTA. The relative importance of industrial exports in 1960 can be explained to a large extent in terms of trading opportunities provided by the colonies. The colonial past together with the high degree of protection and import substitution in the 1940s and 1950s must be two important factors behind the existence of a large industrial sector before the opening up of the economy to international trade.

Portugal has gradually developed into a big importer of foodstuffs and raw materials in its non-EC trade (67·4% of total imports in 1977) while it specialises more in the export of industrial goods. This is not necessarily a sign of success of its industrial sector. It could also be the result of a big failure in the agricultural field. Thus in 1977 imports of food and live animals accounted for 22·5% of total imports from non-

EC countries. Another important item is the import of raw materials for the textiles and clothing industries. Data from Table 1.20 suggest that although exports of textile yarns were very important in 1960, there has been since then a very clear shift towards European markets, initially towards EFTA and later towards the enlarged Community. Portuguese industrial exports to non-EEC countries are also more diversified than in the case of Greece. One important item, virtually non-existent in Tables 1.18 and 1.19, is exports of transport equipment. The fact that this pattern has persisted even after the loss of the colonies and the decline in trade with the old escudo zone is an encouraging sign of the international competitiveness of Portuguese industry.

The question we should now ask is whether foreign trade has had a significant effect on the development of Portuguese industry since 1960. Given the small size of the domestic market one would expect a close correlation between exports and internal rates of growth for individual sectors. The studies undertaken by a research unit of the Ministry of Industry lead to the conclusion that exports have been the principal source of growth for some sectors.[47] This was more pronounced in 1970–4 than in 1964–70. In the 1960s textiles, pulp and paper experienced an export-led growth. For all other sectors, changes in final domestic demand and technical change appeared to be more important.[48] In the 1970s clothing and footwear were added to the previous list, while exports became a very important factor in the growth of the chemical industry. What is very interesting in both periods examined is that import substitution was a negative item, meaning that there was an increasing penetration of the Portuguese market by imported goods. However the leading export sectors of the Portuguese industry have not always been the fastest growing ones. As far as textiles and clothing are concerned there has been a clear shift away from production predominantly oriented towards the home market and the colonies in favour of production for Western European markets. But the relative share of the sector in industrial value added remained relatively stable until 1975 when it was hit hard by the crisis in export markets. It seems therefore that in the case of textiles and clothing booming exports have arrested the relative decline experienced by all other traditional sectors of Portuguese industry. Another interesting case is chemicals, where above-average rates of growth have coincided with a declining share in total exports. On the other hand the rapid growth in the production of machinery and transport equipment has been clearly reflected in Portuguese exports, although the bulk of the production is still destined for domestic consumption.

Table 1.20 Portugal: Structure of Trade with the Rest of the World (in percentage terms)

Product classification	SITC No.	1960 Imports	1960 Exports	1965 Imports	1965 Exports	1970 Imports	1970 Exports	1973 Imports	1973 Exports	1977 Imports	1977 Exports
Food and live animals	(0)	14.2	13.1	10.6	13.2	14.2	10.1	21.4	10.0	22.5	9.7
Beverages and tobacco	(1)	1.8	7.8	1.2	7.0	0.9	7.2	1.2	7.3	0.5	6.1
Beverages	(11)	0.1	7.8	0.1	6.9	n.a.	7.1	0.5	7.2	—	6.1
Tobacco	(12)	1.8	—	1.1	0.1	0.8	n.a.	0.7	0.1	0.5	—
Crude materials, inedible except fuels	(2)	27.3	14.6	25.1	9.1	15.2	10.0	19.8	7.2	20.4	7.6
Wood, lumber and cork	(24)	1.3	8.5	1.0	5.5	1.2	4.7	1.9	4.0	2.5	3.6
Pulp and paper	(25)	1.5	1.9	0.6	2.1	0.4	3.2	0.4	1.5	0.9	1.8
Textile fibres (not yarns)	(26)	15.4	0.5	15.8	0.2	9.0	n.a.	12.0	0.1	8.6	0.1
Mineral fuels, lubricants and related materials	(3)	16.3	3.9	10.7	1.3	11.7	2.2	9.2	1.4	23.3	3.2
Petroleum and petroleum products	(33)	14.3	3.9	9.4	1.3	10.2	2.2	8.5	1.4	22.3	3.2
Animal and vegetable oils and fats	(4)	1.5	1.4	3.2	1.2	1.2	1.3	2.1	1.3	0.7	0.9
Aggregate SITC sections 0–4		61.1	40.8	54.2	31.8	43.2	30.8	53.7	27.2	67.4	27.5
Chemicals	(5)	6.8	7.4	6.3	6.7	8.0	6.4	5.8	6.2	6.5	5.1
Manufactured goods; classified by material	(6)	10.0	42.3	18.1	47.1	23.0	38.4	15.2	33.5	10.7	33.0
Leather, leather manufactures, NES	(61)	0.1	0.1	0.1	0.2	n.a.	n.a.	0.2	0.3	0.3	0.4
Wood and cork manufactures	(63)	0.1	11.8	0.1	7.2	n.a.	3.9	0.1	4.7	—	5.0
Paper, paperboard	(64)	0.7	0.9	0.9	0.9	1.5	1.0	1.3	0.9	1.0	1.6
Textile yarn, fabrics, made-up articles	(65)	2.6	22.0	4.1	22.9	3.9	19.5	2.9	18.8	1.6	14.6

Non-metallic mineral manufactures	(66)	0·4	2·4	5·2	10·2	8·3	8·6	4·8	3·1	1·3	4·2
Iron and steel	(67)	n.a.	n.a.	2·9	0·9	4·0	1·2	3·0	0·9	3·9	3·8
Non-ferrous metals	(68)*	2·3	0·4	2·4	0·3	3·0	2·8	1·4	0·3	1·6	0·2
Manufactures of metal, NES	(69)	1·2	2·0	2·1	3·2	1·5	n.a.	1·2	3·5	0·7	3·8
Machinery and transport	(7)	19·2	3·4	18·8	4·0	22·2	8·9	21·3	16·4	13·3	14·6
Machinery, not electric	(71)	9·5	1·7	9·0	2·2	9·5	2·7	6·9	6·0	5·9	5·4
Electrical machinery	(72)	3·1	1·4	3·2	1·4	5·1	5·0	3·5	6·3	2·5	2·9
Transport equipment	(73)	6·6	0·3	6·6	0·5	7·6	1·2	11·0	4·1	4·9	6·3
Miscellaneous manufactured articles	(8)	1·9	4·2	2·4	8·7	3·7	13·8	3·9	15·3	2·1	17·1
Furniture	(82)**	—	0·3	0·1	0·2	n.a.	n.a.	0·1	0·2	—	0·1
Clothing	(84)	0·1	1·9	0·3	0·1	0·6	10·0	0·9	10·3	0·3	11·4
Footwear	(85)	—	0·4	—	5·1	n.a.	1·6	0·1	1·5	—	3·1
Aggregate SITC sections 5–8		37·9	57·3	45·6	66·5	56·9	67·5	46·2	71·4	32·6	69·8

* In 1960 SITC 67 is included in SITC 68.
** SITC 82 includes only SITC 821 from 1973.

Sources: OECD, *Trade by Commodities: Series B* (Paris: OECD, various issues); own calculations.

The fact that growth of industrial production in Greece in the 1960s and early 1970s seems to have been more export-led than was the case in Portugal can probably be explained in terms of the different stage of industrialisation in which the two countries found themselves during this period. Greece started from a near zero point. The development of industries which relied on low wages and domestically produced raw materials coincided with Greece's comparative advantage and the availability of free access to Community markets. In contrast the Portuguese manufacturing sector was already relatively developed in 1960. Therefore the opening of the economy coincided with a shift towards the production of intermediate and capital goods in which Portugal could only slowly become internationally competitive.

Because of the very restrictive policies towards foreign investment until 1965, transnational enterprises account for a much smaller percentage of total output than in Greece or Spain. The other major difference that exists is the relatively low share of US companies, which is compensated for by a strong Community presence, particularly in the form of British and German investments (Table 1.21).

Table 1.21 **Stock of Foreign Investment in Portugal by Country of Origin (1978)**

Country	%
EC-9	49·9
UK	(12·5)
Germany	(11·6)
France	(8·9)
Netherlands	(7·6)
USA	19·3
EFTA	18·9
Switzerland	(14·5)
Spain	5·6
Others	8·3
	100·0

Source: Foreign Investment Institute, Stock of Foreign Investment (Lisbon, May 1979).

In 1959 foreign investment represented only 1% of gross capital formation but by 1970 it had reached the level of 27%.[49] The total inflow of foreign investment has been small in balance of payments terms (576 million dollars in 1964–78, Bank of Portugal data) but this figure may give a misleading picture of the role of foreign companies in

Portuguese industrial development and exports. By 1975 companies
with foreign participation accounted for 16·6% of total value added in
the manufacturing sector (Table 1.22). This however included
companies with a minority foreign participation, which represented
about 60% of all firms mentioned above. Foreign investment played a
major role in sectors such as electrical and non-electrical machinery,
rubber products, transport equipment, basic metals and chemicals and
a marginal one in textiles and clothing. The pattern is therefore very
similar to that found in Greece where local entrepreneurs tended to
concentrate on traditional sectors and foreign companies on goods
with a larger capital and technological input.

Available evidence seems to suggest that foreign companies are on
the average much more export-oriented than Portuguese ones.[50] This

Table 1.22 **Companies with Foreign Participation in
Portuguese Manufacturing Industry (as a percentage of
total value added), 1975**

Sectors	Value Added
Food	14·5
Beverages	10·4
Tobacco	4·0
Textiles	5·6
Clothing, footwear	4·1
Wood, cork	6·3
Furniture	2·8
Paper	19·2
Printing, publishing	3·7
Rubber	43·8
Chemicals	24·3
Petroleum products	·—
Non-metallic minerals	11·7
Basic metals	27·4
Metal products	2·1
Non-electrical machinery	23·2
Electrical machinery	68·0
Transport equipment	31·4
Others	25·3
Total manufacturing sector	16·6

Source: Ministério da Indústria e Tecnologia, Estatística da actividade industrial (July, 1979).

applies particularly to clothing, footwear, electrical and non-electrical machinery and pulp and paper, where the foreign-controlled sector is dominated by firms which export most, if not all, of their production. In 1973 exports of electronics and clothing accounted for slightly less than half of the total value of exports by foreign-controlled firms. Thus even in a traditional sector such as clothing the export lead was not taken by local entrepreneurs, as happened, for example, in Greece. The strong export orientation of transnational enterprises, together with the concentration on assembly plants (electronics, automotive industry) with low value added and traditional sectors such as clothing make the Portuguese experience more similar to that of South-East Asian countries or Mexico, than that of Greece and Spain. Vaitsos concludes that the fundamental factor for Portugal's place in the European division of labour, as far as manufacturing export activities are concerned, rests on its low wage level.[51]

In the last two decades Portuguese industry has undergone a major structural transformation, moving slowly away from small firms in traditional sectors towards modern plants producing intermediate and capital goods. At the same time Portugal has become more integrated in the Western economic system through trade as well as through the increasing participation of foreign companies at the production level. Structural changes and the opening-up of the economy were closely interconnected since the old development model based on import substitution and high protection had reached its limits in the 1960s. In the first years of the EFTA agreement it was mainly the traditional sectors which took advantage of the positive discrimination they enjoyed *vis-à-vis* third country producers in the markets of member countries. In later years there has been an increasing diversification of exports which is also manifested in Portugal's trade with the enlarged Community. However there is still a clear intersectoral division of labour, with Portugal's comparative advantage being almost exclusively based on relatively low wages.

The fast rate of growth of Portuguese industry has contributed very little towards solving the problem of unemployment or underemployment in the economy. Between 1960 and 1971 employment in industry increased by 1·5% per annum, while employment in the economy as a whole fell by 0·5%.[52] Massive emigration to Western Europe provided a safety valve, while remittances from migrant workers have been an important item not only for the balance of payments but for GDP as a whole. In the late 1960s Portuguese industry was already faced with a shortage of skilled workers, which was certainly accentuated by the four-year conscription of men in the army. The Portuguese experience with migration in the 1960s was very similar to that of Greece, but the problem in Portugal has acquired a new dimension again with the inflow of *retornados* from the colonies. In 1978 the rate of registered unemployment was 8% (OECD data). Since massive emigration will be impossible in the 1980s, both for internal political reasons as well as for economic and social reasons in the host countries, industrial growth will have to continue at a rapid pace but with more emphasis this time on the labour side.

The three main problems of the 1960s were unemployment/emigration, the stagnation of the agricultural sector and the heavy drain on resources resulting from the colonial wars. After 1974 unemployment worsened for the reasons mentioned above. Agricultural output, together with industrial output, fell while the government deficit kept on swelling. One could argue that this was almost an inevitable result of the crisis which ensued after the collapse of the dictatorial regime, decolonisation and the international economic recession.

The new regime also inherited a large number of other problems which are still waiting to be tackled. We have already talked about the high degree of dualism in industry. At the same time an effective regional policy is urgently needed in a country where per capita income in Lisbon is at least four times higher than that in the poorest district and where about 95% of industrial production is concentrated on a coastal strip that goes from some forty miles north of Oporto to Sines, south of Lisbon. In Portugal we also find an underdeveloped financial system, while the capital market is virtually non-existent. But these are characteristics of many other developing countries.

The stabilisation programme adopted in 1978 under pressure from the IMF clearly more than met its objective on the balance of payments front one year later, but at the expense of growth, employment, real wages and even inflation, given the effects of devaluation in countries with open economies. The above effects were highly undesirable for a country which would have to close slowly the gap separating itself from the rest of the Community if membership were to be a success. They were also dangerous in a country which had only recently emerged from a long period of dictatorship and where parliamentary democracy was still unstable.

Portugal has a relatively low degree of protection which will be reduced even further as a result of the 1972 Agreement signed with the Community. In this respect accession should be less of a problem than for a country like Spain. But Portugal may need more protection rather than less or, alternatively, effective policies at the micro level and a comprehensive set of incentives for the development of new industries. Reliance on one factor, namely, low wages, can be neither desirable nor feasible as a long-term solution. On the other hand it could be argued that the flexibility in the choice of policy instruments needed for the restructuring of Portuguese industry and the negative effects expected from the incorporation of the agricultural sector into the CAP (Chapter 5) make the economic case for immediate membership relatively weak. But this will have to be discussed later within a wider political context.

Spain

Spain and Europe – The Long Flirtation

Spain and Portugal share, together with geographical borders, similar experiences in their recent political history. Both countries underwent long periods of dictatorial rule based apparently on the same ideology, with the corporate state and Catholicism providing the foundation stones. However in the last fifteen years of the two regimes the experience was remarkably different both in terms of the role played by the state in economic development and the external orientation of the ruling classes. In this section we shall examine Spain's relations with Western Europe during the last phase of the Franco era. The main conclusion will be that Franco's European policy cannot be explained in purely economic terms nor can it be divorced from internal political and economic developments. Europe was a constant theme in the long fight between the liberals and the Falangists and always an important factor behind major policy changes, although it often appeared to be a justification rather than the cause of those changes. Discussion about Europe and Spain's role in it extended beyond government circles; isolation from Europe was also used by the democratic opposition as an effective weapon against the Franco regime. In this respect the Spanish experience is very similar to that of Greece. The difference with Portugal can be explained, at least partly, in terms of the geographical position of the two countries – Spain being more closely connected with the rest of the continent – and the fact that Spain was fortunate(!) enough to lose most of its colonies at an earlier stage.

After the end of the Second World War Spain found itself in a state of international quarantine which, however, did not last for long because of the Cold War and the change in attitude of the major Western powers. The main turning points were the UN resolution of 1950 lifting the economic and diplomatic sanctions against Spain, the 1953 Agreement which comprised a package of economic aid and the creation of US military bases in the country, and the Concordat signed in 1953 with the Holy See. The latter provided Franco with the support of the powerful Catholic Church, while the agreement with the Americans marked the unofficial entry of Spain into the Western alliance. One could argue that from 1953 onwards we witness a gradual shift of allegiance away from the United States and towards Western Europe. This shift has both an economic and political justification.

The war years and the period of international isolation justified a policy of self-sufficiency. Once the external reasons were removed economic liberalisation both internally and externally had to wait for a shift in the balance of forces within the regime itself. This came about in 1957 with the entry of various Opus Dei technocrats into the government, following a serious economic crisis. This in turn led to the 1959 Stabilisation Plan which, according to Donges, marked the first big step towards an outward-looking industrialisation policy in Spain.[53] The internal crisis combined with external factors to bring about this major economic reform. There was a strong American influence which was also exercised indirectly through international organisations like the IMF, the International Bank for Reconstruction and Development (IBRD) and the OEEC.[54] At the same time many Spanish officials, who have always been sensitive to French ideas, were following with great interest the experience with indicative planning on the other side of the Pyrenees. It may not after all be only a coincidence that the Spanish economic reform which started in 1959 combined liberalisation and planning. Last but not least, the creation of the EEC seems to have played a very important role. There was widespread feeling among the new technocrats, many government officials as well as businessmen, that there was a growing gap between Spain and Europe and that this was one of the last chances for the country to take part in the European integration process.[55] For this to become possible, internal economic changes were considered as absolutely necessary. It could however be argued that the Opus Dei technocrats used the support of international organisations and European integration as a means to an end, the end being the liberalisation of the economy. But it is also true that a man like Ullastres, who was the architect of the Stabilisation Plan and later appointed ambassador to the EEC, had a strong pro-European conviction.

In the beginning there seemed to be some hesitation in Spain between the EEC and EFTA which was quickly resolved in favour of the former. The first reason was the long-term political objectives enshrined in the Treaty of Rome. The fact that such objectives were espoused by some members of Franco's government was also an indication of the changes that had taken place in the regime itself. However, one should not take this point too far because most of those technocrats who entered the government in the late 1950s were not prepared to consider any far-reaching political reforms which would have made Spain a respectable partner for the Six. The second reason was the inclusion of agriculture in the Rome Treaty. Finally, the UK application of 1961 ended any hesitation that remained, given the dependence of Spanish agricultural exports on the British market. In

February 1962 the Foreign Minister, Castiella, requested the opening of negotiations with the EEC with the aim of signing an association agreement. This decision was the result of fifteen successive meetings of the Spanish cabinet.[56]

Three different sides can be identified inside Spain on the EEC issue. First of all, there were the Opus Dei members of the government, with wide support in the civil service and business circles, who were in favour of close links with Western Europe which was closely associated with economic and, for some people, political liberalisation in Spain. In the view of the democratic opposition, however, an association agreement with the EEC without serious political changes would have further legitimised Franco's regime. Isolation from Europe was therefore used as a means of pressure against Franco and his government. In June 1962 more than a hundred opposition figures from inside Spain and in exile met at the fourth Congress of the European Movement in Munich and approved a declaration on the political conditions which the Six should demand before signing any agreement with Spain. This declaration, together with the fact that many of the participants were arrested on their return and sent into exile, reinforced the anti-Spanish lobby within the EEC. Finally, the Falangists and the old diehards of the regime were against any close link with 'decadent Europe' and in favour of the 'splendid isolation' of the country.[57]

The Spanish application of 1962 was met with complete silence from the Community for about two years. A decision in principle to start exploratory talks with the other side was taken only in April 1964. Real negotiations did not start before September 1967 and an agreement was signed in Luxembourg in June 1970. Thus it took the Community more than eight years to agree to the signing of a preferential agreement of a purely commercial nature, which was certainly miles away from the association agreement that Castiella and Ullastres had had in mind.

The Spanish application received strong political support from the French and General de Gaulle himself, who saw the agreement with Spain as a way of extending the Community's influence towards the south. But geopolitical considerations went hand-in-hand with a strong reluctance to make any concessions which might prejudice the economic interests of France and particularly the French farmers. Thus French reactions in the 1960s were only the first taste of what was to follow later with respect to the Spanish application for membership. The Federal Republic of Germany was for political and economic reasons a protagonist of the pro-Spanish lobby. The Germans also favoured Spain's integration into NATO, an issue which had surfaced around 1959 but was later withdrawn because of strong opposition from the Scandinavians and the Dutch. The latter were also leading the opposition against Spain in the Community, followed by the Italians who were much more concerned with the negative effects of an agreement with Spain on their farmers. Meanwhile the European Parliament had issued the Birkelbach Report which stressed the political conditions that should be imposed not only for Community membership but also for association agreements. This immediately excluded Spain as a possible candidate.[58] In the end negotiations with Spain became closely linked with the Community's negotiations with another Mediterranean country, namely, Israel. It was yet another one of those interesting package deals which aimed to reconcile the interests of countries like France and the Netherlands, which supported each other's favourite 'enemy'.[59]

The 1970 Agreement set two stages in the creation of a free trade area between the two sides. But detailed provisions were only made for the first six-year stage, the contents of the second being subject to further negotiations. For the first stage the Community undertook to eliminate quantitative restrictions on substantially all imports coming from Spain and to reduce its common external tariff by 60% from January 1973. There were also some exceptions with respect to sensitive products like textiles, clothing and footwear, where Spain was clearly more competitive. As far as agriculture was concerned, the proposed tariff reductions were often inferior to those previously and subsequently offered to other Mediterranean countries. But the variable levy remained a more effective means of protection of Community farmers. Spain proposed tariff reductions of 25–60%, with the large majority of imports falling in the 25% category. These were to be implemented in the course of six years. The preferences granted by Spain covered about 60% of all Community exports to the country in 1968, with most of agricultural trade being virtually excluded.

Although the agreement was based on the principle of reciprocity between the two sides Spain was offered more favourable treatment. This is even more true if one takes into account Spain's higher level of tariffs and the extensive use of quotas and other non-tariff barriers. On the other hand the Spanish negotiators had obtained in economic terms much less than they had originally hoped for but, as Gamir argues, the preferential agreement was more of a political operation for both internal and external reasons.[60] Tamames, a well-known economist who later also appeared as a leading member of the communist party, criticised the agreement as weighted against Spain, using the rather spurious argument that since Spain started from a much higher level of tariffs, it ended up offering bigger concessions than the Community.[61] A more serious criticism was that Spain could have been better off with the

Generalised Scheme of Preferences which also involved no reciprocity.[62] It is interesting that a few years later the Commission was to complain that the 1970 Agreement was weighted against the Community. The argument was that this was no longer justified, given the rapid development of Spanish industry.[63]

After the signing of the 1970 Agreement there followed two years of peace which was finally interrupted by the first round of enlargement in 1973 and the adoption of the 'global Mediterranean policy'. With the entry of three new members into the Community, the 1970 Agreement had to be renegotiated. This was particularly important for Spain because of the free access to the British market which Spanish agricultural exports used to enjoy. In the context of the global Mediterranean policy, the Community proposed the creation of a free trade area in industrial goods with a longer timetable for Spain, extending to 1985, and limited concessions in agricultural trade. This was for obvious reasons unacceptable to the Spaniards.[64] Since no compromise could be reached, the two sides agreed to apply a standstill to tariffs on trade between Spain and the three new members which was to last until June 1977. When a final compromise seemed to have been reached between the two sides the negotiations were suspended by the Community following the execution of Basque prisoners by Franco in September 1975. After his death the negotiations were resumed in April of the following year but by then the picture had changed drastically on the Spanish side. With the disappearance of Franco and the first steps towards the restoration of democracy nobody in Spain was any longer interested in a free trade area agreement with the Community. The only objective now was full membership.

Liberalisation and Planning

Between 1939, which marked the final victory of Franco's forces over the Republicans, and 1959, the year of the Stabilisation Plan, the institutional and legal framework under which the Spanish economy operated was similar to the one in Portugal under Salazar. The imposition of the corporate state meant the creation of vertical syndicates in different sectors of activity, with employers and employees under the same umbrella. Their main function was the direct control over workers which had as a consequence the constant deterioration in real wages until 1955. The law for the regulation and defence of national industry made all industrial investment subject to government authorisation. This was coupled with government control over prices and wages. Foreign investment was allowed only if it did not exceed 25% of the assets of any national enterprise, with a theoretical maximum of 45%. This regulation, together with heavy restrictions on the repatriation of profits and capital, kept foreign investors out of Spain. On the other hand Franco's government kept an armoury of weapons directed against international trade. This took the form of severe exchange controls, high tariffs (although being specific they gradually lost their punch because of inflation), quantitative restrictions and a multiple exchange rate system. Self-sufficiency was a national slogan and industrialisation was based on import substitution.[65]

There was one important aspect in which the Franco regime differed from its Portuguese counterpart, namely, in the direct involvement of the state in industry. In 1941 the Instituto Nacional de Industria (INI) was created with the objective of strengthening defence industries and promoting self-sufficiency in areas where private resources were insufficient. INI was modelled on the Italian IRI and came to play an important role in industrialisation, a fact which differentiates the Spanish experience from that of either Portugal or Greece.

The advent of the Opus Dei technocrats and the Stabilisation Plan which followed in 1959 marked the beginning of a new era in Franco's Spain. We have already referred to the serious internal and external factors which brought about this change. It led to the gradual disappearance of industrial licensing laws, the elimination of physical controls, the opening of the economy to foreign investment and tourism and the gradual liberalisation of international trade through the elimination of direct controls and many quantitative restrictions. In most cases the Stabilisation Plan contained measures constituting the first step in a gradual process of economic liberalisation which was to continue through the 1960s and 1970s. More immediate measures were also announced, such as severe cuts on public expenditure aimed at reducing inflation, the devaluation of the peseta and the abolition of multiple exchange rates as well as a freeze in wages. According to Carr and Fusi 'the remedy was taken from the recipe book of orthodox capitalism'.[66] However, liberalisation measures were accompanied by a strong emphasis on indicative planning, with the state playing a guiding role in industrial development. Thus Spain was to follow the French postwar example and capitalism appeared to be more enlightened than orthodox.

Referring to the past fifteen years of Franco's rule, Wright concludes that 'the Spanish economy is a mixture of state and privately run business. In this it is not different from other West European countries, although proportions vary.'[67] The first part of the sentence is almost a platitude since *laissez-faire* has long ceased to exist in Western Europe. Let us then examine the second part of the sentence and draw some comparisons with the Portuguese and Greek experience. It would be useful to distinguish here between internal measures and those intending to influence or regulate the interaction between Spanish and foreign firms at the level of production or trade.

The Stabilisation Plan meant the end of the period of self-sufficiency and led to the growing importance of the balance of payments for the national economy, which has been manifest not only through trade but also through invisible earnings and capital movements. Nevertheless it is perhaps too easy to exaggerate the degree of openness achieved by the Spanish economy in comparison with the 1950s. Spanish industry still enjoys a much higher degree of protection than either its Portuguese or even its Greek counterparts, one important reason being that Spain only signed a limited trade agreement with the Community in 1970.[68] After 1959 many quantitative restrictions were abolished and the average level of effective tariff protection was considerably reduced. The 1970 Agreement led to a further tariff reduction in trade with the Community countries of 26% on average. But still, many industries remain heavily protected. The Spanish tariff structure is similar to both the Greek and the Portuguese ones, namely, the rate of protection falls as one moves from consumer to intermediate and capital goods. This is certainly to be expected in countries which started with consumer goods industries and also needed cheap capital imports. High tariff protection has been combined with important quantitative restrictions which apply particularly to imports of transport equipment, textiles, clothing and food products. One should also add the existence of taxes on imports in the form of fiscal duties, although their real effect is more difficult to establish. On the export side Spanish governments have introduced a series of incentives including tax rebates (*desgravación fiscal de la exportación*) and a very effective system of official credit and insurance. These measures are in addition to the whole gamut of industrial and regional incentives incorporated in the development plans.[69]

The licensing of industrial investment by domestic firms was completely abolished in 1963. But the state was not left without power to influence the development of the economy. With indicative planning, the emphasis was more on the noun rather than the adjective. The state had many instruments at its disposal, including tax incentives, control over credit – directly through official credit institutions and indirectly through private commercial banks – control over the system of external protection and, to a large extent, over prices and wages. At the same time it remained the single biggest industrial producer through the enterprises controlled by INI.

During the Franco period there were three Development Plans, in 1964, 1968 and 1972 respectively. Government intervention took the form of the *acción concertada*, when firms agreed on certain targets like production levels, training of workers, and so on, in return for state credit and tax benefits. Similar incentives were used to encourage mergers and investment in sectors of special interest. Regional policy was also one of the main aspects of planning in Spain. Regional development relied much on the French concept of *pôles de croissance* or *polos de desarrollo* in Spanish. The banking structure, dominated by seven private commercial banks, was preserved at least partly by restrictive government legislation on the opening of new branches. The Bank of Spain was nationalised in 1962. The growing importance of official credit through state banks, as a source of investment funds for private industry, meant that the state had another important policy instrument at its disposal in order to influence investment decisions.[70]

After 1959 there was a dramatic change in government policy towards foreign investment which led to a big inflow of funds. Any investment which would lead to more than 50% foreign participation in a firm required government authorisation which was granted in most cases. After the late 1960s governments became more selective. They were particularly interested in the export potential as well as the technology input of new investments.

One area where government intentions and policies did not change fundamentally after 1959 was in relation to the control over workers and wages. The syndicates remained but their power gradually dwindled with industrial growth and the emergence of independent, illegal trade unions (*comisiones obreras* – CC.OO). Thus wages slowly slipped away from the control of the government and since 1965 they have been rising faster than in either Greece or Portugal (ILO data). At the same time, faced with massive emigration to Western Europe, Franco's officials tried to make a great national project out of a necessary evil. On this subject, Ullastres exclaimed: 'Europe and the world call us and if we go to them it is not to escape a possible deficit in the balance of payments but because it is our universal mission.'[71]

In 1976 enterprises controlled by INI accounted for 11% of total value added in the manufacturing sector and 14% for industry and mining as a whole. The corresponding numbers were 23% for chemicals and 19% for the metallurgical sectors.[72] Given the relatively big size of those enterprises, the role played by INI in Spanish industry is much more decisive than the figures mentioned above might suggest. If we take the 700 biggest industrial firms in 1975 then the twenty-six INI-controlled enterprises accounted for 20·02% of total sales, 19·70% of investment and 28·61% of exports.[73] With the end of the policy of self-sufficiency and the fact that the Spanish army became increasingly dependent on imports of arms from the United States, INI's development changed from that originally intended when it was set up in 1941. Its activities now cover a wide area including basic industries such as iron, steel and shipbuilding, advanced technology (computers, aeronautics), mining (mainly coal), oil exploration, tourism and regional development. INI has often been accused of running unprofitable enterprises without using any commercial criteria in its operations and starving private industry of scarce investment funds.[74] In 1978 INI-controlled enterprises accounted for about one-third of total industrial investment. It is however fair to point out that INI has a high share in industrial sectors like iron, steel and shipbuilding, which have been hit by the international recession and which are heavily subsidised all over Western Europe.

Although it is doubtful whether the three development plans as such provided an effective strategy for development, it is true that government policies and the changes initiated in 1959 have been a determining factor in the high rates of growth of the 1960s and early 1970s. With the advent of parliamentary democracy after the death of Franco a series of major reforms have been initiated. The Moncloa Pact of October 1977, based on the agreement of the three biggest national parties, the centre party, the socialists and the communists (UCD, PSOE and PCE), was the real starting point. Apart from measures aimed at correcting the short-term disequilibria of the Spanish economy, an agreement was reached for a reform of the monetary and financial system – with the aim of strengthening the role of market forces and dismantling the complex system of government intervention – the social security and the taxation system. As far as the latter was concerned, the objective was to increase efficiency and equity in a country where government revenue was remarkably low compared with other OECD countries and where the taxation system was substantially regressive. After the March 1979 elections the new Suárez government introduced liberalisation measures for the banking system and the external sector, including Spanish direct investment abroad. Such measures were usually justified in terms of the imminent accession to the Community. But given also the experience of the Stabilisation Plan of 1959, one could remain doubtful as to whether relations with the Community were the cause rather than a convenient justification for measures which were desirable *per se*. Exactly the same thing seems to be happening in Greece since 1974.

Economic Growth, Diversification and Import Substitution

There are two main aspects in which Spain's industrial development in the past two decades differs from that of Portugal and Greece. One is that Spain only signed a limited preferential agreement with the Six, and this did not happen until 1970. This meant that Spanish firms could work behind protective walls which in turn had another effect, namely, the creation of an anti-export bias in the system. The second was the relatively large size of the Spanish market which gave an import substitution policy a longer lease of life. From an economic point of view it could be argued that it has been a fortunate coincidence for Spain that no far-reaching trade agreement was signed with either European trade bloc during the period of rapid industrialisation of the 1960s and early 1970s. It is however true that although Spain did not sign any preferential agreement in the 1960s the lowering of tariffs in the Western world and the booming economic conditions of that period had a major impact on the Spanish balance of payments and economic development in general.

During the period examined Spain experienced a major transformation of its economic structure, with a big decline in the share of the agricultural sector and increases in industry and services. Within the manufacturing sector there have been two remarkable changes in terms of the magnitudes involved, namely, a decline in traditional sectors like food, beverages, tobacco and textiles, and a tremendous increase in metal industries, particularly in capital goods and transport equipment. But despite its high rates of growth, Spanish industry was unable to solve the unemployment problem in the country, which was at least partly due to the rapid exodus from the countryside. Between 1960 and 1974 employment in the manufacturing sector increased by 1·5% per annum as opposed to 7·7% increases in productivity.[75] The contributions to employment were much higher in the construction sector and services. The capital-intensive nature of industrialisation, which also reminds us of the Portuguese and Greek cases, can be attributed to a number of factors. First of all, the structural transformation of Spanish industry and the rapid growth of the capital goods sector. Secondly, the level of interest rates which were kept artificially low by the government. Thirdly, labour legislation, initiated under Franco and preserved until now, which made lay-offs of workers extremely difficult. Last but not least, the large-scale emigration of Spanish workers to more developed countries of Western Europe and especially to France. Although estimates vary a great deal, it appears that more than one million workers left the country in the 1960s. In relative terms the size of international emigration is much smaller than that experienced by Greece and certainly Portugal. But one should also add the large-scale internal migration on a permanent basis of the order of four and a half million people, moving mainly towards Madrid, Barcelona and Bilbao.

The size of the internal migration also gives an indication of the relative lack of success of regional policy. Industry remained concentrated very much in the Basque and Catalan provinces and around

Madrid. On the other hand the small reduction in income differentials between regions was the result of internal migration rather than the spread of economic growth.

The abandonment of the policy of self-sufficiency, which coincided more or less with the adoption of outward-looking policies in Greece and Portugal, led to the increasing importance of international trade. Thus both exports and imports of goods grew much faster than total output. But being without any preferential agreement with the Community and EFTA until 1970 and 1979 respectively, Spain has not experienced a big shift in the geographical distribution of its foreign trade. As far as the 1970 Agreement is concerned one should bear in mind its limited nature and the fact that its application coincided with the first enlargement, the international recession and the oil crisis. The first observation one can make, and which in a sense almost contradicts the foreign policy orientation of all Spanish governments since the end of the 1950s, is the decline in importance of Western European markets (EC and EFTA) as an outlet for Spanish exports. From 63·2% of total exports in 1961 they fell to 53·0% in 1977 (Table 1.23); but the EC share has remained relatively stable

Table 1.23 **Spain: Geographical Distribution of Foreign Trade as a Percentage of Total Trade (goods only)**

	Imports					Exports				
	1961	*1965*	*1970*	*1973*	*1977*	*1961*	*1965*	*1970*	*1973*	*1977*
EC–6	26·1	37·4	32·5	—	—	37·6	36·2	36·1	—	—
EC–9	—	—	—	43·2	33·8	—	—	—	47·8	46·3
EFTA	14·0	16·9	14·4	6·9	4·8	25·6	23·1	18·0	8·3	6·7
Latin America	10·1	8·9	9·7	8·3	9·1	7·5	12·7	13·2	8·8	10·2
Middle East	n.a.	5·8	6·4	9·1	21·6	n.a.	0·7	1·1	2·9	4·6
Centrally Planned Economies	1·2	2·3	1·4	1·9	2·0	2·1	2·5	2·8	2·2	2·8
USSR	n.a.	n.a.	n.a.	0·4	0·7	n.a.	n.a.	n.a.	0·3	1·0
USA	25·2	17·5	19·0	16·3	12·1	9·9	12·0	14·1	13·9	9·8
Japan	0·3	1·1	3·1	2·6	3·2	1·8	1·4	—	1·4	1·2
UK	n.a.	n.a.	7·1	6·2	4·7	n.a.	n.a.	8·8	8·0	6·3
Germany	n.a.	n.a.	12·7	13·8	10·2	n.a.	n.a.	11·8	11·8	10·6
France	n.a.	n.a.	9·4	10·3	8·5	n.a.	n.a.	10·3	12·8	16·0
Italy	n.a.	n.a.	5·2	6·1	5·1	n.a.	n.a.	6·6	5·3	5·1

Sources: OECD, *Trade by Commodities: Series B* (Paris: OECD, various issues); own calculations.

during this period. The share of Latin America and the United States grew sharply until 1970 and then fell. France now constitutes the single most important market for Spanish exports. On the import side there is a considerable decline of the share of imports from the United States which, however, still remain the single most important supplier followed by the Federal Republic.

With the exception of 1960, Spain has always run trade deficits which in most years were more than balanced by surpluses in invisibles. As we see in Table 1.24 tourism has been by far the most important export industry. From 1974 Spain entered into a new period of regular deficits in the current account and growing deficits in the basic balance, which reflected the rise in oil prices, the stagnation of export markets and the growing disequilibria at home. This trend was, however, quickly arrested and in the late 1970s the current account moved again slowly into surplus. After the 1959 devaluation the exchange rate of the peseta remained stable until November 1967 when it was devalued *vis-à-vis* the dollar. In February 1973 the peseta was floated, originally upwards with respect to the US currency, and then devalued by about 20% in July 1977. As shown in Table 1.11, the peseta depreciated less than either the drachma or the escudo; however it lost much of its value with respect to all former snake currencies.

Table 1.24　**Spain: Balance of Payments Profile (in percentage terms)**

	1960	1965	1970	1973	1977
Exports[a]/Imports[a]	108·3	36·7	57·0	60·4	63·5
Tourism/Exports[a]	39·7	108·4	67·7	60·3	37·7
Migrant Remittances/Exports[a]	7·4	29·2	18·8	16·9	n.a.
Transportation/Exports[a]	5·6	11·1	14·9	13·7	14·0

[a] Goods only.

Source: OECD, *Balance of Payments of OECD Countries 1960–1977* (Paris: OECD, 1979).

As with Portugal and Greece the transformation of Spain's economic structure has been clearly reflected in its trade with the EC and the rest of the world (Tables 1.25 and 1.26). Spain is entering into the 1980s with a much more diversified structure of exports than either Portugal or Greece and a division of labour with the industrialised world which is more intra-sectoral than intersectoral. On the export side we have a big shift from foodstuffs and raw materials to manufactured goods. But the latter are not dominated by traditional labour-intensive goods. The share of textiles has actually fallen to 2·5% of total exports, while clothing and footwear – two dynamic export sectors – account for only 6%. Relatively big increases are registered by non-metallic minerals, iron and steel after 1965, and metal manufactures. But the revolution in Spanish industrial exports takes place in the sector producing machinery and transport equipment, the share of which rises from 2% in 1961 to 27% in 1977. Within this sector transport equipment alone accounts for more than half of total exports. This must be at least partly due to the establishment in Valencia of the Ford car plant with a strong export orientation. As with Portugal and Greece, the structure of Spanish imports from the Community has not changed substantially. The percentage of total imports taken by industrial goods has remained the same, with machinery and transport equipment representing slightly less than half of industrial imports.

The structure of Spain's trade with the rest of the world is remarkably different compared with its trade with the Community. We start with a situation in 1961 when the exchange of foodstuffs and raw materials predominated in Spain's trade with non-EC countries. On the export side agricultural products (SITC 0–1) accounted for 42·1% of total exports; on the industrial side the main exports were chemicals, textiles, iron and steel, basic metals and non-electrical machinery. On the import side raw materials and mineral fuels accounted for 45·7% and machinery and transport equipment, presumably coming from the industrialised world, for 15·7%. Still on imports, two important changes have taken place since then: (a) the big rise in oil prices, which raised the share of oil imports, and (b) the first round of enlargement of the Community in 1973, which diverted part of industrial imports to the EC category. The change on the export side has been even more drastic and thus, on the basis of the 1977 figures, Spain appears as an importer of raw materials from non-EC countries and an exporter of industrial products.

One of the main characteristics of Spanish industrialisation, which is in clear contrast to the experience of a country like Greece, has been the rapid growth in the production of capital equipment. This growth has also been reflected in the export performance of the sectors. Thus while in 1961 exports of capital equipment accounted for only 5·5% of total domestic production, this had risen to 27·4% by 1974. During the same period the share of domestic production in apparent consumption (domestic production plus imports) remained more or less stable (68·2% and 67·2% in 1961 and 1974 respectively).[76]

Table 1.25 Spain: Structure of Trade with the EC (in percentage terms)

Product classification	(SITC No.)	1961 Imports	1961 Exports	1965 Imports	1965 Exports	1970 Imports	1970 Exports	1973 Imports	1973 Exports	1977 Imports	1977 Exports
Food and live animals	(0)	5·5	46·3	7·9	54·7	4·5	32·9	4·6	26·6	3·6	21·5
Beverages and tobacco	(1)	0·1	2·2	0·1	3·3	0·2	2·1	—	5·7	0·9	3·2
Beverages	(11)	0·1	2·2	0·1	3·3	0·1	2·1	—	5·7	0·7	3·2
Tobacco	(12)	—	—	—	—	0·1	—	—	—	0·2	—
Crude materials, inedible except fuels	(2)	5·9	13·4	4·7	9·3	6·0	5·6	6·8	3·6	7·6	4·1
Wood, lumber and cork	(24)	0·6	0·8	0·3	0·5	0·2	0·4	0·3	0·2	0·7	0·2
Pulp and paper	(25)	0·2	—	0·1	0·2	0·4	—	0·3	0·2	0·4	0·5
Textile fibres (not yarns)	(26)	2·0	0·4	1·5	0·3	2·0	0·1	1·4	0·9	1·3	0·8
Mineral fuels, lubricants and related materials	(3)	3·4	1·0	3·3	1·6	2·0	5·2	1·5	6·6	3·2	2·1
Petroleum and petroleum products	(33)	1·6	1·0	0·7	1·9	0·8	2·8	0·7	5·3	1·5	2·1
Animal and vegetable oils and fats	(4)	1·1	14·5	0·7	1·4	0·3	10·7	0·4	4·1	0·3	1·4
Aggregate SITC sections 0–4		16·1	77·4	15·1	72·0	13·1	56·5	14·0	46·6	15·6	32·4
Chemicals	(5)	22·6	3·5	14·2	6·1	17·8	4·4	17·5	4·0	18·5	4·6
Manufactured goods, classified by material	(6)	16·8	14·7	26·3	13·4	20·1	17·9	18·7	21·5	18·3	24·2
Leather, leather manufactures, NES	(61)	0·1	0·6	—	1·3	—	1·5	—	1·9	—	2·1
Wood and cork manufactures	(63)	0·2	1·2	0·1	0·7	—	1·2	0·2	1·8	0·2	1·5
Paper, paperboard	(64)	0·7	—	0·7	0·1	1·1	0·3	0·9	0·6	1·1	1·2
Textile yarn, fabrics, made-up articles	(65)	1·4	3·6	2·9	2·9	2·3	3·0	2·8	2·6	0·6	2·5

Non-metallic mineral manufactures	(66)	1·5	0·2	2·6	0·7	2·2	1·5	2·6	1·8	3·0	2·2
Iron and steel	(67)	9·8	7·1	14·8	0·9	8·7	2·5	6·2	6·6	6·2	6·0
Non-ferrous metals	(68)	1·2	1·6	2·7	4·9	2·7	3·2	2·9	1·2	2·4	2·1
Manufactures of metal, NES	(69)	1·5	0·2	2·0	0·9	2·0	2·1	2·2	2·4	2·4	3·5
Machinery and transport	(7)	41·2	2·0	39·8	3·3	42·8	14·7	42·3	17·1	39·2	27·0
Machinery, not electric	(71)	27·8	1·2	27·3	1·6	29·8	5·3	28·1	5·2	22·9	7·8
Electrical machinery	(72)	6·3	0·7	7·8	0·9	8·1	3·2	8·3	4·2	9·8	3·8
Transport equipment	(73)	7·1	0·2	4·7	0·8	4·8	6·3	5·9	7·8	6·5	15·4
Miscellaneous manufactured articles	(8)	3·2	2·3	4·6	5·1	6·3	6·4	7·6	10·7	8·4	11·7
Furniture	(82)*	—	0·2	0·2	0·9	n.a.	1·0	0·4	1·4	0·5	1·2
Clothing	(84)	0·1	0·4	0·4	0·7	0·5	1·5	0·6	2·6	0·6	2·5
Footwear	(85)	—	0·2	—	0·3	—	0·8	0·1	2·4	0·1	3·5
Aggregate SITC sections 5–8		83·8	22·5	84·9	27·9	86·9	43·4	86·0	53·4	84·4	67·6

* SITC 82 includes only SITC 821 from 1973 onwards.

Sources: OECD, Trade by Commodities: Series B (Paris: OECD, various issues); own calculations.

Table 1.26 **Spain: Structure of Trade with the Rest of the World (in percentage terms)**

Product classification	SITC No.	1961 Imports	1961 Exports	1965 Imports	1965 Exports	1970 Imports	1970 Exports	1973 Imports	1973 Exports	1977 Imports	1977 Exports
Food and live animals	(0)	17·9	36·3	18·4	32·2	12·1	21·8	18·9	15·9	14·2	11·5
Beverages and tobacco.	(1)	3·5	5·8	2·6	5·9	2·2	4·1	2·2	3·0	1·6	2·4
Beverages	(11)	0·1	5·8	0·3	5·8	0·2	3·9	0·4	2·8		2·2
Tobacco	(12)	3·3	—	—	—	0·2	n.a.	1·8	0·2	1·6	0·2
Crude materials, inedible except fuels	(2)	24·9	6·2	18·3	5·7	22·6	3·0	21·5	2·2	17·7	2·1
Wood, lumber and cork	(24)	1·7	1·1	2·6	0·8	2·8	0·5	2·4	0·3	2·3	0·4
Pulp and paper	(25)	2·1	—	1·4	—	1·5	n.a.	1·3	0·2	0·8	0·1
Textile fibres (not yarns)	(26)	9·2	1·0	3·1	1·5	2·8	0·4	3·0	0·5	2·0	0·5
Mineral fuels, lubricants and related materials	(3)	20·8	8·9	15·1	4·3	18·7	5·6	22·1	2·9	41·6	5·1
Petroleum and petroleum products	(33)	20·3	8·6	13·7	4·2	16·2	4·9	20·1	2·9	38·8	5·0
Animal and vegetable oils and fats	(4)	5·3	6·7	3·3	2·2	0·7	3·1	0·6	3·9	0·6	2·8
Aggregate SITC sections 0–4		72·4	63·9	57·7	50·3	56·3	37·6	65·3	27·9	75·7	23·5
Chemicals	(5)	4·7	5·6	6·0	9·5	7·1	5·7	6·1	5·2	4·3	7·9
Manufactured goods, classified by material	(6)	5·3	17·8	13·3	13·9	14·2	16·8	7·8	21·9	6·0	29·6
Leather, leather manufactures, NES	(61)	0·1	0·8	0·2	0·8	0·2	0·7	0·4	0·9	0·5	1·2
Wood and cork manufactures	(63)	0·1	1·9	0·1	2·0	n.a.	1·5	0·1	1·0	0·1	0·7
Paper, paperboard	(64)	0·7	0·2	1·0	0·4	1·1	0·8	1·1	1·1	0·8	1·5
Textile yarn, fabrics, made-up articles	(65)	0·4	7·0	1·2	5·2	1·0	3·9	1·2	3·9	0·8	3·8

	SITC										
Non-metallic mineral manufactures	(66)	0·3	0·7	2·0	0·7	0·6	1·5	0·6	2·4	0·4	5·9
Iron and steel	(67)	1·6	3·6	5·0	1·2	7·0	1·9	2·0	5·6	1·5	7·9
Non-ferrous metals	(68)	1·5	2·6	2·9	0·9	3·2	1·3	1·7	0·8	1·2	1·0
Manufactures of metal, NES	(69)	0·4	0·7	0·7	1·9	0·7	3·8	0·7	3·7	0·5	5·0
Machinery and transport	(7)	15·7	4·5	19·9	14·4	17·8	22·2	16·7	25·7	10·1	24·4
Machinery, not electric	(71)	9·2	2·8	13·7	6·0	10·6	7·8	8·7	7·4	6·2	9·8
Electrical machinery	(72)	2·2	1·0	3·7	1·4	3·2	3·7	3·2	3·2	2·9	4·1
Transport equipment	(73)	4·3	0·7	2·4	7·0	4·1	10·7	4·7	15·1	0·9	10·5
Miscellaneous manufactured articles	(8)	1·8	8·1	3·1	11·8	3·7	17·3	4·1	19·2	4·0	13·8
Furniture	(82)*	—	0·2	0·1	0·8	n.a.	0·7	0·1	0·9	0·1	0·6
Clothing	(84)	0·1	1·5	0·3	1·4	0·2	2·5	0·3	1·8	0·3	1·7
Footwear	(85)	—	0·7	—	1·4	n.a.	6·4	—	8·0	—	4·4
Aggregate SITC sections 5–8		27·5	36·0	42·3	49·6	42·8	62·0	34·7	72·0	24·4	75·7

* SITC 82 includes only SITC 821 from 1973 onwards.

Sources: OECD, Trade by Commodities: Series B (Paris: OECD, various issues); own calculations.

The opening of the Spanish economy to foreign capital has played a crucial role in terms of the balance of payments, its contribution to fixed capital formation and employment as well as the transfer of technology. Between 1960 and 1977, the net inflow of long-term investment reached 12,686 million dollars.[77] But one should also allow for the outflow resulting from the repatriation of profits and the payment of royalties and technology transfers, which amounted to about 47% of the total capital inflow.[78]

Foreign penetration at the production level differs from sector to sector. If we take the amount of capital subscribed or acquired by foreigners as a percentage of the total nominal value of shares issued by Spanish companies, we end up with the following figures: 47·8% for chemicals, 27·8% for machinery and transport equipment, 24·8% for paper and printing, 21·8% for mining and 20·0% for the food industry.[79] These figures can be compared with the data in Table 1.27

Table 1.27 Role of Foreign Capital in the 700 Biggest Companies in Spain, 1975 (as a percentage of total value added)

Sectors	Foreign participation ≥ 50%	Foreign participation < 50%
Mining	16·26	—
Food, beverages, tobacco	36·17	24·02
Textiles	39·71	—
Leather, footwear, clothing	7·29	—
Wood, cork, furniture	—	—
Paper, publishing	11·70	7·76
Petroleum products	—	56·03
Chemicals	40·71	35·35
Non-metallic minerals	22·01	40·81
Iron and steel	2·69	34·21
Basic metals	22·63	49·42
Metal products	20·06	26·70
Non-electrical machinery	18·28	40·07
Electrical machinery	57·59	23·57
Shipbuilding	—	—
Transport equipment	18·76	29·20
Construction	4·67	6·94
Electricity, water, gas	—	2·07
Other industries	56·18	14·85
Total	19·85	21·60

Source: Las grandes empresas industriales, op. cit., tables IV–6 and IV–11.

which show the relative importance of firms with foreign participation among the top 700 in Spain. They give some indication of the role played by foreign capital in Spanish industrialisation. We should however add that foreign penetration would appear smaller if we had data for each sector as a whole and not just for the biggest firms. The picture we get from Table 1.27 is certainly not as clear as in the case of Portugal and Greece. Here there is no obvious correlation between high degrees of foreign penetration and the so-called modern sectors. Above-average penetration is found in electrical machinery and chemicals, but also in food industry and textiles. Thus there is a less clear division of labour between local and foreign entrepreneurs, which should be at least partly attributed to the role played by INI in capital- and high technology-intensive sectors.

As regards the origin of foreign investment, the data in Table 1.28 show that US firms have led the way, followed by European firms, from Germany and the UK in particular. Behind Swiss investment we should expect to find mainly US and European firms which establish their headquarters in Switzerland because of the tax and banking facilities offered there. It is interesting that until 1975 Japanese investment was virtually non-existent, which was also true in both Portugal and Greece.

There has been a great deal of criticism in Spain, which is also familiar in other developing countries, that growing dependence on transnational companies leads to the perpetuation of the country's dependence on imported technology because subsidiaries will tend to rely on research and development being carried out in the industrial metropolis. Most studies undertaken seem to confirm this fear. Several economists in Spain have also argued that multinational companies tend to increase the country's dependence on foreign imports because

Table 1.28 **Foreign Investment in Spain by Country of Origin, 1975 (companies with ⩾50% foreign participation)**

Country	%
USA	40·61
EC–9	35·03
Germany	(10·54)
UK	(10·13)
France	(5·42)
Netherlands	(4·37)
Italy	(2·10)
Switzerland	16·65
Others	7·71

Source: Muñoz, Roldán and Serrano, op. cit., table 16, p. 130.

most direct investment takes the form of assembly plants with low value added and a high import content of inputs which often come from other subsidiaries of the same company.[80] Things can become much worse for the balance of payments if the foreign subsidiaries are restricted in their export activities by the parent company.

It is certainly impossible to generalise about foreign investment in Spain or in any other country for that matter. If we take the 700 biggest companies in the country, it appears that on average exports as a percentage of total sales do not show any substantial difference when we compare Spanish with foreign-owned companies. The figures for 1975 were 11·61% for Spanish companies, 12·12% for companies with majority foreign participation and 9·35% for those with minority participation. But when we take individual sectors within the manu-facturing industry we find that it is only in clothing, leather and footwear (49·96%), paper (40·95%), iron and steel (29·50%) and non-electrical machinery (22·60%) that exports represent a relatively big share of the total sales of companies with majority foreign partici-pation.[81] It seems therefore that the local market provided the main incentive for most of foreign direct investment in Spain. In those sectors where there has been the largest concentration of foreign investment, namely, chemicals, machinery and transport equipment, we find that the figures are not very different from the average figure mentioned above (12·26% for chemicals, 12·12% for electrical machinery and 13·31% for transport equipment). On the import side the fears expressed seem to be more justified since firms with either majority or minority foreign participation rely much more heavily on imported inputs than domestic firms (35·37%, 69·90% and 25·35% respectively).[82]

We should not fail to mention that since the mid-1960s Spain has become an important exporter of capital. The accumulated outflow of capital between 1963 and 1978 reached the sum of 57,171 million pesetas, of which 47·75% had gone to Latin America.[83] There has also been growing Spanish investment in the south of France. This has been a means of jumping the Community tariff barriers. In the recent liberalisation measures applying to Spanish investment abroad the argument was often put forward that this would also help to promote Spanish exports.

External protection and the size of the internal market have been determining factors in Spanish industrialisation since the economic reform of 1959. This also seems to apply to a good deal of foreign direct investment undertaken in the country. Given the relatively low level of protection of Community markets, it is expected that the liberalisation of trade between the two sides, following Spain's accession, will have a serious negative effect on Spain's trade balance (see below, Chapter

4).[84] Apprehension about the future has been strengthened by recent economic trends. The Spanish economy started feeling the effects of the economic recession around mid-1975. This was later than most OECD countries. Since then Spain has experienced relatively slow growth, falling investment and growing unemployment, hand-in-hand with high inflation rates. The sharp acceleration of inflation was partly attributed to rapidly rising wage costs which in turn were not unrelated to the internal political changes which took place during the same period. In this respect, the Spanish experience was very similar to that of Greece and Portugal, at least during the first years after the revolution. In the years 1975–7 wages in Spain rose much faster than in any Community country.

Despite its diversified industrial structure Spain's 'revealed' comparative advantage still seems to lie in labour-intensive and resource-based products.[85] Thus after trade liberalisation most benefits are expected to accrue to exporters of foodstuffs, shoes and leather products. Motor cars are the main exception to the rule and this is because Spain has become integrated in the process of internationalisation of production.

Although exogenous factors have played a major role in Spanish industrialisation, relations with the Community as such have not been as determinant a factor as in the case of Greece or even Portugal. At least, the static effects of trade liberalisation with the Nine are expected to be negative but this should not lead to an immediate policy conclusion. Even if we do concentrate on trade only and abstract from all other considerations, the real choice is not between the status quo and full membership, because the former is no longer accepted by the Community. In view of its fast economic development and the attraction of its internal market, Spain is now asked to pay the price of reciprocity. Given the importance of its agricultural sector and the fact that the cost of being cut off from the international division of labour is almost prohibitive, membership of the Community can appear as the only solution, even in purely economic terms. But this solution will necessitate important structural changes and possibly a new model of economic development for the future.

Conclusions

This has been a comparative study of the process of economic development in the three Mediterranean countries during the last two decades. We have concentrated our attention on two main explanatory variables, namely, the role played by governments and the external economic environment. We have found many similarities in the experience of the three countries despite the large distance in geographical and cultural terms – to mention only two – which has separated them. This is especially true as regards the two Iberian countries on the one hand and Greece on the other. This distance can also be explained in terms of the direction of communication flows – political, economic and cultural – which is usually along a vertical rather than a horizontal axis. Thus there has been very little exchange of goods or ideas between the Mediterranean countries, although each one of them has been slowly drawn in by the industrialised core of Western Europe. Similarities should not however conceal the large number of differences which still exist and which make the experience of each country almost unique.

During the period examined we witnessed the gradual opening of the three economies to international economic exchange. The timing was very similar and was certainly not coincidental. Governments were influenced by the advice offered by international organisations, the process of economic liberalisation which was taking place in the Western system and European economic integration. The opening of the three economies was greatly facilitated by the economic boom of the 1960s and early 1970s. Their integration into the Western economic system played a determining role in the rapid industrialis- ation of Greece, Portugal and Spain. It provided them with markets for their exports, which in many cases were of fundamental import- ance given the small size of domestic markets. Invisible earnings and capital inflows provided the foreign exchange necessary for the balancing of trade deficits. Investment by transnational enterprises added to domestic savings while it also provided access to technology and oligopolistic markets. Export of capital to the three countries was matched, so to speak, by an export of labour to the North which played an important political and economic role.

There is certainly an alternative way of presenting the effects of outward-looking policies in the three countries.[86] If we approach the problem from a more critical angle, we can talk of an industrialisation process which has led to an increasing dependence on foreign trade and technology. This has in turn created a dualistic economy, serious regional and structural disequilibria and a highly unequal distribution of income. It has also brought about the adoption of foreign consump- tion habits which do not correspond to the standard of living already achieved in those countries. Last but not least the rapid process of industrialisation did not solve the problem of unemployment and this forced hundreds of thousands of workers to leave their country in search of jobs abroad.

The two pictures presented above do not actually contradict each other. The development of the three Mediterranean countries has not been autonomous, whatever this word actually means in the postwar economic system. The development model adopted has not led to the creation of an integrated industrial structure and it has often implied a high price in social terms. Having said that, we can go on to question, together with Muñoz, Roldán and Serrano,[87] the feasibility of 'autonomous miracles' in our time. We can also add some qualifications to the conclusions reached by centre-periphery theorists. On the export side the three countries are still below the world average in terms of their dependence on exports (their share of world exports of manufactures being lower than their share of world industrial production – Table 1.29). As regards their dependence on foreign capital, this is certainly not higher than that found in small member countries of the Community, such as Belgium. What is more worrying is that the three countries have until now relied to a very large extent on imported technology, their expenditure on research and development being almost insignificant. For industrial growth to become a more self-generating process in the future, domestic development of technology and skills will be absolutely crucial.

Table 1.29 **Greece, Portugal, Spain: Share of World Industrial Production and Export of Manufactures**

Country	1963 World Production	Exports	1973 World Production	Exports	1977 World Production	Exports[a]
Greece	0·19	0·04	0·30	0·15	0·33	0·22
Portugal	0·23	0·30	0·30	0·35	0·32	0·21
Spain	0·88	0·28	1·37	0·92	1·56	1·07

[a] 1976 data.

Source: OECD, *The Impact of Newly Industrialising Countries*, op. cit., tables 1 and 2, pp. 18–19.

Centre-periphery theory would be very useful if it enabled us to make predictions about the future. Does it imply that the division of labour between the centre and the periphery will remain frozen? Even more, does it suggest that differences will be aggravated by time? What else could the concept of unequal development mean? The experience of Greece, Portugal and Spain suggests rather the opposite. The three countries have enjoyed high rates of growth and rapid industrialisation, which led to a substantial increase in their share of world industrial production and exports of manufactures (Table 1.29). This applies especially to Greece and Spain, two countries which also sustained high levels of investment until the early 1970s. The change in Portugal was less dramatic. Moreover the combined effect of the international recession and the various political problems at home had a serious negative effect on the Portuguese economy. This was, for example, reflected in the remarkable decline in Portugal's share of world exports of manufactures in 1977. This was, however, partly reversed in the following year.

It is certainly true that there is still a vertical division of labour between the Three and existing members of the Community, although here again there is a large difference between Spain on the one hand and Greece on the other. But it would be rather absurd to expect them to specialise immediately in the production of high technology equipment. Instead, these countries could take advantage of their relatively low labour costs and of the 'product cycle' which with the growing internationalisation of production is being transformed into a 'process cycle'.[88]

In all three countries the state has played a decisive role in economic development. In Spain its area of activities has been the most extensive, with the state engaged in indicative planning and also adopting an important entrepreneurial role. In Greece its main power lay in its control over the financial system. As far as Portugal is concerned, the Salazar–Caetano regime almost totally identified the national interest with the interests of an economic oligarchy. After the revolution the public sector was considerably increased and now the state has a direct control over the financial sector and a major part of the manufacturing sector. In both Spain and Greece the state has also played an important supporting role by providing the economic infrastructure and also offering a series of different incentives and subsidies with the aim of encouraging domestic and foreign investment. We could enter a lengthy debate on whether the low level of research and development (with the consequent high dependence on foreign technology), the regional disequilibria and the inequality of income distribution, to mention but a few of the problems associated with economic development in the three countries, were inevitable in view of the development model adopted or were mainly a function of political decisions taken or rather political inertia. One obvious failure in all three countries has been the low labour absorption in the course of the industrialisation process. In this respect, and ignoring the human cost involved, labour migration may have played a very negative role by providing a safety valve for the governments concerned.

We have tried to show that the three countries have become gradually integrated into the Western economic system and this integration has played a major role in the process of their economic development. Although institutional relations with the European

Community have differed from one country to the other, the degree of dependence reached in trade with the Nine is very similar. In 1977 exports to the Community as a percentage of total exports of goods ranged from 46·3% to 51·7%, with an average of intra-Community trade for existing members of 50·7%. Their import dependence was considerably lower, ranging from 33·8% to 43·6% compared with an average of 49·4% for intra-Community trade.[89] This difference can be explained in terms of the much higher rates of protection in the three countries. Greece's association agreement with the Community played an important role in the growth of its dynamic industries. An almost similar outcome seems to have come from the Portuguese experience with EFTA. Spanish industrialisation has depended less on access to foreign markets. The size of the domestic market in Spain made a policy of import substitution viable for a longer period of time.

The six founding members of the Community were almost caught unprepared when they found themselves bombarded with applications for the conclusion of preferential agreements coming from different Mediterranean countries. Given the economic size of the Community, this was a very natural response from countries left out on the periphery of a new trade bloc. The various agreements signed with the Mediterranean countries up to 1972 were a series of uncoordinated responses to external pressures. The Greek and Turkish agreements, concluded in times of euphoria, were not repeated. Later agreements were of a more limited nature. Dissatisfaction with the old piecemeal approach, French and Italian worries about having to make increasing concessions in the agricultural field, the first round of enlargement and American hostility to the proliferation of preferential agreements, all led to the development of a new 'global Mediterranean policy'. It was in the context of this new policy that the enlarged Community tried to negotiate a new agreement with Spain. The problems which emerged during those negotiations are only one example of the difficulties encountered by the Nine in their attempt to implement the new global policy. The Community had important political, strategic and economic interests in the Mediterranean area, but its policy instruments were only limited to trade and aid. Moreover it became extremely difficult, particularly for countries like France and Italy, to reconcile external pressures and internal demands, the latter coming from producers of Mediterranean products and the so-called sensitive industries.[90]

The two main issues which arose in the negotiations with the Mediterranean countries were the question of reciprocity in the dismantling of tariff barriers and the concessions to be made by the Community for Mediterranean agricultural exports. Spain was the only country among the three applicants which was directly involved in such negotiations. But the subject has a great relevance for all Three. The agreements signed by the Three with the Community, and Portugal's membership of EFTA, had one characteristic in common. Reciprocity in trade concessions was limited, at least during the first stage of those agreements. Both Greece and Portugal have already started feeling the effects of trade liberalisation under the existing agreements. This would have to continue until the creation of a customs union and a free trade area by 1984 and 1985 respectively. The same would happen to Spain, even if it did not apply for membership, because the preservation of the status quo was unacceptable to the Community. Thus none of the three countries could have obtained free access to Community markets for its industrial exports without trade liberalisation on its part. The Community had agreed to sign trade agreements based on non-reciprocity only with countries of the southern littoral. Moreover these agreements were full of safeguard clauses and exceptions which applied to the most important industrial exports of the countries concerned. Therefore for Greece, Portugal and Spain, tariff disarmament was the price to pay for free access to Community markets, irrespective of whether they applied for membership or not. Moreover, as far as agricultural trade was concerned, a very important area for both Greece and Spain, neither the association agreement nor any agreement signed within the context of the global Mediterranean policy could have guaranteed equal treatment with Community farmers.

Together with all existing members of the Community, the three applicant countries have been hard hit by the world recession and the energy crisis. On the one hand they are all heavily dependent on imported energy resources, while on the other they cannot balance the negative effect in their terms of trade by passing on the price increases to foreign consumers of their own products. Foreign demand for their exports of traditional consumer goods is more price-elastic than the demand for capital and high technology goods which are characteristic of the exports of advanced industrialised countries. The economic crisis led to a worsening of their balance of payments which was met by a series of devaluations of the national currency, especially *vis-à-vis* the currencies of the snake. Devaluations in turn contributed to the inflationary spiral. The crisis was most strongly felt in Portugal which in the end was forced to accept the full rigour of the IMF therapy in order to obtain much needed international credit. For the other two countries, and especially Greece, the balance of payments could very quickly become a serious constraint on economic growth. Large trade deficits are only one side of the problem. The other is that invisible earnings may also be adversely affected in the future because of labour migration in Europe slowly coming to an end and the stagnation in world trade which in turn could affect earnings from shipping. As for the future of tourism in the three countries, predictions are less easy to make. For all those reasons, the effect which Community membership will have on the balance of payments of the Three will be crucial.

The fall of the dictatorships has also led to internal political and economic changes. The fact that world recession found the three countries in the middle of a transitional period meant that the real options for policy response were very limited. Moreover the three Mediterranean countries now have parliamentary democratic regimes and organised trade unions which make them very different from most other NICs. Thus after the fall of dictatorial regimes wages in Spain and Greece were rising faster than in Community countries. The models which have been implicit in their recent economic development did not attach a high price, or at least they could afford not to, to such things as regional disequilibria, income inequalities or massive migration. Open democratic systems cannot ignore the social pressures arising from such problems. Policies will have to be designed which not only satisfy pressing social needs but help the society 'to adapt, obviously late in the day, its peculiar ancestral ways and political and economic institutions to the needs of the international system into which it is already inserted'.[91] Membership of the Community, therefore, strengthens the challenge for adjustment.

Part Two

THE PROCESS OF ENLARGEMENT

2

Internal Debate

Greece, Portugal and Spain have recently emerged from dictatorial rule which, in the case of the two Iberian countries, has lasted for several decades. Dictatorial regimes had turned the three countries into pariahs of the international system and isolation was an inevitable consequence. The desire for international recognition is now combined with the need to strengthen the new democratic institutions which sometimes appear to be too shaky for the comfort of many democrats in the three countries. All governments concerned seem to believe that membership of the Community will lend an aura of respectability to new regimes and also help to strengthen fledgling democracies. However, this view is not shared by all political formations in the three Mediterranean countries.

The second round of enlargement involves the nine member countries of the European Community as well as the three applicants. Nevertheless it has become a political issue of major importance in only two countries, namely, France and Greece. In all the others enlargement has remained a secondary issue which does not provoke a real political debate. This is either because political parties and pressure groups feel that the effect would only be marginal for their country or because there is a general political agreement about the desirability, or even inevitability, of the actual event. Either explanation, however, sounds paradoxical when applied to an applicant country.

In this chapter we propose to study the political debate about membership in the three applicant countries. This will be followed in the next chapter by a study of Community reactions and the reactions of individual member countries in the context of negotiations between the two sides. Here we shall examine the interests and expectations associated with membership as they have been expressed in policy statements and analyses made by political leaders and representatives of interest groups as well as in interviews conducted in the three countries. We are particularly interested in finding out how Community membership has been linked with domestic issues and with the overall foreign policy of the country. We are also concerned with the level of information and knowledge about the Community in the three prospective members.

When we study the political debate in the three countries we should bear in mind that Greece is about two years ahead of both Spain and Portugal. Greece's Treaty of Accession was signed in May 1979 and ratified by the Greek parliament the following month. In contrast, at the beginning of 1980 both Portugal and Spain were still in the early stages of their negotiations with the Community. It is therefore inevitable that the internal political debate has not as yet had time to develop fully. Moreover Greece has had a much longer history of close links with the Community, which means that the public, not to mention the Greek political class, has been exposed longer to the problems involved. Relations with the Community have already been debated by the Greek parliament in the context of the association agreement. Last but not least, Greece has a long-established political class which was only ostracised for the relatively short period of seven years. None of these things apply to the two Iberian countries. However, as we shall try to explain below, the above reasons only partly explain why the application for membership became such a major political issue in post-1974 Greece, but not in Spain or Portugal.

Greece: The Politics of Exaggeration

The Treaty of Accession was ratified by the Greek parliament on 28 June 1979 with more than the three-fifths majority required by the constitution. There were 191 votes cast in favour, two against and three blank votes. All 175 deputies of the government party, New Democracy (ND), voted in favour, together with the four KO.DI.SO (Party of Democratic Socialism) deputies, the four National Rally ('extreme right') deputies, two members of EDIK (Union of Democratic Centre), the leader and only representative of EDA (United Democratic Left) and five independents. The only two votes cast against the treaty were those of the representative of the Communist Party of the Interior and an independent, while the blank votes were cast by the three remaining members of EDIK. Thus political support for Greece's accession covered a wide spectrum, from the extreme right to various small parties of the left. But more than one-third of all MPs, namely, the ninety-five deputies of PASOK (Panhellenic Socialist Movement) and the eleven deputies of the orthodox Communist Party (KKE), following orders from the party leadership, decided to boycott the session. The leader of PASOK, Andreas Papandreou, stated that the participation of his party would have legitimised the government's contravention of popular sovereignty and he promised to ask for a referendum on coming to power. But there was also the suspicion that participation in the debate and the voting might have revealed the party's lack of unity on this issue.

Greece therefore appears to be a divided country with the two main opposition parties (PASOK and KKE), which together gained about 35% of the popular vote in the 1977 elections, being strongly and consistently opposed to membership. The science of public opinion research is relatively underdeveloped in Greece and we therefore have little indication of what popular feeling is on this issue. According to one opinion poll conducted in 1978, 45·2% of the sample were in favour, 24·1% against and 30·7% were undecided.[1] A similar opinion poll conducted a year later showed that the percentage of 'don't knows' had risen to 46% at the expense both of those who declared themselves to be in favour and those against.[2] This in fact may suggest that the Greek public was beginning to know more about the Community and therefore found it increasingly difficult to give a simple 'yes' or 'no' answer. The conclusion would then be that more information leads to widespread perplexity, which is not altogether surprising.

There are three important background factors which have tended to colour Greek political debate since 1974. One is the experience of the military dictatorship which has often been associated with foreign intervention, or at least with more than tacit support by the United States and NATO countries in general. The second is the Cyprus crisis and the continued tension in relations with Turkey. The third is the charisma of Constantine Karamanlis who has certainly dominated Greek politics since the fall of the dictatorship. It is very characteristic of modern Greek history that one factor is directly, and a second is indirectly, related to foreign policy. In Greece more than in probably any other Mediterranean country foreign policy issues have always occupied a central place in the domestic political debate.[3]

Given the geographical position of the country and the way in which the Greeks achieved their independence from the Ottoman empire in 1828, it may not be altogether surprising that Greece has been subjected to so many foreign interventions during its recent history. As Jean Siotis has so succinctly put it, there is a strong feeling in the country that Greece has always been the object rather than the subject of international diplomacy.[4] This feeling has been intensified by the recent experience of the dictatorship and the invasion of Cyprus by Turkey, particularly since there is a tradition of blaming foreigners for everything. Since the Second World War and the political division of Europe, the geographical position of the country no longer coincides with its political and military alliances, not to mention the cultural aspirations of the Greek élite. Thus Greece is considered as a Western country. There is, though, a strong feeling of isolation caused by the fact that the country is surrounded by neighbours such as Albania, Yugoslavia, Bulgaria and Turkey, with very different political regimes or religions. After Turkey's invasion of Cyprus and the tension in bilateral Greek–Turkish relations, there has been political unanimity on at least one issue, namely, that the main danger is no longer perceived to come from the North but from the East.[5]

The lessons drawn from history can differ widely. Thus for the pro-marketeers, and Karamanlis in particular, membership of the Community will mark the end of a long period of political isolation, strengthen Greece's independence and bargaining power *vis-à-vis* third countries, while enabling the country to take part in the political construction of Europe.[6] For most pro-marketeers in Greece the political integration of Western Europe is both desirable and inevitable and this is where the main emphasis is placed. In contrast, strong nationalism is one of the main characteristics of the PASOK ideology, which also contains many populist elements. The coexistence of populism and nationalism is certainly not a new phenomenon. For Papandreou and his supporters Community membership means that many decisions will be taken in Brussels which, inevitably, will lead to a loss of national sovereignty.[7]

Support for or opposition to the Community is only part of a clear divergence in the general foreign policy orientation of the two biggest parties in Greece. For the ND, disillusionment with the Americans and the withdrawal from the military wing of NATO in 1974 did not mean that the old maxim 'Greece belongs to the West' had ceased to hold true. A united Europe, with a role independent of the two superpowers, has been seen as the obvious alternative. It is characteristic that political groups to the left of the ND have expressed their support for a European defence community.[8] With the exception of the extreme right, nobody disagreed with Karamanlis's partial withdrawal from NATO and most opposition parties have been in favour of a complete withdrawal. Thus, Greece's reintegration into the military wing of NATO in October 1980, which followed protracted negotiations with the alliance constantly under the threat of a Turkish veto, seems to have widened the gap between government and opposition on foreign policy. It is however worth adding that the decision taken by the ND to return to NATO did not signify any change of heart about the Atlantic alliance on behalf of the government but only the belief that it would thus be easier to preserve the balance of power with Turkey.

This combination of a strong emphasis on the independence of Western Europe, coupled with a rather hesitant, or qualified, support for NATO, explains why many Greeks have looked to France as a model to follow. The admiration and partial imitation of General de

Gaulle by Karamanlis and the excellent personal relations between the latter and Giscard d'Estaing have meanwhile created a 'special relationship' between the two countries. For Greece the application for membership has coincided with an era of active foreign policy. According to Roy Macridis, since 1947 'Greece has had no foreign policy, other than to follow American directives'.[9] This ended in 1974 with the fall of the dictatorship, and Greek governments have been busy ever since trying to recover lost ground. Détente was discovered and, in consequence, better relations have been established with the Soviet Union and China. Moreover Karamanlis took an ambitious initiative in trying to promote economic co-operation among the countries of the Balkan peninsula. At the same time, long-established co-operation with the Arab states was given a new impetus. Thus the government has tried to prove that membership of the Community is not incompatible with a multidimensional foreign policy. This has, after all, been the experience of existing members.

All Greek political parties agree that the main foreign policy issue is Cyprus and relations with Turkey. For PASOK it is clear that Western powers have been constantly supporting the latter in its conflict with Greece. Until very recently the Community was always identified with NATO and this was beautifully summarised in the political slogan 'EEC–NATO – the same syndicate'. It was also obvious to PASOK supporters that both organisations were dominated and controlled by the United States.[10] Therefore the argument that the Community will lead to the creation of an independent Europe seemed to be absolute nonsense. Moreover it was often argued that complete reintegration of the Greek armed forces in NATO would be a precondition for Greece's entry into the Community. A common fallacy in the arguments used by anti-marketeers was that the Community countries were actually keen to see Greece accede. As we shall see in Chapter 3, this assumption was certainly far from the truth.

PASOK has a *tiers-mondiste* ideology and would like to follow the example set by a neighbouring non-aligned country, namely, Yugoslavia. It has played a very active role in the three conferences of Mediterranean progressive and socialist parties, held so far in Barcelona (1976), Malta (1977) and Athens (1979).[11] In Malta Papandreou argued against the participation of Southern European countries in the European Community and suggested as an alternative the co-ordination of investment plans and commercial policies of Mediterranean countries, leading in the long run to a common market and even a Mediterranean economic community. Such ideas did not meet with much enthusiastic support from the other participants. However, they were followed two years later in Athens with proposals for technological co-operation and the setting up of a Mediterranean bank, but again with little success. As an alternative to accession, PASOK put forward the idea of a special agreement with the Community along the lines of that negotiated with Norway. But then it was discovered that this agreement did not contain any provisions for trade in agricultural goods which is so important for Greece. More recently, PASOK turned its eyes towards the agreement signed between the Community and Yugoslavia in 1980 as a possible model to follow. This was also accompanied by the adoption of a more qualified stand towards the Community which was very different from the attitude of outright rejection shown in the first years after the fall of the dictatorship.[12]

For pro-marketeers Greece's membership of the Community would help to consolidate democratic institutions and avert the danger of another *coup d'état* in the future. They always refer to the freezing of the Association Agreement and the Community's denunciation of the military regime. It is however true that the strengthening of democratic institutions is sometimes identified with keeping one political party in power. Accession to the Community has been all along the *cheval de bataille* of the ND and one of the main issues on which it fought the 1977 elections. This is most likely to be true of the forthcoming elections which will have to be held by November 1981. As far as PASOK is concerned, membership of the Community will help to preserve the political and social status quo in the country and therefore reduce the possibilities of a socialist experiment. This view seems to be shared also by many people on the other side of the political fence. At the same time Andreas Papandreou casts some doubts on the attachment of Western European governments to democratic institutions and refers to NATO policies during the military dictatorship. This again explains why a great deal of the debate in Greece is about the kind of distinction one can draw between the Community on the one hand and NATO and the United States on the other.

We can also explain the different approaches adopted by the two biggest political parties in Greece in terms of their economic *Weltanschauung*. Pro-marketeers in general tend to adopt an evolutionist model of development.[13] They stress the economic successes of the last two decades and believe that Community membership will help Greece to move closer towards Western European countries in political, economic and social terms. For the reformers within ND and other pro-European parties, membership provides an ideal opportunity to bring about the modernisation of the Greek state and bureaucracy, which is long overdue. This will be the result of a process of osmosis but also a necessity if Greece is to take an active part in the Community decision-making system. A great deal of internal legislation has already been passed 'in view of accession'. In many cases accession seems to serve more as a justification rather than a real cause for changes. Pro-marketeers also argue that the Greek economy is likely to gain from access to markets and Community funds and from a fresh wind of competition blowing from Western Europe. As a last resort one can argue that full membership is more advantageous than the status of an associate because of the benefits likely to accrue to Greek farmers, the transfer of resources and the ability to participate in Community decision-making.

Andreas Papandreou, himself an academic economist before he turned to politics, has espoused the theories of *dependencia* in his analysis of Greek economic development. According to him, the heart of the problem 'lies in the fact that the growth pattern, the structure of growth of the dependent economy, is channeled in paths that reflect the requirements of the metropolis rather than its own requirements'.[14] With the exception of France and northern Italy, this analysis is supposed to apply to all non-socialist countries of the Mediterranean which have become 'peripheral capitalist formations'. PASOK is certainly the only mass political party in Western Europe – although its leaders might deny that Greece is really part of Western Europe – which has espoused such an economic theory. The only way out of economic dependency is a policy of autonomous economic development, planning and socialisation of some strategic sectors of the economy. But this will be incompatible with the liberal economic philosophy of the Treaty of Rome. The Greek economy will also need tariff protection and protection from the invasion of foreign monopolies which again will be impossible when Greece becomes a member of the Community. Unless Greece adopts a radically different economic policy, 'dependent development' will not allow the Greek economy to improve its position in the international division of labour.

We have so far tried to rationalise what sometimes appear rather irrational or unfounded arguments used by both sides. We have also simplified the picture by presenting, almost in a Weberian sense, two alternative political and economic models. The issue of membership has been closely linked with domestic politics and general foreign policy. In the process of becoming a major political issue, it has been grossly simplified and exaggerated. For many of its supporters the EC has become the panacea which will cure the various ills of Greek society. The standard of living will be raised to Western European levels and funds will flow into Greece. Greek industry will suddenly gain access to very large markets (as if this has not applied since 1968). For the others, Greece will be invaded by the multinationals (as if the latter have not already played a major role in Greek industrialisation). Small and medium-sized farm units will disappear and the agricultural population will be reduced until the proportion of the labour force engaged in agriculture eventually reaches the Community average of 8%. Greek workers will emigrate to the West, while Greece will be flooded by unemployed Turks in search of jobs. For the orthodox communists export opportunities will be reduced because, they claim, it is Community policy to restrict exports to the socialist and non-aligned countries.[15] National sovereignty is also at stake and even the cultural independence of the country. On the other hand some members of the Greek Orthodox Church have been very concerned at the prospect of coexisting with so many Catholics and Protestants and it has been maintained that membership of the Community is yet another attempt, after the capture of Constantinople by the crusaders, to put an end to the Orthodox faith.[16]

According to Juan Linz,[17] in Southern Europe *politique d'abord* is still prominent. Grand political issues are endlessly debated and everything is presented in ideological terms. This observation certainly applies to the political debate in Greece on the issue of Community membership, although slightly less so in the final stages of the negotiations when bread-and-butter issues, such as the price of olive oil and peaches, became of immediate concern to many people. It was only then that more dispassionate analyses of the problems involved were published in Greek newspapers and periodicals. The politics of exaggeration was toned down as the arguments aired by both sides became more sophisticated and also more technical.

One unfortunate result of the tendency of both pro- and anti-marketeers to exaggerate the positive or negative effects of accession is that little attention has been paid to the role which Greek governments should play and the policies – internal and external – which should be adopted in order to maximise the benefits or minimise the costs. This approach has been adopted by a few members of the ND, but has been mainly held by the centre and centre-left political formations, such as the Social Democrats (KO.DI.SO) led by John Pesmazoglou who had negotiated Greece's association agreement with the Community.

With the exception of PASOK and KKE, the latter being one of the most orthodox and Moscow-oriented communist parties in Western Europe, all the other small political formations on the right and left of the ND have supported the principle of accession. Disapproval of the government's conduct of negotiations and dissatisfaction with the terms of entry are almost inevitable in the political game. In the end they accounted for the two 'noes' and the three blank votes cast in the Greek parliament. The enlargement of the Community also served as an ideological justification for the 'enlargement' of the ND with defectors from EDIK, when the latter underwent a process of disintegration after the big electoral defeat of 1977. The argument was that the country was split between 'Europeanists' and 'anti-

Europeanists' and that the former had to rally behind Karamanlis.

The 'civil society' in Greece, to use Gramscian terminology, is relatively underdeveloped. Political parties have traditionally relied on charismatic leaders. This statement should however be somewhat qualified when applied to the post-1974 political system. Although the role of Andreas Papandreou has been absolutely crucial in the development of PASOK one cannot ignore the fact that it also has a mass party organisation and following. Moreover the democratic election in 1980 of George Rallis as the new leader of the ND and automatically new prime minister may in fact indicate that Greek politics has now entered into a new era. In Greece there are few organised interest groups representing important segments of Greek society. We shall here only refer to those which purport to represent industrialists, workers and farmers.

The Confederation of Greek Industries (SEV), probably the best organised and certainly the most active and effective interest group, has been consistently in favour of membership. On the surface this may sound surprising, since free and unlimited access for exports has already been achieved (with the exception of textiles) while import competition will certainly intensify after accession. The enthusiasm of SEV was somewhat tempered after the publication of a report on the consequences of accession for each branch of industry. However the reasons for the position adopted by SEV are not difficult to trace. The Confederation is essentially run by the biggest of Greek industrialists – not an uncommon experience in other countries – who themselves have little to fear from accession. Interest groups representing small firms and workshops have certainly been more cautious in their approach. Moreover many industrialists hope that accession will force the antiquated and cumbersome bureaucracy in Greece to modernise itself. The political dimension of accession has also been an operative factor in determining the position of industrialists. Once the political decision had been taken by the government, it was considered to be both futile and counter-productive to raise any objections about the general principle. Additionally closer ties with the West also were seen as a guarantee against radical changes which were associated with the rapid rise of PASOK, the legalisation of the Communists and also the 'socialist' practices adopted by the ND.

The General Confederation of Greek Workers (GSEE) has also been consistently in favour of accession because of expected improvements in labour legislation, better conditions of collective bargaining and its close ties with the European Trade Union Confederation (ETUC). The rate of unionisation in Greece is low. Moreover the GSEE is not fully representative since many existing unions are excluded from it. Among these, attitudes towards the Community have been determined by one factor, namely, which political party has control over each individual union.

As far as the farmers are concerned, the biggest organisation is the Greek Confederation of Agricultural Co-operatives (PASEGES) which also represents Greek agricultural interests in Brussels. It has always been in favour of entry but has also stressed the need for institutional and structural reforms. For PASEGES accession also provides an opportunity to strengthen the co-operative movement in the country. The long transitional period adopted for agricultural goods was a cause for disappointment. Other farmers' organisations, mainly controlled by PASOK and KKE, have expressed themselves against membership. An interesting example of the prominence of *la politique d'abord* is the case of Crete, which is the region likely to benefit the most from the CAP. None the less there seems to be a large percentage of farmers opposed to the Community because of their political affiliation with PASOK, which is particularly strong on the island.

Probably for the first time in modern Greek history the two biggest political parties maintain a high degree of independence from outside powers. This seems to be less true of either Spain or Portugal. Moreover neither of the two parties belongs to any of the wider political families of Western Europe. The ND does not fit easily in the Christian Democrat or conservative groups of the European Parliament and therefore, by a process of elimination, one can conclude that it may want to join the liberals. This would after all fit very well with the new image that the party wants to present. On the other hand PASOK has so far refused to join the Socialist International, although the decision has been taken in favour of joining ranks with the other socialists in the European Parliament. Another factor which distinguishes Greece from Portugal and Spain is that foreign policy considerations seem to be more important than the strengthening of parliamentary institutions in the minds of pro-marketeers. After all at the end of the 1970s the Greek political system was more stable than that of the other two countries.

The application for membership of June 1975 found most of the Greek political class in a state of Euro-euphoria. There were great expectations attached to the Community membership, often totally unrealistic. During the early stages of the negotiations this gave way to a more sober attitude which was the result of the difficulties encountered in Brussels and also better knowledge of what membership of the Community really meant. This at least applied to the initiated few. Meanwhile the 1977 elections brought about a big shift in the internal political balance of power. The strengthening of the two parties opposed to Community membership destroyed the image of near unanimity on this issue and led to a long and heated political debate which has not always helped to clarify complex, technical issues which make up the largest part of the *acquis communautaire*. The biggest opposition party has remained opposed to membership and has committed itself to ask for a referendum on this issue although it is up to Constantine Karamanlis, the new President of the Republic, to authorise such a referendum. In June 1980, in an interview with the newspaper *Ta Nea*, PASOK's leader, Andreas Papandreou, made some statements which implied a shift in his party's policy. For the first time he saw some real possibilities for the development of a European foreign policy independent from the United States. In fact he had already translated his new analysis into action by establishing closer links with Western European socialists, some of whom had been previously dismissed as serving American interests. He then went on to say that 'there were possibilities for the use of safeguard clauses and the re-examination and revision of certain aspects of the accession treaty'.[18] One may therefore wonder whether a PASOK government might rediscover Harold Wilson's formula of renegotiation or simply accept Community membership as a *fait accompli* and try to increase its margin of manoeuvre in terms of internal economic policies by appealing to the political realism of its EC partners.

Portugal: In the Midst of Indifference

In March 1977 the Portuguese government, led by Mário Soares, lodged its application for membership of the European Community. The Council of Ministers then asked the Commission to present its opinion on the application, which was submitted in May 1978. The official opening of the negotiations then took place in October of the same year. But while the Portuguese were negotiating in Brussels, opinion polls conducted at home showed that the large majority of the population were not really interested in the issue and had no knowledge at all of what the Community was all about.[19] Three years after the application made by Mário Soares there has still been very little discussion about the prospect of membership. The government and the various political parties have limited themselves to some generalities and there has been little analysis concerning the likely effects on the Portuguese economy. The question of membership was a non-issue in both the 1976 and 1979 elections. Parliament debated the matter only once, in March 1977, while the parliamentary committee set up to deal with problems of European integration had never met.

Moreover the Commission on European Integration, a team of experts dealing with the negotiations, had taken a long time to function properly and many of its members did not express any optimism for the immediate future.

This apparent indifference of the Portuguese deserves some explanation, particularly when it is compared with the experience of a country like Greece. It should be partly related to the long period of isolation which the country had undergone under the Salazar–Caetano regime, the high rates of illiteracy and the limited knowledge of the outside world. It is characteristic that even the best national newspapers are extremely poor in terms of their foreign, and particularly European, news coverage. Scanning the Portuguese papers for the period 1976–9, we found very few articles indeed in which there was any attempt to analyse various aspects of Community policies or the likely effects of membership for Portugal. However, the most important fact which explains the apparent indifference of the Portuguese to Community membership was that the country was going through a series of successive political crises, with short-lived governments that were unable to tackle the economic situation. Therefore the issue of Community membership became like a luxury good which could only be purchased once other basic needs had been satisfied. None the less, Portugal's entry into the EC has been very closely linked with domestic politics and it is virtually impossible to understand the changing attitudes of different political parties, unless they are set against the background of a rapidly evolving political situation.

The Democratic Alliance, consisting of the Social Democrats (PSD), the Centre Democrats (CDS), the monarchists and other smaller groups on the right and centre of the political spectrum, which won the December 1979 election with 45% of the votes, was in favour of Community membership. So were the Socialists (PS) of Soares with 27%, who suffered a sharp decline in their electoral strength compared with the 35% registered in 1976. Thus in 1979 the pro-European parties accounted for 72% of the total vote. On the other hand the Communists and their allies, with 19%, were opposed to membership, and so were small parties on the extreme left and the extreme right. The parliamentary elections of October 1980 did nothing but confirm the new trend in Portuguese politics. The Democratic Alliance was returned to power with 47% of the votes, while the Republican and Socialist Front (PS and allies) lagged far behind with 28% and the Communists with their own allies were third with 17%.

The attitude of political parties, with the exception of the Communists, was formed in the aftermath of the 1974 revolution[20] and was a function of internal political events. The initiative for the Portuguese application was taken by Mário Soares who as late as December 1974 had excluded any such possibility and in fact seemed to be in favour of an extension of the 1972 Agreement into an association agreement.[21] According to the PS, which was founded in Bonn in April 1973, the Community was a creation of the multinationals. The aim of the party was not to 'correct the most unjust aspects of capitalism but to destroy capitalism'[22] and this language was in some conflict with the liberal economic principles of the Treaty of Rome. Although their final political objectives were different both the PSD (then PPD) and the CDS, together with the Confederation of Portuguese Industrialists (CIP), were in favour of some form of association agreement with the Community. It was only in 1976 that membership became a real possibility as a result of an initiative taken by the PSP with the support of the two parties on its right. Later on it became quite clear that support was actually given for widely differing reasons. This leads us to examine the position of each political party separately.

For the PS, Community membership was seen as a means of consolidating the new regime which was based on the pact signed with the military in February 1976 and the constitution ratified in April of the same year. These set the country on a path of 'transition to socialism'. Membership was also an important weapon in the struggle against the PCP (Communist Party) and the radical elements in the Armed Forces Movement (MFA). For the other two parties, the need to strengthen the anti-communist alliance was of paramount importance. The CDS voted against the socialist constitution, while we can now say with the benefit of hindsight that the 'yes' vote of the PSD members was more of a tactical move at the time rather than an expression of real support for the principles it enshrined.

The ratification of the constitution and the elections of April 1976 marked the end of the revolutionary phase which after September 1974 had developed into a confrontation between the PCP and its allies in the MFA on the one hand and an anti-communist alliance led by the socialists on the other. The defeat of a left-wing *coup* in November 1975 also constituted a major defeat for the PCP and led to a purge of most radical elements in the army. In 1976 the socialists saw Portugal's entry into the Community, or at least its acceptance in principle, as a means of averting the danger of another *coup* from either left or right.[23]

Internal political stability is also closely linked with the external orientation of the country. Portugal had just lost its colonies and was seeking a new role which Europe could provide. Many members of the MFA had flirted with the idea of closer links with the Soviet Union and Comecon. Even more people seemed to be attracted by a Third World policy which became identified with Major Melo Antunes who had served as foreign minister. Therefore Portugal's economic and political integration into the European Community, coupled with its membership of NATO, would considerably reduce the likelihood of such dangerous experiments in the near future. Members of the PS were keen on drawing comparisons with other countries or regions, the example of which had to be avoided. Thus Mário Soares argued that isolation from the Community would mean that Portugal would end up as the Puerto Rico or the Cuba of Europe, alluding to a complete dependence on the United States or the Soviet Union. In another instance he referred to Mauritania as a model to be avoided, while for António Barreto (PS minister at the time) the danger was that Portugal would be turned into another Côte d'Azur.[24]

Membership of the Community became almost identified with Soares and his party, who were always eager to stress their links with Europe. One of the main slogans of the party in the 1976 election was 'Europa conosco' – 'Europe is with us'. Acceptance by the Community of the application for membership was seen as likely to bring major political gains to the party. One should bear in mind that the PS was heavily dependent, financially and otherwise, on the German Social Democrats and the Socialist International in general. This relationship may have already begun to be counterproductive for the party inside Portugal.

Though the initiative came from the socialist party, the issue of EC membership was approached with some scepticism and hesitation, particularly by the left wing of the PS. The *tiers-mondiste* ideology has strong roots in Portugal and this was again reflected in the policies of the government formed by Maria Lourdes Pintassilgo, which led the country to elections in December 1979. It is characteristic, for example, that a small political group to the left of the PS which later joined the party, namely the Group of Socialist Intervention, played an active role in the first two conferences of Mediterranean socialist parties. Even the PS had participated in the first conference in Barcelona. Although the leadership of the PS has in fact adopted a social democratic model, elements of a more radical socialism with a Third World orientation are still alive within its ranks. As a result it is not always easy for the left wing of the PS to reconcile its political and economic objectives, or even those of the Portuguese constitution, with the liberal philosophy of the Treaty of Rome. Sometimes the approach adopted is that in view of the degree of economic integration already achieved full membership presents itself as the best among very few politically feasible strategies. But there are always two implicit assumptions in the arguments presented by pro-marketeers, namely, that Portugal would be granted a long transitional period and large-scale economic aid; otherwise membership would not make sense in economic terms. Two aspects which have been particularly stressed are the rights of Portuguese migrant workers and access to

Community funds, which was seen as a means of avoiding the imposition of IMF policies in the future.

The pro-European stand of the PSD and the CDS, the two biggest parties within the Democratic Alliance, is based on somewhat different grounds from that of the socialist party. It is true that both share the pro-European and pro-Western ideology adopted by the PS leadership. The CDS, which is a member of the European Union of Christian Democrats, has had the fewest difficulties in following such a line. On the other hand the PSD, which would like to join the Socialist International although the magic key for opening this door is still kept by Mário Soares, has followed a strong nationalist policy under the leadership of Sa Carneiro. This policy could force the party to adopt a more qualified stand *vis-à-vis* the Community, particularly when the real problems start arising during the negotiations.

Support for the Soares initiative in 1976 was part of a wider strategy which aimed to consolidate the anti-communist alliance with European support and hence avoid a repetition of the events of 1975. But the future membership of the Community has also been seen by the PSD and the CDS as an opportunity to recover some of the ground lost during the heady days of the revolution. The European option means opting for a liberal democratic regime. The socialist constitution, which made provisions for extensive nationalisations and the exclusion of private entrepreneurs from the financial sector of the economy, was deemed to be incompatible with Community membership. Accession would necessitate major economic reforms such as the strengthening of private enterprise, the decollectivisation of farms in Alentejo and a more liberal policy towards foreign investment.[25] Community membership was not immediately linked with internal reforms. This link became clearly established around the end of 1978 when both the PSD and the CDS felt strong enough to attack the *acquis de la révolution*. It is very characteristic that one of the first statements made by Rui Almeida Mendes, who was appointed as the new Secretary of State of European Integration after the 1979 elections, was that the government would allow the establishment of private banks and insurance companies in order to meet its obligations as a future member of the Community.[26] On previous occasions the Commission had disappointed many people on the right and centre of the political spectrum by stating that the size of the public sector was certainly not incompatible with the Treaty of Rome, provided that EC competition rules were observed. This argument was also used by the socialists who denounced the *demagogia* of the right.[27]

On the other side of the fence the PCP, which has remained a revolutionary party with strong pro-Moscow leanings and little sympathy for the Eurocommunist policy pursued by its Spanish

comrades, has been adamant in its opposition to Community membership. Entry into the EC represents an important step in the 'capitalist
recuperation' of Portugal. The noises made by the PSD and the CDS
for a revision of the constitution are pointed to as confirmation of this
argument. The PCP naturally wants closer relations with
Comecon and the Third World. In some economic studies published in one of the party periodicals[28] – more than anything
published by the other parties on this subject – members of the PCP
paint a very grim picture of the effects of accession on Portuguese
industry and agriculture. They also do not share the optimism of many
pro-marketeers, which until 1980 still remained to be confirmed, that
membership would lead to massive economic aid from Western
Europe.

The representatives of private industry (CIP) also echo the views
expressed by the PSD and the CDS on the subject of Community
membership. The need to strengthen the role played by the private
sector and clarify the rules of the economic game, coupled with some
nostalgia for the past, was foremost in the minds of Portuguese
industrialists. But it was also realised that there would be many
casualties in the sector as a result of accession. The Confederation of
Portuguese Agriculture (CAP) has also expressed itself in favour of
membership for general political reasons, but has asked for a long
transitional period (ten to fifteen years) in order to protect and reform
this sector of the economy and avoid serious negative repercussions on
the balance of payments and the cost of living. The CAP consists
mainly of small landowners in the north. Its counterpart in the south
(STR) is controlled by the communist party and is, therefore, opposed
to membership. Exactly the same situation prevails in the trade union
movement. Intersindical–CGTP, by far the biggest organisation, is
controlled by the communists and is opposed to the EC for the reasons
given by the PCP, while the UGT, whose power lies mainly among
white-collar workers and is supported by the three other political
parties, has been strongly pro-European for obvious political reasons
and rather unclear – or perhaps hidden – economic reasons.

The decision to apply for membership of the Community was
clearly a political decision taken at a time when the regime was
extremely shaky and the economic situation alarming. This brought
the three biggest political parties together on a pro-European platform. But nobody seemed prepared to face the consequences of such a
decision in terms of public debate, concrete analyses and internal
reforms. The lack of experience of both the Portuguese administration
and the political leadership seemed to be one explanation; but the
internal crisis was by far the most important. There was also a
widespread belief that even a 'yes, in principle' answer from the

Community would help to consolidate the new political status quo in the country and nobody in the PS, PSD or CDS wanted a return to the 1974–5 situation. But this agreement on the preservation of the status quo, represented by the 1976 constitution, did not last for long. Membership of the Community came to be seen by political forces on the right as a means of strengthening their calls for internal change. There was also an implicit assumption in the arguments of all pro-marketeers, namely, that the Community would be generous in its negotiations with Portugal both in terms of the transitional period after accession as well as the size of its economic aid.

Given the political nature of the decision taken, it was also understandable that Portuguese political leaders had to emphasise the political dimension of the Community.[29] This may suggest that once it has become a member Portugal will follow the tradition of most small member countries of the Community and support closer political and economic integration. Pitta e Cunha[30] does not share this view and refers to the strong consciousness of national identity among the Portuguese. One might also add the long period of isolation as another contributing factor.

Sympathetic views towards a Third World policy and the difficulty in reconciling economic radicalism with the ideology of the Treaty of Rome help to explain the reserved attitude adopted by left-wing members of the socialist party, although this has not as yet been translated into outright opposition. The PSD and the CDS appear to be more unified and probably consistent in their support of Community membership. This was in fact confirmed by the big push given to Portugal's negotiations with the Community by the Sa Carneiro government after the 1979 elections. However, strong support of those two parties has been made easier in the absence of any real debate about the effects of accession on various groups of the society, such as small businessmen and farmers in the north. The nationalist line followed by the PSD may also boomerang in the future. There is however one fear which is strongly felt and shared by all parties, namely, the effects on the Portuguese economy of trade liberalisation between the two Iberian countries once both become members of the Community. This fear has long historical roots. For all these reasons, it seems very likely that if the negotiations drag on and the Community does not show enough flexibility then the consensus in the pro-marketeer camp will go through a very serious test.

Spain: The Politics of Consensus and After

After Greece and Portugal, the picture in Spain is almost dull. There is little in terms of internal political debate and the reason seems to be that everybody agrees about the desirability of Spain's accession to the Community. The first time that this subject was formally discussed in the Cortes was in June 1979 when the representatives of all political groups, from the neo-Francoists of Fraga Iribarne (CD) to the communists of Carillo (PCE) and from the Andalusian Socialists (PSA) to the Basque Christian Democrats (PNV), declared their faith in European unification and their eagerness to see Spain take an active part in this process. Agreement among the politicians is also reflected in Spanish public opinion. According to an opinion poll 67% of the people questioned were in favour of Spain's entry to the Community, only 7% were against and 28% fell in the 'don't know' category.[31] Moreover all the major interest groups, including industrialists, trade unionists and farmers, have also taken a favourable stand.

There are at least two important factors which help to explain this extraordinary unanimity in Spain. The first is the simple fact that the European option was decided by the Franco regime back in 1962 when Foreign Minister Castiella requested the opening of 'negotiations with a view to establishing an Association which could lead to full integration in due course'. The democratic opposition was also in favour of the European option but only under the condition that parliamentary democracy would be restored in Spain. Because this view was also adopted by the Community itself, Europe became almost a symbol of democracy for most Spaniards. Furthermore, entry into Europe and the end of international isolation came to be considered almost as an automatic reward which would follow the restoration of democracy. It would be like the return of the prodigal son to the family fold. In this respect the Spanish experience is very similar to that of Greece although as far as the latter is concerned this did not lead to agreement among all the major political forces. We have already referred to foreign policy and its effects on the Greek political scene as one explanatory factor. Differences in the economic structure of the two countries are also considerable. But probably the most important variable has been the direction of political developments in Spain and Greece, particularly on the left of the political spectrum.

Spain's transition to parliamentary democracy which followed Franco's death in November 1975 has been characterised by the politics of consensus among the major political forces of the country. This period was formally ended in May 1980 with the motion of censure against the government deposed by the Socialists. Some people have called this period 'government Italian style', others considered it a typical example of consociational democracy, while others denounced a situation where so many decisions are taken by a small clique of political leaders without any popular participation.[32] But irrespective of preferences or value judgements, it remains a fact that most important political acts in the transitional period were based on an agreement between the political leaders of the different parties. This was manifest in the ratification of the new constitution by the Cortes with 325 votes in favour, six against and fourteen abstentions; the Moncloa Pact of October 1977 which provided a comprehensive programme of economic recovery coupled with structural reforms; and the autonomy statutes for Catalonia and the Basque country, which later received an overwhelming majority in the referenda organised in the two regions. In all these cases the government of the UCD, led by Adolfo Suárez, worked in close collaboration with the two main opposition parties on its left (PSOE and PCE) and also with representatives of the regions.

Accession to the Community has been another example of consensus politics, which has survived the breakdown of the latter. All political parties emphasise the political dimension and objectives of the Community, although each one seems to have different expectations. Thus some people refer to the 'Europe of regions', others talk about the 'Europe of workers' or the 'Europe of peoples' or even the 'Europe of citizens'.[33] Nobody seems to support openly the 'Europe of monopolies', although the UCD, at least, espouses the liberal economic philosophy of the Treaty of Rome. Medina has argued that 'chacun pense qu'il va trouver à la Communauté ce qu'il cherche'.[34] For all political parties, except for the extreme right and left which do not agree with the final objective, Spain's integration into the Community will help to consolidate the new democratic regime. Although many people would argue that Spain needs Europe less than the other two applicants in political and economic terms, it is however true that the Spanish political class has to deal with two extremely difficult issues, namely, devolution in the form of regional autonomy statutes and political terrorism which comes mainly from the Basque organisation ETA. The Basque and Catalan regions have been given autonomy statutes but the elections for the regional parliaments resulted in a big defeat for the main national parties. Andalusian and Galician nationalism are also quite strong. There was a period when the Suárez government was clearly backtracking on its earlier promises on devolution but this seems to have come to an end when the government was forced to rely on the votes of regional parties in order to survive the Socialist motion of censure deposed in May 1980. Meanwhile, terrorist attacks have multiplied. There is a legitimate fear shared by many Spaniards that those factors may lead to an explosive situation which in turn could provoke a reaction from ultraconservative forces in the Spanish army. Membership of the Community is seen as a means of making such an eventuality more unlikely.

The central state in Spain now finds itself being pulled simultaneously in two opposite directions: internal devolution and a transfer of powers to the Community level. Regional representatives from Catalonia, the Basque country and Andalusia believe that regional autonomy will become easier within a wider European framework. Representatives of the poorer regions also hope for a substantial transfer of funds from Brussels or Luxembourg. Some 'enlightened' people in Madrid seem to hold a similar view, thinking that devolution would be politically more acceptable, while at the same time it may be easier to contain extreme centrifugal tendencies. The example of Belgium may have a great deal to teach us here.

Entry into Europe can also provide an opportunity and an excuse for internal economic and social reforms. The nature and extent of such reforms obviously depend on each one's political preferences. Thus the UCD hopes to modernise the economy and rationalise a system which suffers from the heavy burden of state bureaucracy. The socialists, and even the communists, want to bring about a European style of social democracy, at least in the medium term. As for the long term, Keynes's famous maxim may apply. They also hope that questions such as divorce and contraception, which inside Spain provoke great opposition from the Catholic Church, will be solved as Spain becomes involved in the more progressive mainstream of European political life. Moreover one encounters in Spain a real enthusiasm for European political integration which reminds one of the early days of the Community. The language used by many political leaders has not been heard in most member countries for quite some time. Thus the Community is something much more than the *acquis communautaire*. It also represents a political culture and a way of thinking which, through a process of osmosis, may be transmitted to a new member country. In this respect again the attitude is very similar to the one we have already found in Greece, at least as far as the pro-marketeers there are concerned. The main difference is that the left-wing parties in Spain have adopted a reformist ideology (social democracy in the case of the PSOE and Eurocommunism in the case of the PCE), while the Greek socialists and communists believe, or at least pretend to believe, that radical changes are both desirable and feasible. One could also add that the more advanced stage of Spanish industrialisation also explains, at least partly, the adoption of a reformist ideology.

The application for membership was lodged by the Suárez government in July 1977, only one month after the first general election in Spain since 1937. This has also coincided with a very active foreign policy which in terms of its general lines of orientation has not marked a radical departure from the policy followed by Franco. The main difference is that the margin of manoeuvre open to the Suárez government has been much wider. Thus the first democratic Spanish government, although reaffirming its ties with the West and the European Community in particular, has tried to strengthen its links with Latin America, the Arab countries and the Third World movement. Spain moved its membership from the European group in the IMF to the Latin American group, became a member of the Inter-American Bank, permanent observer at the Organisation of American States and the Andean Pact, and also asked for membership of the UN Economic Commission for Latin America (ECLA). It gave full recognition to the PLO while still refusing, together with Greece, to establish full diplomatic relations with Israel. The Suárez government also decided to participate as an observer at the summit of the non-aligned states held in Cuba in September 1979, an action which caused some irritation in Western capitals. All these initiatives have had the support of the parties to the left of the UCD, and were intended to develop fully the Latin American and Arab connections of Spain and thus put an end to the era during which Washington and the Vatican were the twin pillars of Spanish foreign policy.

Even in the heyday of consensus politics in Spain, there were important differences among political parties as manifested, for example, in the foreign policy field. Thus the UCD and the CD on its right have always seen Spain's membership of NATO as a necessary complement to economic integration into the Community. Nevertheless, in view of the socialist and communist opposition to NATO, Suárez is unlikely to rush over a decision.[35] It is also interesting that the PSOE is, not opposed to the renewal in 1981 of the bilateral agreement with the United States which would allow for the continuation of US military bases in Spain. In practical terms, this is more important for the Americans than the integration of the Spanish armed forces into NATO which is often viewed as the only firm guarantee of Spain's alignment with the West. This is exactly what brings about the split along the left/right dividing line in Spain.

The PSOE is sometimes presented as being in favour of a neutralist foreign policy, with a strong Third World orientation. Its support of the PLO and the Polisario Front in Sahara together with its opposition to NATO are taken as clear indications of this tendency. But at the same time there is wholehearted support for European unification and a tacit acceptance of US bases in the country. This apparent contradiction can be explained to a large extent in terms of internal divisions within the party itself which were highlighted by the crisis provoked in 1979 regarding the Marxist or non-Marxist nature of the party's ideology. The left wing of the party is more *tiers-mondiste* in its orientation, denounces social democracy and is also very critical of the Community as it now stands; none the less it adds that changes will have to be made from the inside, an attitude also adopted by the PCE.

It believes in some form of Mediterranean socialism, and it is not a coincidence that the first conference of Mediterranean socialist parties was held in Barcelona in November 1976 and was organised by two small Spanish parties including the PSP of Tierno Galván who later joined the PSOE and became its chairman. The PSOE also sees the second round of enlargement as a means of shifting the balance of power within the Community towards the South. At the same time there is an external countervailing force which together with internal Spanish politics brings the PSOE nearer to European social democracy, namely, the influence exerted by the German SPD and the Socialist International, mainly through financial means.

For the PCE, support for Spain's accession to the Community is part and parcel of the Eurocommunist strategy followed by its leadership.[36] The first time that the party expressed itself in favour of signing an agreement with the Community was in 1964. During Franco's dictatorship Spain's relations with the Community provided a powerful weapon with which the PCE could attack the regime. The position of the Spanish communists on Europe is not very different from that developed by their Italian comrades some years ago.[37] European integration is seen as a political and economic reality. Socialism in one country the size of Spain or Italy is no longer feasible. Thus one should work within Community institutions in alliance with like-minded parties in order to go beyond free trade and negative integration. Carillo, who has been extremely critical of the Soviet Union, would like to see Europe emerging as a third force between the two superpowers, an objective which also seems to be shared by the PSOE. The Spanish communists have also accused their French comrades of opportunism and demagogy in their opposition to Spain's entry to the Community.[38]

The general agreement about the issue of membership and preoccupation with internal problems have meant that the internal political debate about the Community has so far been very restricted. The first debate in the parliament took place almost two years after the application made by the Suárez government which was criticised for this delay on both its left and right. The speeches made by representatives of the different parties showed political realism and sufficient knowledge of the main issues involved. This also seems to apply to the Spanish administration and the business community or at least those directly involved with Community matters.[39] In starting its negotiations with the Community, Spain was better prepared than Greece and certainly Portugal in terms of background work and technical studies. Studies which had already been completed by 1979 on the effects of accession on Spanish industry and agriculture were more advanced than the corresponding work in Greece after the end of its own negotiations and miles ahead of what the Portuguese thought they should undertake in the future. Since the time of Franco the business community has been more closely involved in negotiations with the Community than its counterpart in Greece. The various business organisations such as the Confederación de Organizaciones Empresariales, the CEPYME which represents small and medium enterprises and the chambers of commerce have long since been in favour of membership. However a business survey conducted by the Ministry of Industry has revealed that in many sectors of Spanish industry there is much anxiety about the level of competitiveness and the likely effects of trade liberalisation with Community countries.[40] It is not surprising, therefore, that they have asked for a long transitional period after accession. The two main trade unions, the Workers' Commissions (CC.OO), controlled by the communists, and the UGT, controlled by the socialists, are also in the pro-marketeer camp. Last but not least the farmers' organisations such as the CNAG and the CNJA, as well as the chambers of agriculture, have adopted positions similar to those of the business community. They are in favour of an early accession but naturally enough they would like a long transitional period for sensitive sectors such as meat, dairy products and sugar. The Spanish government has opted for a uniform transitional period for all sectors which would be nearer the ten-year maximum set out by the Commission (see also Chapter 3).

The Spanish public, although ill informed, has been carefully educated to view entry into Europe as a great step forward. It seemed somewhat surprised that the Spanish application is facing so many problems, particularly in neighbouring France, since it was always made to believe by the other Europeans and Spanish democratic forces that the only obstacle to Spain's membership was Franco's dictatorial regime. The statements made by Giscard d'Estaing in June 1980, in which he asked for a 'pause' in the enlargement negotiations, provoked a strong reaction from all political forces in Spain. The UCD spoke of demagogy and political opportunism, while the correspondent of *El Pais* in Paris wrote about the transformation of the political consensus in Spain in favour of entry into a consensus against France.[41] One may wonder at this stage which political party, if any, is likely to qualify its stand on Europe if the negotiations approach some deadlock or seek to give political expression to economically disaffected groups after accession.

Democratic Institutions and Economic Prosperity after Accession

The three applications for membership were among the first foreign policy initiatives taken by the new democratic governments: a fact which indicates the political and economic importance of the Community for the three Southern European countries. Nevertheless one could also argue that once Greece had applied for membership the process became almost self-reinforcing because each Iberian country expected the other to apply and none could afford to be left out of a second round of enlargement, if there were to be one.

Entry into Europe was clearly a high policy decision. It meant a choice of a political and economic regime and a framework within which the foreign policy of each country would be exercised. It also implied a decision to integrate themselves more closely into a family of nations with which the three applicants felt they had a close cultural affinity. Economic issues seemed to be secondary, although the distinction from so-called political issues is rather artificial. It is true that the Community looks much bigger from the outside than from within; it also appears more of a political entity than it may actually be. Moreover the experience of Greece, the only country which has so far completed its entry negotiations, suggests that mundane economic issues become increasingly important as real bargaining about the adoption of the *acquis communautaire* comes to replace general discussions about high principles.

Pro-marketeers in the three countries have associated membership with the strengthening of democratic institutions. But much will depend on the success of integration of the three economies into the Community and the creation of strong groups of interest, representing large sections of the society, which would stand to lose from an abrupt change in relations with other member countries. After all, successful *coups d'état* do not usually come about because a few army officers are dissatisfied with the running of state affairs. As time goes by and the new democratic regimes become more consolidated, the argument about the preservation of democracy will lose much of its strength. In fact what many people often have in mind is the preservation of, or return to, a certain political and economic status quo which is associated with particular political parties. This was evident in Portugal and Greece and to a large extent explained the support given to membership by the business community.

Forces on the right and centre of the political spectrum have not had any great difficulty in supporting the European option which was entirely compatible with their Western orientation and their preference for a mixed economic order. Although the mixture does not have to be and has not actually been identical in all countries, it is however true that membership of the Community as well as the acceptance of economic interdependence and the opening of national economies do impose certain constraints on national economic policy.

In the beginning European integration was mainly based on the support of conservative and liberal forces. One of the major successes of the European experiment has been that parties on the left have become gradually integrated into the whole process. This has meant, for example, that the French socialists and the Italian communists have come to recognise the advantages and accepted the constraints of economic interdependence. As a result they have decided to operate within the system and try to change it from inside. This has usually gone hand-in-hand with the adoption of some form of reformist ideology under the name of social democracy or even Eurocommunism, without the two being necessarily identical.

The economic and political conditions in the three applicant countries are substantially different from those prevailing in the core of Western Europe. Their level of economic development is much lower and their regional disequilibria and income inequalities are wider – probably a function of the dualistic structure of the economy. Such economic ground is not usually very fertile for reformist ideas. Moreover long periods of right-wing dictatorships can breed left-wing radicalism and, in the case of the three applicants, some cynicism about the attachment of other Western countries to democratic ideals when they are applied to foreigners. In addition the political class – at least in the two Iberian countries – is relatively inexperienced, the communist parties have only recently emerged from the underground and the trade union movements remain, after long periods of persecution, relatively underdeveloped. One can argue that in those three countries there is a juxtaposition of a powerful state apparatus and an extremely weak civil society. This means that there are very few transmission belts between the state, including the top political class, and the general public. We should not therefore be surprised that the political process is very different from that found in modern industrialised and welfare societies. As far as foreign policy is concerned, here again, geographical position, recent history and economic factors such as the level of development and the structure of the economy should again make those countries more receptive to Third World ideas than any existing member of the Community.

Such factors as those mentioned above cannot determine political developments in advance, although they could be seen as setting the boundaries within which the political system can operate. A number of other factors should also be taken into account. For example, the type of transition from dictatorship to democracy, exogenous political factors and, probably even more important, the role of personalities such as González, Papandreou or Soares, if we just limit ourselves to the socialist parties.

Europeanism as an ideology apart, it is not immediately obvious why, at least on economic grounds, a socialist or communist party should favour the accession of its country into a Community where the main emphasis still lies on market integration rather than common policies or transfer of resources. Probably the strongest argument is a negative one, namely, that the three economies are already heavily dependent on the Community, mainly in terms of trade and investment. Full membership would enable these countries to translate this economic integration/dependence into political integration and participation in the decision-making system. This argument implies either that the cost of total or partial withdrawal from the international division of labour – where the Community plays such an important role for the three applicants – is prohibitive, or that radical solutions are not politically feasible. The two arguments are overlapping rather than mutually exclusive. As long as the Community remains as it now stands, support from left-wing political forces will continue to be based on negative rather than positive arguments.

One common characteristic we found in all three countries is the importance attached to the so-called bridge theory. Thus the Greeks believe that their country will serve as a bridge connecting Western Europe with the Balkans and, even more important, with the Middle East. The Spaniards believe exactly the same with respect to Latin America and the Portuguese with respect to their ex-colonies in Africa and also Brazil. They all argue that such links with other parts of the world will, after accession, bring benefits to existing member countries as well as to themselves. In typical Mediterranean fashion it is sometimes said that this is an important part of the dowry that each country is bringing to the marriage. But brides often tend to exaggerate the value of their dowry! Greece, Portugal and Spain certainly have an interest in developing their relations with other areas with which they may have geographical proximity or historical ties. It is also quite likely that their bargaining power will be strengthened once they become members of the Community. It is much less obvious why countries such as the Federal Republic of Germany, France or Britain need wait for their accession in order to use them as launching boards for their economic operations in the Middle East, Latin America or Africa. In fact there is precious little evidence to support the various versions of the bridge theory.

The three countries attach much importance to the political dimension of the Community. They are also unlikely to resist a transfer of powers to the supranational level. Political union, as the final objective of European integration, enjoys a more enthusiastic reception in the three Mediterranean countries than, for example, in those which joined the Community in 1973; although this statement needs some qualification when it is applied to Portugal and the Greek left. Another characteristic of the three newcomers is their expectations about the role which Europe should play in the international scene, particularly *vis-à-vis* the United States. In this respect they are likely to be more Gaullist than most existing members of the Community.

Many pro-marketeers have associated membership with internal political and economic reforms which the previous dictatorial regimes have proved unwilling or unable to bring about. The international economic crisis and now accession to the Community add considerably to the urgency of such a task. If membership leads to increased economic prosperity it will also help to strengthen democracy and boost political support for European integration. This will depend on the international economic environment, Community policies and internal developments in the three new members. If it fails then democracy is also likely to suffer, and this would defeat the whole purpose of the second round of enlargement.

3

Negotiations and Community Attitudes

Before the Community had had the time to digest the effects of the first round of enlargement in 1973, when Britain, Ireland and Denmark became full members, it was faced with a second round of enlargement, this time moving southwards. The political and economic characteristics of the three new applicants as well as the particular conjuncture at which it happened made the second round of enlargement very different from the first. The Greek application, lodged in June 1975, caught the Community almost unprepared. It was not until 1977, when the two Iberian countries were already joining the queue, that the first attempts were made at Community level to develop some form of comprehensive policy on the subject. The fall of the three dictatorships on the European side of the Mediterranean drastically changed the political map of Europe. The Nine seemed to have been taken by surprise when they discovered that their Community constituted a strong pole of attraction for its southern neighbours and that it was expected to play an active role in the area. From the two previous chapters it should be clear that Greece, Portugal and Spain are different animals, in political and economic terms, from those countries which joined in 1973, although they should be more easily digestible than Britain. Another characteristic was the different timing of the three applications, which meant that neither global negotiations nor simultaneous entry could be taken for granted. Moreover, unlike the first round of enlargement, none of the three applicants made its membership dependent on the successful conclusion of negotiations of any other country. Last but not least, the three applications came at a time of economic crisis for the whole of the industrialised West. The Community found itself in a state of disarray after the failure of the Economic and Monetary Union (EMU) and the inability of member countries to adopt a joint stand on the energy issue. The much-publicised Tindemans Report on European Union was soon turned into a *tabula rasa*. Although the three applications could be seen as the best form of flattery for a Community which was undergoing a period of stagnation, it is also true that the time was not very opportune for a new enlargement.

The Community's decision-making system is a continuous process of negotiation frequently based on complicated package deals which produce a very delicate balance of profits and losses on each item for every member country or pressure group. The entry of new members is bound to upset these delicate balances of interest and lead to a redistribution of costs and benefits. Therefore, on every issue there will be both defenders of the status quo and those who would like to use enlargement as an opportunity to bring about desired changes. We propose here to examine the reactions of the member countries to the three applications, the interests involved and how these were expressed in terms of Community policies. Enlargement can provide us with an interesting case-study of EC external relations and the role which the Community now plays on the international scene, particularly in Southern Europe. There is however an important qualification, namely, that enlargement is on the boundary between external relations and domestic politics, since negotiations lead to full membership and the adoption of the *acquis communautaire*. We also propose to examine the issues which have arisen in relation to enlargement and the various linkages made by member countries and interest groups.

This chapter is in one sense an interim report on the second round of enlargement. It is written at a time when Greece's Treaty of Accession has been ratified by all national parliaments. Thus unless there is a dramatic political change in Greece itself the Community of Ten is already a political reality. As far as Spain and Portugal are concerned the applications for membership have been welcomed in principle but negotiations are still in the preliminary stage. The most optimistic prediction is that negotiations will be completed by the end of 1981 so that the two Iberian countries could become members in 1983. Thus the second round of enlargement, unlike the first, will be a gradual process, the full impact of which, including the transitional periods after accession, will extend into the 1990s.

The Setting of the Stage

In the beginning there was only Greece. The two Iberian countries did not enter the scene as potential candidates for membership until after Franco's death in November 1975 and the Portuguese elections of April 1976, thus changing the picture completely. Therefore for almost two years the only question under consideration was Greece's entry into the Community and, because of the small size of the country, it was expected to have a marginal effect on the Community itself.

The Karamanlis government of national unity expressed for the first time its intention to apply for membership in August 1974, less than a month after the dramatic events in Cyprus, provoked by the *coup d'état* engineered by the Greek junta which led to the Turkish invasion of Cyprus, the fall of the dictatorship in Greece and the partial withdrawal of Greece from NATO. Greece's declared aim to apply for membership immediately presented the Community with two problems, which were most acutely felt by the Federal Republic of Germany and the UK. Greece's entry would upset the delicate balance which the Community had always tried to maintain between the two 'uneasy allies' in the Eastern Mediterranean since the two association agreements signed in 1961 and 1963 respectively.[1] Given the tension in Greek–Turkish relations over the Cyprus issue and the Aegean, this was seen as a particularly inopportune moment to upset the balance, especially since the Nine were trying to play an active role as a moderator in the Cyprus dispute. Moreover the Karamanlis government seemed to consider Europe as an alternative to NATO and the country's previous dependence on the United States. Neither the British nor the Germans were keen on encouraging such an approach. *Le Monde* was particularly cynical when it referred to France's leaning towards the Greek side:[2]

> Mais cependant le recours qu'il [M. Giscard d'Estaing] offre à M. Caramanlis retient les Grecs dans le camp occidental, pendant que les Etats-Unis, plus intéressés par la grande importance que présente la Turquie pour la défense en Mediterrannée orientale, dispersent leurs faveurs à Ankara. On peut donc parler autant de partage des rôles que de rivalité.

Such an analysis was consistent with conspiracy theories developed in Greece itself.

The possibility of Greece's membership of the Community was met with some incredulity and an obvious lack of enthusiasm by all member countries. The only exception was France which acted all along as Greece's main supporter within the Community. The decision was taken to reactivate the association agreement but there was little that the Nine could offer, since they were not prepared to meet Greece's demands in the agricultural field. Karamanlis, in his tour of European capitals which preceded the submission of Greece's application and was to become a regular pattern in subsequent years, managed to persuade the leaders of member countries on one important point, namely, that Community membership was the only way of keeping Greece in the West and ensuring political stability in the country. The application was submitted on 12 June 1975, after the British referendum.

The Community countries became closely involved in political developments in Portugal after the 1974 revolution. They tried to co-ordinate their policies within the European Political Committee (EPC) and used the 1972 Agreement and economic aid as a lever with which to influence political events. This became particularly important after the first elections of April 1975 during the period of major confrontation between the communists and radical elements in the MFA on the one hand and the socialist-led alliance on the other. This was the time when European policies towards Portugal differed substantially from the policy followed by Henry Kissinger, who seemed rather to have given up hope of preventing the Portuguese communists from taking power and was falling back on the thought that this might frighten the rest of Western Europe away from Eurocommunism. The leading role within the Community was played by the Federal Republic which on this occasion preferred a multilateral to a bilateral framework. Nevertheless the Socialist International and the German Social Democrats in particular seem to have played the most decisive role. In 1974 it was Commissioner Spinelli, François Mitterrand and the Dutch prime minister who expressed the hope that Portugal would eventually join the Community. But this became politically feasible only after April 1976. Meanwhile negotiations with Franco's Spain had been broken off in September 1975 following the execution of Basque political prisoners.

The Commission's opinion on the Greek application,[3] put forward in January 1976, was in clear contrast to the positive responses and the assurances given to Karamanlis by political leaders in the nine countries. The Commission proposed some form of pre-accession period of indefinite duration for the introduction or acceleration of necessary reforms. The emphasis was placed firmly on the economic difficulties likely to arise both for the Community and for Greece. The Commission also expressed concern over the consequences of Greek membership for the Community's relations with Turkey. There were rumours that the idea of a pre-accession period and the references to the political situation in the Eastern Mediterranean were added at the last minute by the Cabinet of Christopher Soames. If this was so it is difficult to imagine that such an initiative did not have the backing of the British government. The Commission was divided and the four French and Italian members, who were in a minority in favouring early Greek entry, expressed their opposition in public.

The Commission's opinion on the Greek application was the first attempt to postpone Greece's accession. It is not clear whether and to what extent the majority of Commissioners were influenced by the prospect, still uncertain, of a Spanish and a Portuguese application in the future. But they certainly shared the hesitation and scepticism of most member governments which for political reasons could not afford to express their feelings in public. The French and the Italians were very critical of the majority decision in favour of a pre-accession period. *Corriere della Sera* argued that their decision marked another step towards the creation of a Community of two tiers, explained the implications for Italy and continued in Dantean fashion: 'La strada del paradiso europeo passa necessariamente per un purgatorio mediter- raneo.'[4] In Greece the Commission's opinion was seen as blackmail and prevailing attitudes were summarised in the headlines of the newspaper *To Vima*: 'NATO and Turkey shut the door of the EEC.'[5] Karamanlis threatened to withdraw Greece's application and exer- cised direct pressure on member governments. The French govern- ment strongly criticised the Commission's opinion and called for the rejection of the idea of a pre-accession period. Other member governments immediately followed suit with public statements sup- porting Greece's immediate entry. Finally the Council of Ministers unanimously rejected the Commission's proposals despite the objec- tions which had been initially raised at the meeting by Britain, Denmark and Belgium.[6] According to many journalists the lack of enthusiasm for Greece's entry was compensated for by the simple fact that no member government wanted to be seen as opposing it. Reginald Dale of the *Financial Times* drew this to its logical conclusion when he wrote: 'If Greece becomes a member, it will be largely by default.'[7]

The Plot Thickens

Soon after the political decision had been taken to open up negoti- ations with Greece, people in the Community realised that an application from Spain, as well as from Portugal, was no longer a remote possibility. Instead it became an imminent danger and suddenly policy makers woke up to the reality of a second round of enlargement. The rhetoric on Western democratic ideals gradually gave way to heated discussions about the price of peaches and olive oil as farmers' organisations, and subsequently others, began reacting to the new reality. This in turn made governments sensitive to the immediate implications of enlargement. The first people to voice their fears were farmers in the south of France and Italy who felt threatened by competition from the low-priced products of the applicant countries, particularly those from Spain. Those fears can be under- stood only if they are seen in the context of the market organisation which applies to most Mediterranean products and which has been the cause of serious grievances in the past (see also Chapter 5). Enlarge- ment offered an opportunity to redress an old imbalance between temperate and Mediterranean products by strengthening the market organisation for the latter and increasing protection *vis-à-vis* third countries.

At the same time the debate on Mediterranean agriculture raised a much wider issue, namely, the disequilibrium between northern and southern regions in the Community, which would be worsened by enlargement. This involved discussions about regional and industrial policy and also about the general economic philosophy behind European integration. Once the first file was opened, others quickly followed. In the end enlargement provided 'a convenient new peg on which to hang old arguments'.[8] Governments and pressure groups started creating a linkage between enlargement and their own favourite issues concerning changes in Community policies and institutions. Moreover, as the files were opened and studied, grand gestures and long-term geopolitical considerations gave way to second thoughts and concentration on immediate issues. In France, where the farmers' reaction was very strong and where political parties were entering a long-drawn-out electoral campaign, enlargement soon became a major political issue. Both the Rassemblement pour la République (RPR), the Gaullist party led by Jacques Chirac, and the Communists (PCF), came out openly against the entry of the three Mediterranean countries. But although enlargement did not become an overt political issue in other Community countries, it was soon obvious that there was growing apprehension almost everywhere. Because very few political leaders were prepared to adopt a clear negative stand in public, various ingenious formulas were invented which sought to postpone enlargement or at least delay some of its economic effects.

The French were the first to talk of *préalables* (preconditions); their favourite subject was naturally Mediterranean agriculture. They were also the first to introduce the idea of 'globalisation', which for many people came to mean joint negotiations with the three applicants and simultaneous entry. For the Greeks this meant that their accession would be put off *ad calendas Graecas*. What the French rather insisted upon was a *globalisation de réflexion* or, as some cynics would put it, 'globalisation under the table'! The French argued that the Community needed to study the cumulative effects of the entry of three new members on Community institutions and economic policies and try to find solutions to the problems created. Such solutions would be a precondition for enlargement. Another idea put forward was that transitional periods, following accession, would be of indefinite duration while negotiations leading to the full integration of a new member into the Community would take place by stages. This idea was first put forward by Pierre Uri in an article in *Le Monde*[9] and later taken up by Commissioner Natali in a report to his fellow Commissioners in September 1977. The Belgians suggested the idea of an intermediate status between associate and full member for the three applicants, with participation in the EPC, while as late as October 1979 the RPR in France thought that participation in the European Council might be more attractive to the applicants and thus persuade them to wait longer for full membership. The Irish wanted to make institutional reforms a precondition for enlargement and they received strong support from their Benelux partners and the Commission. The British Foreign Minister, David Owen, called for an amendment to the Treaty of Rome which would give a clear definition of pluralist democracy and would make provision for the expulsion of a member country if and when the necessary democratic conditions ceased to apply. The relaunching of EMU was also linked with enlargement. The first step was taken by Roy Jenkins in his Florence University speech in October 1977. It was later taken up by the Commission in its so-called 'fresco' (see below). This created a feeling of *déjà vu*, since EMU had already been linked with the first enlargement in 1969–73. Last but not least, the Community's relations with Turkey were directly connected with the second round of enlargement and especially with Greece's application for membership.

The first opportunity that the foreign ministers of the Nine had to discuss in some depth the problems raised by enlargement and try to define a common policy was at the Leeds Castle meeting in May 1977. This was one month after Soares had submitted Portugal's application for membership, despite the attempts made by some governments, particularly the French and the Belgian, to discourage him from this move.

Greece had a very slow start in its negotiations with the Community, which were finally opened in July 1976. The Greeks asked for a five-year transitional period, with the precedent of Britain, Ireland and Denmark in mind. But early in 1977 they suddenly discovered that the formula adopted for the first enlargement was no longer taken for granted. People were suddenly talking of flexibility and transitional periods of indefinite duration. At the same time the spectre of globalisation loomed in the background. In January 1977 the Greeks changed their negotiating team as well as their negotiating tactics. The urgent need to speed up the negotiations was combined with the growing realisation that Greece's insistence on the *acquis d'association* would not lead very far because this approach was strongly challenged by the Community.

In June 1977 French representatives vetoed a rather innocuous Commission paper addressed to the Greeks and the French Minister of Agriculture, Pierre Méhaignerie, insisted on changes in the market organisations for fruit, vegetables and wine prior to Greece's accession. This veto was lifted ten days later when the French changed the emphasis and talked about agricultural reforms which would take place *parallèlement* with Greece's negotiations. There were some indications that the famous co-ordination of French Community policy was under stress again, with high policy considerations on the one hand and concern about domestic economic interests on the other, pulling it in opposite directions. The same problem appeared in Italy where the Minister of Agriculture, Giovanni Marcora, expressed himself strongly against enlargement unless there was a radical reform of the policies applying to Mediterranean agriculture, while the prime minister and the minister of foreign trade made every effort to persuade their corresponding numbers in the three Southern European capitals that this was not the official policy of Italy.[10] However, despite the fact that the various preconditions did not apply to Greece's accession while globalisation had been rejected in theory very little progress was made in the negotiations until the end of 1977. The November elections in Greece, which witnessed the big rise of PASOK, and Karamanlis's tour of the European capitals in January 1978 finally persuaded member governments that negotiations could not drag on indefinitely. It was only then that the real negotiations began.

The Spanish application, submitted in July 1977, met with a very cautious welcome. The Belgian President-in-office, Henri Simonet, said: 'We must not deceive ourselves that negotiations will be easy. The path ahead is strewn with pitfalls.'[11] The debate about enlargement had already reached its climax in France and Italy, although Italy's internal political situation made its treatment of this subject substantially different from that of France. The reform of the CAP applying to Mediterranean products was at the top of the agenda, with proposals from farmers' associations and the Commission as well as the French and Italian governments already lying on the Council's table (see also subsequent sections and Chapter 5). Moreover, as we have already seen, other governments had joined in the discussion about enlargement with their own contributions and preconditions. Thus at the time when the Spanish application was submitted the Community gave the impression of an orchestra in which each member was playing a different tune with little hope of achieving harmony.

In a meeting of the college of Commissioners in September 1977 enlargement was one of the main topics of discussion. Commissioner Natali submitted a report which was the first real attempt to adopt a global approach to the three applications for membership. Natali argued that a long transitional period would be needed for full membership and he adopted Uri's idea of *une négociation par étapes*. He then went on to argue that a co-ordinated effort would be needed during the intermediate period to reduce the economic gap between the existing member countries and the three applicants and to solve some of the problems arising from enlargement. He called for the setting up of a special fund for all Mediterranean regions of the Community of Twelve as well as for other countries in the area which had in the past signed co-operation agreements with the Community. The resources would be used to boost industrial investment, with the emphasis on complementarity between northern and southern regions. The objective was to avoid an expansion in sectors such as textiles, steel and shipbuilding where Community industry already suffered from surplus capacity. In agriculture the emphasis was laid on structural aid, diversification of production and improvement of infrastructure, as opposed to price support which might lead to more surpluses. Thus Natali leaned towards the Italian rather than the French proposals; he was after all an ex-minister of agriculture in Italy.

Natali's report was rejected by the other Commissioners, while causing fury in the applicant countries and leading to threats of resignation by the Italian Commissioner. The indefinite postponement of accession was certainly not welcomed by the three applicants; nor were existing member countries prepared to undertake the economic burden which Natali considered as necessary for the success of the whole operation. The idea of a solidarity fund for the Mediterranean regions was also discussed in SPD circles, while Geoffrey Rippon talked about a European Marshall plan for the areas. As William Wallace has put it, such an initiative would help to transform a zero-sum game of bargaining into a completely different political exercise.[12] At the time of writing none of these ideas for special economic aid have so far materialised into anything concrete.

In Search of a Happy Ending

The French parliamentary elections held in March 1978 constituted a turning point. Until then it had proved virtually impossible to reach a clear political decision at the Community level since enlargement had become an important issue in the electoral campaign. One month after the victory of the 'majority' in France, the Commission published its so-called fresco on enlargement, which consisted of three separate documents.[13] These documents were a compromise after long and difficult negotiations within the Commission itself. The Brussels executive emphasised the need to give a positive answer to the three applicant countries and also not to delay unduly the time of accession.

The duration of transitional periods would be a minimum of five and a maximum of ten years, possibly in two stages. This meant that all proposals which had been put forward in the course of 1977 and which were intended to delay enlargement or at least some of its economic effects were finally rejected. It is true that the formula of a single five-year transitional period was also abandoned; but this was compatible with the demands of the Spaniards and the Portuguese. As for the contents of the transitional periods, they could only be decided during the accession negotiations. The Commission was especially concerned to propose solutions which would enable the Community to escape the dilemma of *élargissement* versus *approfondissement*. Enlargement was closely linked with progress towards EMU, with structural reforms particularly on the applicants' side and with some modest institutional reforms. Some of the ideas had first appeared in the Natali Report. As far as aid was concerned, the Commission thought that the Community instruments already available would be sufficient to deal with Greece's and Spain's accession. Special aid would only be needed for Portugal whose level of development was much lower. The Commission analysed many of the problems which were likely to arise for both sides as a result of enlargement. In view of the conflicts of interest involved it saw two broad alternatives: (i) the systematic use of safeguards during and after the transitional periods and (ii) the adoption of a global strategy and a multi-annual action programme which would aim at reconciling the Community's medium-term economic objectives with the structural measures required as a result of enlargement. The first alternative was undesirable because it would lead to the dilution of the Community. As far as the second was concerned, the Commission steered clear of any specific suggestions.

The Commission's fresco meant that the political decision on enlargement had finally been taken. This was also confirmed by the two opinions on the Portuguese and Spanish applications, which followed shortly after. The first major hurdle, namely, the French elections, had already been overcome. In May 1978 the Council of Ministers adopted a package of measures on Mediterranean agriculture which were intended to meet French and Italian demands halfway (see also Chapter 5). At the same time the whole atmosphere in the Community began to change as the French and German governments took the initiative for the setting up of the European Monetary System (EMS). This combination of events meant that enlargement ceased to be the emotive issue it had been a few months before.

The Commission's opinion on Portugal was submitted in May 1978.[14] This, together with the opinion on Spain, was prepared in consultation both with the applicant countries and the existing members in order to avoid a repetition of the Greek experience. The

Commission stressed the need for an unequivocal 'yes' to the Portuguese application, and then went on to emphasise the urgency of radical economic and social reforms which would enable the country to withstand the consequences of membership. The 'yes, in principle' was actually given by the Council of Ministers and negotiations were formally opened in October 1978.

The tone of the Commission's opinion on Spain, submitted in November 1978,[15] was substantially different. Although the Commission recommended the opening of negotiations leading to accession, the emphasis was clearly on the problems of adjustment for both sides. It was obvious that only Spain's accession could have a sizeable effect on various sections of Community industry and agriculture and this was accentuated because of the recession. The Council of Ministers agreed to have the formal opening of the negotiations in February 1979 but took the unusual decision, at the insistence of the French government, that there would be no substantive talks before the two sides agreed on a 'common basis' for the negotiations. This ensured that the real negotiations would not start before the European Parliament elections in June 1979.

Negotiations with Greece reached their most active phase in the second semester of 1978, when the Commission started to present the Community position on the transitional period, particularly as regards agriculture. It was only then that the real political negotiations took place. In the final compromise a five-year transitional period was adopted, with three exceptions, namely, peaches, tomatoes and free movement of labour (a very interesting combination indeed), for which a seven-year period would apply. It was also agreed that Greece must not become a net contributor to the budget during the transitional period. Given the atmosphere in which the negotiations had taken place and the nature of the Community proposals until December 1979, the final outcome was an almost unexpected success for the Greek side. The three exceptions from the five-year transitional period, which had become almost an obsession for the Greeks, seemed to be intended more as a precedent to be used by the Community with the other two applicant countries than as specific cases important in their own right.

The ratification of Greece's Accession Treaty was almost unanimous in the nine parliaments, with one exception of special significance for the two Iberian countries. The French National Assembly ratified the treaty with 264 votes cast in favour and 204 against, after an extraordinary debate during which references to the Acropolis, Solon and Greek culture were mixed with expressions of fear about pears, aubergines and courgettes.[16] The Giscardians (UDF), together with the large majority of the Gaullists (RPR), faced the solid opposition of the socialists and the communists. It is true that the opposition of the PS was remarkably lukewarm and some people thought that the socialists had decided to vote against Greece's accession only because they knew that there were sufficient votes in the ranks of the majority for the treaty to be ratified. However this was not a good omen for the two Iberian countries, especially if one takes into account the repeated statements made by Jacques Chirac who said 'no' to enlargement but 'yes' to Greece. The prospects for an early completion of the second round of enlargement started looking even grimmer in June 1980 when Giscard d'Estaing, addressing the annual meeting of the French chambers of agriculture, linked the future accession of Spain and Portugal with the problems presented by the renegotiation of Britain's budgetary contribution. He then argued that the Community should bring the first enlargement to completion, implying that Britain at least was not as yet fully integrated, before it deals with the second.[17] Although a French veto on Spain's or Portugal's accession may in the absence of General de Gaulle seem rather unlikely, it is still very possible that accession negotiations may be extremely complicated and unduly prolonged.

In the meantime political changes inside Turkey produced the possibility that the Community would soon be faced with yet another applicant country. We have mentioned that Greece's application for membership meant for many people – it was explicitly stated by the Commission itself – that the delicate balance which the Community had always tried to keep between Athens and Ankara would be completely upset. The Turkish Prime Minister, Suleyman Demirel, denounced the Greek move as 'a political act aimed at getting a new international platform against Turkey'.[18] Once the principle of Greece's membership was accepted the Commission tried to link the opening of negotiations with Greece with new talks which would lead to the reactivation of the Ankara Agreement of 1963. But the inability of Community countries to meet Turkish demands, including economic aid, further concessions for agricultural and industrial exports and the free entry of more Turkish migrant workers, coupled with the growing deterioration of the Turkish economy, led to a continuous worsening of relations between the two sides. In September 1978 the Ecevit government finally decided to freeze the association agreement. Meanwhile Turkey had asked to be admitted to the EPC in order to avoid a situation in which Greece, as a full member, would use this forum to promote its interests as far as the Greek–Turkish dispute was concerned. The British Foreign Minister, David Owen, with strong American support, asked for Turkey to be admitted to meetings where subjects of interest to both countries would be discussed. This was strongly resisted by France and finally rejected by the majority of foreign ministers of the Nine in June 1978. Instead a compromise was reached whereby Turkey would be informed of any decision affecting its interests. The 'troika' formula was then invented, which meant that the country which held the presidency, together with its successor and predecessor, would jointly inform the Turks. This was to avoid a situation in which the Greeks alone would have to represent the Community in such meetings.

The return of Demirel to power in November 1979 changed the picture again. His switch towards an unqualified pro-Western policy was coupled with the adoption of drastic IMF prescriptions, calls for liberalisation of the economy and massive Western aid, and clear hints that Turkey would apply soon for full membership of the Community. One was told that Turkey wanted to apply before January 1981 so as to avert any possibility of a Greek veto. However this argument did not hold true because even if the application were submitted on time, Greece could still have exercised its veto power at any stage of the negotiations. A cynical observer might add that the Greeks, assuming that they wanted to keep Turkey out, could safely leave it to their future partners to do the dirty work.

In July 1980 the Community and Turkey agreed on a revision of the 1963 Agreement. This included improved concessions on Turkish agricultural exports, increased financial aid and a better deal for Turkish workers already in Community countries. The Community's final offer fell far short of Turkey's requests, especially as regards the free movement of labour and the amount of financial aid. However an agreement was eventually reached between the two sides. In February of the same year the Nine had also agreed that Turkey was entitled to apply for membership 'at a later date', although it was obvious that an immediate Turkish application would have been highly embarrassing for all member countries. There was no possibility at all that Turkey could adopt the *acquis communautaire* in the foreseeable future. Thus, any application for membership would also have been an application for special treatment. Moreover, the economic and political problems posed by an eventual Turkish accession to the Community would make the problems raised by the second round of enlargement so far look minuscule by comparison. According to *The Economist* 'much ingenuity [was] being used to devise a polite formula for saying "no"'.[19] This ingenuity of the Europeans was not finally put to the test, thanks to the military *coup* which took place in Turkey in September 1980. Therefore the issue of Turkey's membership will remain shelved at least as long as the army stays in power.

The Leading Actors

Although the Community is basically an economic organisation, the motivations and reactions on both sides as regards the second round of enlargement have been predominantly political.[20] For Community members the positive but not enthusiastic response to the three applications was due to the realisation that it would be politically almost impossible to exclude any European democracy prepared to adopt the *acquis communautaire*. Membership of the Community was also seen as a factor of stability in the area and a means of strengthening parliamentary democracy. Political stability was in turn a prerequisite for economic and military security. According to Beate Kohler, '[S]ecurity for Western Europe is today regarded less as a matter of defence against external aggression than as the maintenance of a workable social and political order'.[21] If order is also associated with democracy and social progress, as Kohler goes on to argue, then we have made tremendous progress since the time of *Pax Americana* in the region. Some people actually see the Community, and the Federal Republic of Germany in particular, as reinforcing or replacing waning American power in Southern Europe.[22] To the extent that this is true, the term 'civilian power',[23] often ascribed to the Community, may have acquired some real meaning.

The applications from the three Mediterranean countries came at a time when the German economic giant had ceased to be a political dwarf and the federal government started playing an active role on the European scene. The rise of German power also coincided with a further shift away from old Gaullist policies in France. The latter was reflected both in the attitude adopted by French representatives within the Community as well as in relations with the United States. The result was close co-operation between the two countries which thus became the main driving force behind almost every Community initiative.

With the fall of the three dictatorships, the *Federal Republic of Germany* assumed an active role in Mediterranean Europe, which became very pronounced in the case of Portugal and to a lesser extent Spain. France had always acted as the champion of Franco's Spain within the Community but when the application for membership came from the new democratic regime, Giscard's margin of manoeuvre had already been considerably reduced by internal economic pressures. On the other hand Giscard d'Estaing had volunteered and finally succeeded in acting as Greece's godfather in the Community. Thus one might speak of a perfect division of tasks between the two leading countries in Western Europe. This also applied extremely well to the Eastern Mediterranean where the Schmidt government maintained the traditional close links with Turkey, provided arms and military aid during the American embargo and played a very active part in trying to raise an economic loan for a country which found itself on the verge of bankruptcy. It is characteristic of the new balance of power that had slowly emerged that Britain played only a secondary role in the political developments in Southern Europe. The exception was Cyprus, where Britain became directly involved as a guarantor power immediately after the 1974 events and indirectly through the EPC in which, on this issue, it played the leading role.

The Federal Republic has been the most consistent supporter of the second round of enlargement. Membership was closely linked with political stability and the strengthening of the Atlantic alliance, which in the case of Greece meant the country's reintegration into the NATO military command and, in the case of Spain, the transformation of a bilateral agreement with the United States into full membership of the alliance. This would be the perfect marriage of high and low politics. But although the Germans were keen on closely linking the two issues they finally discovered that any overt pressure would be counter-productive, given national sensitivities and the internal opposition in the two countries concerned. Moreover the issue of Greece's return to NATO became further entangled when Turkey threatened to use its power of veto.

The support for the three applications was a clear high policy decision. But this also implied a political and economic price for the Community as a whole and the Federal Republic in particular. The dilemma between consolidation and enlargement was a real one for German policy-makers. The choice of the second alternative seemed, however, inevitable. The report prepared by a committee of state secretaries in 1977 emphasised the budgetary cost of enlargement, which would mainly derive from the incorporation of the three farming sectors into the CAP. The cost would increase further if enlargement led to changes in the market organisation for Mediterranean products and if compensation were paid to third countries. The Germans were fully aware of the fact that they would be expected to pay a large part of the net budgetary cost. This would be in addition to what they were already spending on bilateral aid to Portugal, not to mention Turkey, and through the SPD to the two Iberian socialist parties. The net cost would increase much further if the idea of a solidarity fund for Southern Europe which, after all, originated from the German Social Democrats and formed part of their political platform in the European elections of June 1979, were eventually translated into concrete action.

The other major concern of the federal government and the trade unions in particular, is the danger of an influx of foreign workers following the accession of the three Mediterranean countries. The idea of a guided or controlled free movement of labour was mooted.[24] In the negotiations with Greece, the Federal Republic insisted on a long transitional period and finally settled for seven years, although this was seen more as a precedent for the negotiations with the Iberians, and with the Turks in the context of their association agreement.

At the same time trade liberalisation was seen as a great opportunity for German industrialists, particularly as regards exports to Spain. Germany is already the biggest exporter to the three applicants and hence the member country likely to benefit most from the opening of their markets. The specialisation of German industry in high-technology goods and capital equipment and its ability to adjust meant that its export potential was higher but also that the Germans were less worried by competition from low-priced, labour-intensive goods from the three applicant countries. German industry also had big invest-ment interests in the Three and membership was seen as a guarantee for the future. In addition, as a net importer of Mediterranean farm products the Federal Republic expected to gain from enlargement by gaining access to low-cost supplies. This was, however, based on the assumption that the Community market organisation would not change substantially.

Enlargement has also raised another fundamental question, namely the long-term development of a Community of Twelve.[25] Here, as expected, the attitude adopted depended much on the economic interests and ideology of the people involved. There was first of all the fear that enlargement might lead to the dilution of the Community, particularly its free trade principles. Growing government interven-tion and infringement of free competition rules were seen with horror by the Christian Democrats and the industrialists. There was yet another danger perceived by virtually all sides of the political spectrum, that of increased pressures for protectionist policies *vis-à-vis* third countries. Given the export dependence of the German economy, its ability to adjust relative to other Community members and its growing reliance on low-cost, international supplies of semi-finished and finished goods, the creation of a protectionist, regional bloc in Western Europe would be highly undesirable for German interests.

Despite the fact that enlargement was associated with some short- and long-term economic costs, it never became a political issue in the Federal Republic. The three political parties and the main interest groups seemed to agree that enlargement was inevitable for security and political reasons.

The Mediterranean enlargement was originally seen by Giscard d'Estaing and the Quai d'Orsay as a means of shifting the centre of gravity towards the South and thus making *France* the pivotal axis of the enlarged Community. The French have always tried to avoid the creation of a Northern-dominated Community and believe in the existence of interests and a philosophical approach common to all

Latin countries (through some historical sleight of hand Greece could also be included in that category).[26] France has been the main driving force behind the various Mediterranean agreements signed by the Six and the subsequent so-called global Mediterranean policy which was an attempt to provide some general guidelines and a coherent framework for future negotiations (French diplomacy has always been very Cartesian in its approach). Already at the time the French were asked to pay a price for the Community's Mediterranean policy, mainly in the form of agricultural concessions. Thus the dilemma faced by the French government in the context of the second round of enlargement is not really new. In all cases the French have been trying to achieve one simple goal, that is maximise the long-term political and economic benefits and minimise the short-term costs.

Giscard d'Estaing was the only European leader who strongly encouraged the Greek government to apply for membership and who was a consistent and active supporter of the Greek cause during the negotiations. There is nothing inconsistent or schizophrenic about the fact that the French were at the same time very tough negotiators in the agricultural field. Excellent relations with the government in Athens and a strong personal connection between the leaders of the two countries, established during the long years of Karamanlis's exile in Paris, help to explain the positive attitude adopted by France.

The policy adopted *vis-à-vis* Portugal has been remarkably different. The French government tried to discourage Soares from applying for membership and it rarely showed any enthusiasm for Portugal's application. This cannot be explained in terms of the farmers' reactions in France since Portuguese agriculture never presented any real danger. Nor does it seem plausible that Portugal's economic backwardness is the main explanation. Portugal has been considered as an Atlantic rather than Mediterranean country and part of the British sphere of influence. This combination reduces its attractiveness as a partner for France. Moreover Giscard d'Estaing had very little sympathy for the Portuguese socialists or the revolution, while it is indicative that Mitterrand has made repeated statements in favour of Portuguese entry. We have to wait and see whether the roles will be reversed if the conservative forces remain in power in Portugal.

French governments had for many years been active supporters of Spain's gradual integration into the Community and General de Gaulle had several times referred to Spain as a country which should join a European confederation. In 1974, when Franco was still alive, French ministers spoke in favour of Spanish entry,[27] but when the application for membership came in July 1977 French enthusiasm had already been considerably tempered. For geopolitical reasons Giscard d'Estaing and the foreign ministry were ready to encourage Spain's

European vocation. However the strong reactions of the farmers' lobby, the attitude adopted by the Gaullists and the communists and the prospect of parliamentary elections in March 1978 left the government with a very narrow margin of manoeuvre. Moreover it has been argued[28] that there is now yet another cause for French scepticism *vis-à-vis* Spain's entry. It is no longer taken for granted that convergence will prevail over the divergence of economic interests, thus providing the basis for Mediterranean solidarity within the Community. Farmers have denounced the likely 'complicité Nord–Sud' between a producer country such as Spain and consumer countries in order to keep prices low.[29] The active foreign policy followed by Madrid since the death of Franco and its flirtation with Third World and Arab countries may offer a rival recipe in Latin diplomacy which is not compatible with French interests.

Enlargement created a serious dilemma for Giscard d'Estaing and his government as they tried to reconcile long-term geopolitical considerations with conflicting short-term economic interests. The latter could be translated into hundreds of thousands of votes and the immediate prospect of an election, which in the event was actually decided by a very small margin, added to the government's difficulties. They sought to resolve the problem by political manoeuvring at home, putting forward various ingenious proposals which aimed at delaying indefinitely the economic effects of enlargement, linking the latter with a reform of the CAP and also by delaying the whole process until the crucial election of 1978 was over. The same thing was repeated again with the European elections of June 1979. Given that the presidential elections will be held in 1981 and the next parliamentary elections are planned for 1983, it may actually prove rather difficult to squeeze the ratification of the two remaining Treaties of Accession in between.

The strong reaction of farmers in the south west brought about an unequivocal 'no' to enlargement from the PCF which launched a big campaign in all the areas likely to be affected. Throughout 1978 and 1979 *L'Humanité* continued to bombard its readership with an unending series of articles in which all the evils of enlargement were constantly denounced. The PCF campaigned in the French countryside with the typically internationalist slogan 'rester au pays, produire français'.[30] The attitude of the communists on this subject contributed to the worsening of relations with their socialist partners of the United Left and led to an acrimonious exchange with their fellow communists on the other side of the Pyrenees. The French communists also pretended that enlargement would lead to a more extensive use of majority voting within the Council of Ministers and this gave them the opportunity to appear again as the best defenders of national sovereignty.

The Gaullists adopted a more qualified stand. They said 'no' to enlargement but 'yes' to Greece, presumably because Greek farmers were only marginal suppliers of most agricultural products and also because of good relations with the Karamanlis party. Moreover the Gaullists would probably not be opposed to Spain's entry as long as the economic effects could be postponed indefinitely. They certainly had no objection on political grounds to the two Iberian countries joining what should ideally be a loose, intergovernmental organisation. The attitude of the RPR was probably best summarised in a statement made by its deputy secretary-general, Nicole Chouraqui: 'Oui a cette Europe élargie, mais pour plus tard.'[31]

Given the opposition of the RPR and the PCF to Spain's accession, the attitude adopted by the socialists is likely to be crucial. So far they have had to reconcile the pressures coming from their voters and their organisations in the south with their moral obligations towards their Spanish and Portuguese counterparts and their membership of the Socialist International. In this respect the problems they face are similar to those faced by Giscard and his party. The solutions put forward have also been fairly similar. The PS set the reform of the agricultural policy applying to Mediterranean products as a precondition for enlargement. Moreover, the party viewed this reform as part of a new active policy towards the southern peripheral regions of the Community.[32] For the socialists at least, this was consistent with their general policy towards European integration. Some members of the PS have also spoken of the need for flexibility in transitional periods and long duration (Pierre Uri is a member of the party). At the same time French socialists have had many meetings with their opposite numbers within the International and bilateral meetings with the parties of Mediterranean Europe in order to discuss the issue of enlargement and define a common policy.

The first report on the agricultural aspect of enlargement was published by the Conseil National des Jeunes Agriculteurs (CNJA) in April 1976 with the rousing title *Espagne: un choc pour l'Europe*. The debate quickly gathered momentum with the farmers' organisations taking a strong stand against enlargement. The CNJA Report was followed by two more reports on the subject, one published by a working group set up by the ministry of agriculture (Desouches Report), where it was argued that France needed to build a new Maginot line for its agriculture(!) and a Senate report (Pisani–Sordel).[33] The Senate report in particular, written by one socialist and one Giscardian Senator, provided the catalyst for further developments. It took a favourable stand on enlargement for political reasons and then examined the positive and negative effects for French agriculture. It called for long and phased transitional periods after accession and for reforms to the CAP applying to Mediterranean products. Many of these ideas were later adopted by the French government (see also Chapter 5). At the same time the government announced a new programme of national credits to help producers improve their orchards and vines. Later on Giscard asked the government to prepare a ten-year plan for the south-west regions. In the end the measures taken at the national and the Community levels, together with the insistence by Giscard on the political benefits of enlargement, brought about a more qualified attitude from some representatives of the farmers.[34] This could only come about after the 1978 elections, when the leverage which some interest groups could exercise on the government was considerably reduced. However, whether Giscard will finally succeed in overcoming the internal opposition to Spain's entry still remains to be seen.

Although the debate in France on enlargement was dominated by agricultural aspects, there were also other important interests at stake. French industry has been strongly in favour. The objective is to obtain access to the Spanish market and thus enjoy the benefits of reciprocity missing from the 1970 trade agreement. There is also serious concern about the free movement of workers, but it has been safely left to the Germans to defend the interests of host countries. On the institutional front the French have played an active part in the discussions. Back in February 1976 there were what appeared to be inspired leaks in *Le Monde*[35] about the need to form a directorate of big countries in the Community in order to avoid total paralysis after the second enlargement. This idea reappeared later in the same newspaper, although in a somewhat milder form.[36] In 1978, following a French initiative, the Committee of the Three Wise Men was set up with the task of reporting on Community institutions after enlargement. However there were rumours that the policy proposals finally adopted in the report[37] did not meet entirely with the approval of the French president.

Italy should be even more concerned over enlargement than France since a much higher percentage of its total farm production consists of products likely to be affected by competition from the new members. Until very recently Italian governments were alone in their stand against the existing imbalance between temperate and Mediterranean products. However, despite the similarity of the economic problems faced by the two countries, the political response to developments was remarkably different. The Italian farmers did react against the imminent danger of competition from the applicant countries and the Minister of Agriculture, Giovanni Marcora, supported the farmers' cause but was overruled by his prime minister. Enlargement never became a political issue in Italy because all parties were agreed on its desirability. The single most important difference between France and Italy, which explains to a large extent the different political approaches to enlargement, is the attitude of the two communist parties. This is not only reflected in the policy adopted on enlargement but also in their approach to European integration in general. The Italian communists, the second biggest party in the country, were among the most enthusiastic supporters of enlargement. They associated accession to the Community with the consolidation of democracy in the three countries. They also linked enlargement with reform of the CAP, for which they have been fighting for many years. On the other hand countries would help to bring the Community's North–South problem into the limelight. They also hoped that by changing the balance of forces enlargement would make internal reforms politically more feasible. But they were not prepared to make reform a precondition for enlargement since the latter was the first priority.[38] Political consensus on this issue, and on European integration in general, made Italy an active supporter of enlargement despite the adverse economic effects expected for the farming sector. The Italian memorandum submitted in July 1977 and the negotiations which followed on the Mediterranean package also showed that French and Italian interests diverged in many respects (see also Chapter 5).

Among the Big Four, *Britain* is the country likely to be the least affected by the second round of enlargement.[39] Its agriculture is largely complementary to that of the three applicants, while as a net importer Britain has an interest in securing access to low-cost supplies of food. The question of fisheries has not yet appeared on the surface because of the standstill in intra-Community negotiations on the one hand, and the fact that negotiations with the two Iberian countries are still at a preliminary stage; Greece's fishing fleet is too small to present a problem. The Confederation of British Industry (CBI) called for the quick removal of tariff and non-tariff barriers in the applicant countries but it did not show the same degree of optimism and aggressiveness as its German counterpart at the prospect of new markets to be conquered. On the import side, industrialists in sensitive sectors such as textiles, footwear and steel were especially worried about Portuguese and Spanish competition and asked for long transitional periods and safeguard clauses. The greatest concern for the British government has been the budgetary cost of enlargement. According to Treasury estimates, which did not differ much in terms of the total amount estimated by the Commission, the net additional cost for Britain would be £90–115 million per annum at the end of the transitional periods (1977 figures).[40] But these were only static estimates and there was the fear that the final bill could be considerably higher.

According to the late Foreign Minister, Anthony Crosland, enlargement was 'an investment in the democratic future of Europe of which the benefits would in the long run far outweigh the cost'.[41] Britain under a Labour or Conservative government has attached great importance to political stability in the area and enlargement has been closely linked with the strengthening of the Atlantic alliance. Its special interest in the Eastern Mediterranean and the strongly felt need to preserve a balance between Greece and Turkey led Britain to propose the latter's participation in the EPC. In February 1978, when the French wanted to set a firm date for the conclusion of the negotiations with Greece, the British foreign minister asked for parallelism in negotiations with the three countries and expressed his government's anxiety that his partners were only interested in bringing about a Community of Ten. Such statements and proposals, coupled with the role played by Christopher Soames in the preparation of the Commission's opinion on the Greek application, did not add to the popularity of the British in Athens. Britain showed a special interest in the Portuguese application which can be explained in terms of the long history of close relations between the two countries and the support given by the Labour Party to the Portuguese socialists. Moreover in a Community of Twelve one might expect the emergence of an Anglo-Lusitanian alliance in favour of a radical reform of the CAP, since the existing policy does not suit the interests of either country.

Another initiative that came from Britain was for an amendment to the Rome Treaty which would make parliamentary democracy a precondition for Community membership. On the other hand, there were widespread fears on the continent that the then Labour government saw enlargement as a means of diluting the Community. James Callaghan's letter to the national executive committee of the party seemed to confirm such fears.[42]

The Remaining Cast

Membership of a Community with common institutions, well-established legal procedures and an efficient decision-making system makes much more sense for small countries than it does for big ones. Participation in such a Community enables them to avoid excessive dependence on a single big power with all the inevitable political repercussions that this may have and serves to increase their bargaining power in international forums. This seems to be true of all small countries of the European Community. The most obvious and recent example is the case of the Republic of Ireland which through its membership of the Community has managed to escape from isolation and its one-way dependence on Britain. Moreover all small countries have so far succeeded in receiving major economic benefits from European integration, not only through free industrial trade but also through the Agricultural Fund (Netherlands, Denmark, Ireland), other intra-Community transfers (Ireland) and also by providing the seat for Community institutions (Belgium, Luxembourg). For all the above reasons it is natural that these countries should be particularly preoccupied with any threat to the *acquis communautaire*, the efficiency of the decision-making system and the danger of moving towards a more intergovernmental Community which might provide fewer guarantees for the interests of small member countries.

The entry of three new members with unstable political systems and a low level of economic development presented a serious problem for the cohesion of the Community. At the same time it was bound to aggravate an already difficult situation as far as Community institutions were concerned. Thus enlargement was viewed with some apprehension by the small countries, while at the same time an attempt was made to link it with institutional reforms which were long overdue. Despite these common characteristics, the reaction was certainly not identical. Among the five countries concerned, only *Ireland* faced the likelihood of having to pay an economic price for enlargement. In a Community of Twelve, Ireland would have to compete with other poor countries for limited funds (regional, social policy, and so on). Given a similar level of economic development, Ireland would also have to compete with the three applicant countries in sensitive sectors such as textiles, clothing and footwear. Irish ministers have tried to secure a guarantee from other member countries that Ireland would not be worse off after enlargement, at least as far as net receipts from the budget are concerned. During its presidency, it also tried to make more extensive use of majority voting in the Council of Ministers. In this respect Britain was singled out as the main culprit resisting such attempts.[12] The *Benelux* countries have been particularly reticent about the entry of new members. This applies much more to Belgium and Luxembourg than to Holland. Dutch ministers, and particularly those from the Labour Party, have been very sensitive to the argument that membership of the Community would help to consolidate the three new democracies. Van der Stoel, the ex-foreign minister, had carried a very active campaign against the Greek colonels and later gave strong support to the Greek and Portuguese applications for membership. The initial reticence about Spain was a function of the old policy against the Franco regime and some incredulity about the democratic intentions of the first two governments after the death of Franco. *Denmark* is different from the other four. The existence of a large section of the population with strong anti-market feelings and the Scandinavian connection makes it impossible for any Danish government to try to link enlargement with major institutional reforms leading to more supranationalism or to welcome a shift in the balance of power towards the south. Nevertheless Denmark did not take a negative stand on enlargement. On the contrary, during its presidency in the first half of 1978 it tried to break the deadlock which the Community had reached on the subject.

The *Commission* has shared with the small countries the same worries about the danger of dilution and a possible paralysis of Community institutions. Faced with the state of general confusion which characterised early Community responses on the subject, the Commission tried to promote a more coherent and rational policy by emphasising the long-term consequences and making proposals reminiscent of what Ernst Haas has called the 'upgrading of common interests'.[44] It was reasonable for the Commission to be in favour of the globalisation of the negotiations and the simultaneous entry of the three applicants.[45] This would make adjustment easier, particularly for Community institutions. The Commission also wanted to escape from the dilemma of *élargissement* versus *approfondissement* through the adoption of concrete measures at the Community level. But the Commission was faced with three important constraints, namely, lack of internal cohesion, lack of human resources and lack of political will on behalf of the member states. The college of Commissioners had lost the internal cohesion which characterised it during the 1960s. In many cases internal divisions reflected the different attitudes of member governments. Examples which immediately come to mind are the opinion on the Greek application, the Natali Report and the preparation of the fresco on enlargement. Furthermore the Commission often appeared to have lost the comparative advantage which it should, at least theoretically, possess over national administrations: greater expertise and better human resources for the subjects it covered. Last but not least, it had to cope with the fact that most member governments were not prepared to pay either a political or an economic price with respect to enlargement. They felt that they were unable to say 'no' to the three applications but at the same time they were not ready to go ahead with far-reaching reforms in Community institutions or policies or to give economic aid to the three applicant countries. The above constraints were closely interrelated. They were a function of a continuous trend towards more intergovernmentalism, the weakening of the Commission and the end of the economic honeymoon of the 1960s.

The Commission's opinion on the Greek application left a mark on the negotiations, with the Greeks constantly suspecting the Commission of being an unfriendly partner. This mistake was not repeated with Spain and Portugal and one now has the impression that the Commission constitutes the main driving force for the speedy conclusion of the negotiations. The fresco on enlargement, despite the fact that it finally appeared in a rather diluted form with very few concrete proposals, represents the only attempt to adopt a global approach and think ahead in terms of the Community of Twelve in the future. In relation to enlargement, the Commission picked four main areas in which concrete action was considered to be most urgent: industrial policy, Mediterranean agriculture, EMU and institutions. On the first one, very little has happened so far. On the second, French and Italian pressures, followed by Commission proposals, led to the adoption of new directives and regulations by the Council of Ministers. As regards the third area Roy Jenkins's initiative on EMU was quickly taken up by Schmidt and Giscard. This Franco–German marriage gave birth to the EMS. On the institutional front, we are now at the stage where policy recommendations (Three Wise Men and Spierenburg Reports)[46] wait to be translated into political action. In the present political climate, it seems that they may have to wait for a long time.

The attitudes of member governments to the three applications ranged from moderate enthusiasm to serious apprehension, with the balance tilting towards the latter. The decision was taken at the top political level and was the result of high policy considerations. In many cases there seemed to be a gap between the statements made by the heads of government and the attitude adopted by their ministers and civil servants in Brussels, probably because the latter were less impressed by arguments referring to political stability and democracy in the Mediterranean. Enlargement did not become a political issue within member countries because it was not seen as affecting any vital interests; also because different parties agreed about the political imperative. The only exceptions were France and, to a lesser extent, Italy. National parliaments remained largely indifferent, again with the exception of the National Assembly in France. On the contrary, the European Parliament extensively debated this issue but it was limited by its inability to influence the negotiations. In view of the above it is not surprising that public opinion did not react much to enlargement either. Opinion polls showed that there was a high percentage of 'don't knows' and that the Germans, Italians and Irish were most favourable to the accession of the three candidates, the Danes least so. Among the candidates, Spain was the marginal favourite.[47] As far as transnational politics is concerned, the nine socialist parties have played the most important role by holding periodic meetings, trying to co-ordinate their policies and also by establishing regular contacts with their counterparts in the two Iberian countries – PASOK did not participate because of ideological differences and its opposition to Greece's accession. In addition, enlargement served to highlight once again the division which has gradually developed between the communist parties of Western Europe, with the Italians and Spaniards on the one side, the French, the Portuguese and the Greeks on the other.

A word should also be said about the attitude of outsiders and especially the most important one, that is, the United States. Until the fall of the dictatorships the three countries had close political, economic and military relations with the United States, which stood in some contrast to their relative isolation in Western Europe. Until 1974 US relations with Greece differed little from those of a big power with a client state. During the Franco regime close relations with Washington (including bilateral military and economic agreements) and the Vatican constituted the two main pillars of Spanish foreign policy. Despite the Salazar dictatorship, Portugal was a founding member of NATO. It also had a bilateral agreement with the United States, providing the latter with defence facilities in the Azores.

The fall of the three dictatorships in a period of détente and the subsequent applications for membership of the Community marked for some people the end of *Pax Americana* in Southern Europe. A study mission of the US Congress Committee on Foreign Affairs concluded that American influence in the area would decline and that these countries would try to establish closer ties with Western Europe. 'The United States should welcome this development by encouraging their closer cooperation with and eventual membership of the European Community.'[48] This attitude was finally adopted by the Carter administration. Enlargement was seen as a means of stabilising the political situation in the area and keeping the three countries in the Western alliance. It was argued that a return to the old bilateral relation of dependence was virtually impossible, and for many people also undesirable. Only under Henry Kissinger was there a great reluctance to accept the new status quo.[49] Despite American support for enlargement, there has been a great dearth of official statements on the subject from the other side of the Atlantic. The explanation given was that the new administration did not want to interefere with what was an internal Community decision. Moreover such statements might be counterproductive, particularly in the applicant countries.

It is interesting that while American officials were saying, mostly in private, that accession to the Community would ensure that the three countries remained in the Western alliance, socialists in France, Portugal and Spain, and some pro-marketeers in Greece, argued that the socialist transformation of the society would be extremely difficult to implement if these countries were left outside the Community, since the other alternative was dependence on the United States.[50]

Enlargement raised only one important question mark for the United States regarding the effect on relations with Turkey. It is not therefore surprising that the State Department strongly supported the proposal for Turkey's participation in the EPC. On the economic side enlargement is expected to lead to some trade diversion, particularly with respect to agricultural trade, which would be at the expense of third countries. This time, orange producers in Florida have not succeeded in determining American foreign policy! Trade diversion effects will be more serious for other Mediterranean countries which have already registered their demands for compensation.[51] On the other hand the Soviet Union has been predictably against enlargement, although a report in *Pravda* in September 1974 seemed to suggest that a distinction was finally drawn between NATO and the EC.[52] Again predictably, China was in favour.

The Moral of the Story

The experience so far with the second round of enlargement confirms once again that despite the divergence of interests and the loose structure of the European Community, decisions are sometimes taken and policy enacted. In a period of prolonged economic recession and growing unemployment, it is remarkable that the *acquis communautaire* has been preserved; even more so, that the Community is prepared to open the doors to three semi-industrialised countries on the European periphery. It is also confirmed that the Community practises diplomacy by reaction to external events instead of trying to shape the external environment in which it lives. At the same time, it appears to the other side an 'inefficient and unsympathetic negotiator'[53] because of the slowness and the unwieldiness of its internal decision-making system.

With respect to the process of enlargement it may be useful to distinguish between two separate phases: that which covers the negotiations with the applicant countries and ends with the ratification of the treaties of accession; and that which involves changes in Community policies and institutions, as well as inside the member countries themselves, as a result of, or in anticipation of, the entry of new members.

The negotiations between an applicant country and the Community are only about the type and length of the transitional period which follows accession. The *acquis communautaire* itself does not come into question during those negotiations. But though the economic and other effects of accession may be postponed as a result of the transitional period each new member enjoys full political rights from the very first moment of its accession. Since the *acquis communautaire* is in constant evolution a new member country is immediately allowed to participate in the decision-making process, despite the fact that it is not yet ready to accept the full obligations resulting from the adoption of the *acquis* as it stood on the day of accession.

The above argument implies that the formula adopted in the 1973 enlargement would be broadly valid. Nevertheless both the proposal for a pre-accession period and the one for negotiations by stages went completely against the main principle adopted in the first enlargement. In the case of Greece both ideas were finally rejected and the Community went back to the old formula. Assuming that the Commission's proposals, as they appeared in the 1978 fresco, also apply to the two Iberian countries, then the same formula will hold true for the second round of enlargement in general. Two qualifications should be added here: one that transitional periods will be longer than five years and the other that prolonged negotiations could be seen as a second best alternative to a pre-accession period.

At the time of writing, the first phase of the enlargement process has been completed only as far as Greece is concerned. Negotiations with Spain and Portugal are still going on and are likely to continue for some time. At this stage we may venture some preliminary conclusions about the first phase. On the surface at least, it would appear that negotiations take place between two very unequal partners. On the one hand there is a powerful club of industrialised countries which can exercise considerable political and economic leverage and on the other, a small and relatively poor country (this applies with some qualifications in the case of Spain) which comes to the negotiations as a *démandeur*. It may even seem surprising that the negotiations actually start since there is little in terms of tangible and immediate benefits that existing members expect to gain by increasing the membership of the club.

Experience so far suggests that this potential inequality does not really manifest itself in the negotiations because of the context within which they take place and the objective constraints under which both sides operate. To start with, the fact that negotiations lead to full membership immediately excludes a zero-sum-game mentality. It is not in the Community's long-term interest to allow in a new member for whom accession proves to be an economic disaster. Moreover, since the strengthening of parliamentary democracy and the consolidation of the new status quo in the three countries appears to be one of the main objectives on both sides the destabilisation of the system or the strengthening of radical political forces, which may reject the European option and a pro-West foreign policy, would defeat the whole purpose of enlargement. A cynic would argue that Papandreou and Cunhal have been the strongest negotiating cards for the Greek and the Portuguese governments respectively. By the same token, one would expect the political consensus in Spain to weaken the hand of the Suárez government, although it may prove to be a major advantage in the regular, everyday negotiations which form part of Community membership. Similarly, it seems to be recognised on the Community side that accession talks should not be prolonged indefinitely if the growth of anti-European feeling in the applicant countries is to be avoided.

We have argued here that the negotiating strength of the applicant countries lies in their economic weakness and in the threat of a radical reorientation of their foreign policy, an argument which has apparently been used by the Karamanlis government and which becomes even more credible when it is espoused by big opposition parties. What it really boils down to is the political and strategic importance of the three countries for the whole of Western Europe. Given the economic character of the European Community and the nature of the accession talks, high policy considerations have to be translated into bargaining about customs duties and support prices for agricultural products. After all, the history of the Community is full of examples where high and low politics are closely intertwined.

The negotiations between Greece and the Community provided a sharp contrast between a single-minded government exercising a highly centralised authority on the one hand, and a heterogeneous group of countries with divergent interests seeking to achieve unanimity on the other. On the Greek side, interest groups played a minor role in the negotiations, which were conducted in great secrecy. The Greek government decided that it was the best judge of the country's interest and acted accordingly. In parenthesis one might add here that the Spanish government is unlikely to follow the Greek example because of the many domestic constraints. On the European side, more time was spent in intra-Community negotiations trying to agree on a mandate for the Commission than in direct negotiations with the Greeks. But after all this is the usual Community practice. There was also another important difference between the two sides: what was for Karamanlis the *cheval de bataille* of his foreign policy was inevitably a fairly low priority for the Community as a whole.[54] There was therefore a serious danger that the accession talks would be unduly prolonged. The danger became very real when Greece's negotiations were caught up in the debate about enlargement which started early in 1977. The Greeks then used all possible means to speed up their negotiations and avoid a *de facto* globalisation. Unavoidably they tried to minimise all problems arising in the negotiations. Karamanlis himself embarked on regular tours of the European capitals trying to break the various bottlenecks in personal discussions with Giscard or

Schmidt over the heads of the technocrats involved in the negotiations. This policy bore fruit in the end. Greece's Treaty of Accession was signed slightly less than three years after the formal opening of the negotiations. This was at least one year longer than would have been necessary if everything had gone smoothly. However, given the various obstacles that had appeared since Greece's application in June 1975, it was a remarkable achievement for both sides.

The importance of the accession talks has often been exaggerated out of all proportion. People in Greece – the same thing is also likely to happen in Spain and Portugal – attached great importance to what they referred to as 'terms of entry' without actually realising, or pretending not to realise, that these terms of entry applied only to the transitional period. After all, some of them read English newspapers and had learnt something from the Wilson government. Greece's terms of entry were probably the best that could be achieved under the circumstances, although this is in any case an impossible argument to prove. What is rather puzzling is that the two sides spent months negotiating about the elimination by stages of industrial customs duties during the five-year transitional period: as if tariff protection were the most important and non-tariff barriers – many of which are most likely to survive after membership – had not been discovered yet, or as if changes in the exchange rate could have no significant effect on the competitiveness of national industry. Membership of the Community does not deprive a country of the right to devalue or revalue its currency nor does it entail the obligation to join the EMS. Changes of the exchange rate which are certain to continue in the future, both inside and outside the EMS, make nonsense of attempts to compare agricultural prices before accession and on that basis decide the length of the transitional period.

Transitional periods are only meant to provide both sides, particularly the new member, with a breathing space in order to make the necessary adjustments. If these adjustments do not take place, then transitional periods only serve to postpone the final shock. This may be very convenient for politicians who are unlikely still to be in power in five or ten years' time. Moreover the experience of the first enlargement suggests that changes in the economic environment as well as Community policies can make transitional arrangements irrelevant and cost-benefit analyses completely out of date even before the new member accedes. It could be, though, that the accession talks are part of the Community ritual of initiation.

It is certainly unrealistic to think that institutions and policies intended for a Community of Six, or even Nine, can remain unchanged after the entry of three new members with different interests and problems. It would be disastrous to believe that adjustment will not be necessary on both sides, although most of the effort will surely have to be made by the applicant countries. In this respect, very little has happened until now. By concentrating on the transitional periods both sides have often lost sight of the wider and long-term implications of enlargement, or it may be that they have preferred not to think about them. In Part Three of this book we shall examine some of the problems which are likely to arise from the accession of the three Mediterranean countries, concentrating particularly on industry and agriculture. We also propose to discuss alternative solutions and the likely pressures for changes inside the Community of Twelve. In other words Part Three will be a small contribution to the search for a new package deal which will be compatible with the new economic and political characteristics of the enlarged Community.

Part Three

THE COMMUNITY OF TWELVE

4

Industrial Sector and Division of Labour

In 1978 the industrial sector accounted for 30·7% of civilian employment in Greece, 34·8% in Portugal and 37·3% in Spain. In the Community of Nine, Denmark was at one extreme with 30·3% of the civilian labour force engaged in the industrial sector and the Federal Republic of Germany at the other with 45·1% (OECD data). The second round of enlargement will undoubtedly have important repercussions for the whole sector and for manufacturing industry in particular in the three new members as well as the Community as a whole. One can go as far as to say that developments in this sector will really determine whether the second enlargement is a success or not. This sounds like stating the obvious but repetition of this fact is probably necessary because from the debate arising from enlargement one often has the impression that Community membership is almost identical with participation in the CAP.

Producing sophisticated estimates of the likely effects of enlargement in industry is beyond the scope of this chapter or even this book. One would have to study each sector or subsector of industrial activity separately in order to be able to produce any meaningful results. Moreover economic science has not yet reached that level of sophistication which would enable economists or econometricians to produce fairly reliable forecasts for the future. Available studies of the likely effects of enlargement in industrial trade between the Three and the Nine, although useful in providing some indication of the direction which these effects may take, have to be treated with much caution. Here we only propose to paint with a broad brush and it is therefore inevitable that the discussion will remain at a high level of generality which may prove unsatisfactory to many readers.

There is at least one other reason why we cannot be very specific in discussing enlargement and the industrial sector. Unlike agriculture, there is no well-defined, clear-cut policy for industry at the Community level. Usually people study the likely effects of trade liberalisation and the adoption by the new members of the Common External Tariff (CET) on industrial trade. But Community membership means more than that. Moreover there is a host of measures which governments can take in order to influence the industrial process at home. Many of those measures will continue to be at their disposal after accession and there is no way we can predict what will be made of them. We refer here to the whole bundle of policy instruments which usually come under the name of industrial policy. They include financial and fiscal incentives (such as subsidised loans and preferential tax treatment), public procurement policies, subsidisation of inputs, control over mergers and anti-trust policy, provision of infrastructural investment, and so on.[1] These measures vary from one country to the other and from one period to the next, depending on political preferences and the needs of the economy, to mention only two factors. What distinguishes this long list of measures from macroeconomic policy is that the former are supposed to deal with structural change while the latter is what the French call 'la politique conjoncturelle', although it is true that the dividing line between the two is rather blurred.

Industrial policy, probably more than macroeconomic policy and the use of the exchange rate, is an important factor in influencing industrial development in each country. We have certainly seen that in our discussion of the industrialisation process in the three Mediterranean countries. This certainly should not be taken to imply that governmental policies are the only thing that counts or that one set of policies will produce the same result in each country. Wolfgang Hager has referred to the state as the midwife of industrialisation.[2] True. But it is also true that no two babies are alike.

In this chapter we start with a discussion of the various attempts made at the Community level to go beyond negative integration. We then examine some of the problems presented by the international recession of the 1970s and the policies developed to deal with them. We concentrate particularly on the so-called sensitive sectors. The three prospective members are then introduced into the picture and the likely effects of enlargement for both sides are discussed. This leads us to the final section of this chapter which contains some suggestions about the policy measures which will have to be taken at the Community as well as the national level in order to meet the challenge of enlargement.

Attempts to Develop a Common Industrial Policy

The Paris Treaty which led to the establishment of the European Coal and Steel Community (ECSC) gave the High Authority extensive powers. These included the raising of levies on production, extending loans to firms for capital investment, financing research and development and retraining redundant workers. The supranational institution was also empowered to co-ordinate investment plans, although the authors of the treaty did not go as far as giving the High Authority the right of veto over investment decisions. Some mild form of long-term planning was envisaged, while in a period of 'manifest crisis' the High Authority had the power, with the agreement of the Council, to establish a system of production quotas. Mergers were subject to authorisation by the High Authority and all state aids and subsidies were prohibited. However, member states reserved the right to pursue independent commercial policies *vis-à-vis* third countries.[3]

Although the philosophy of the Paris Treaty was fundamentally liberal, the High Authority was expected to play an active role in both the coal and steel sectors. This was almost inevitable given the strategic importance of the two sectors in national economies, the supranationalist fervour of the Schuman era and also the fact that one of the main objects of the whole exercise was to avoid the re-emergence of cartels among steel producers; hence the policing powers given to the High Authority.

In contrast, industrial policy was barely given a place in the Rome Treaty signed in 1957. This certainly applies only to the treaty which led to the establishment of the EEC, since the Euratom treaty signed at the same time did contain distinct elements of an industrial policy. With respect to the EEC treaty, the emphasis was on the creation of a customs union and there were precise timetables for the elimination of tariffs, quotas and other obstacles to trade. Provisions were also made for the liberalisation of labour and capital movements and the freedom of establishment. The only common policies referred to in the treaty were in the fields of agriculture, transport and external trade, the common commercial policy being a necessary consequence of the eventual creation of the CET. Even here the founding members had to content themselves with an agreement on some general objectives. The actual content of these common policies was to be decided later.[4]

Jacquemin and de Jong[5] draw a distinction between government intervention which is intended to eliminate distortions to competition and intervention which is inspired by sectoral or regional considerations which often results in some form of planning. This implies that the state may have different priorities or objectives from those which result from the free interplay of market forces. The Rome Treaty only touched upon the first aspect of industrial policy. Articles 85–90 dealt with restrictive business practices, the abuse of dominant positions and the role of state enterprise, Article 91 provided for measures against dumping practices and Articles 92–4 dealt with government aid and subsidies. Strictly speaking, all this forms part of the Community's competition policy which has been administered by a distinct directorate-general in the Commission. The directorate-general for industrial affairs was formed as late as July 1967, after the merger of the three executives.

The treaty implied a free market economy and said very little about the role of government in industrial development. It was certainly much easier to make provision for the elimination of tariffs and other trade barriers than to argue on the principles, not to mention concrete measures, of economic policies which would be conducted at Community level. There was however another factor or rather a combination of two factors which basically explain the strong liberal bias of the treaty. German economic liberalism was combined with French nationalism. What we mean by this is that although France, following a long-established tradition, favoured *dirigiste* measures and experimented with indicative planning at the national level, it was not prepared to accept any form of planning at the Community level. However the group of planners in France soon realised the limitations imposed on national economic decisions by the creation of the customs union and started promoting the idea of Community planning.[6]

The premises of the treaty stood in clear contradiction to the trend which emerged during the 1960s in all EC countries of increasing government intervention in the economy. But this contradiction did not become so acute because the second decade of European integration coincided with a honeymoon period for all Western European economies, characterised by high rates of growth, balance of payments surpluses, low rates of inflation and near full employment. It is so much easier for liberal policies to survive in such times.

The contradiction referred to above is not unique to the European Community but applies to the Western economic system as a whole. The advance of the nation-state into an ever wider range of economic activities has coincided with the preservation, if not strengthening, of a liberal international economic order and a rapid growth of economic interdependence which in turn has imposed serious constraints on the ability of governments to manage the economy. This potential conflict remained in abeyance until the early 1970s. Andrew Shonfield actually wonders why 'it has taken so long for the potential conflict between these two forces which have moved the economic policies of Western countries in the second half of the twentieth century to emerge as an actual threat'.[7]

During the 1960s France and the Commission were the driving forces behind the development of a Community industrial policy, although each had rather different reasons and different goals in mind.

The French had two objectives close to their heart: close co-operation between governments and firms in specific sectors, especially high technology sectors where Europe was faced with the *défi américain* and the control of foreign investment. Both were strongly resisted by the liberal-minded Germans. In 1970 Colonna di Paliano, the Commissioner responsible for industrial affairs, submitted a memorandum which constituted the Commission's programme of action on industrial policy. It started with the need to create a single market within the Community and therefore eliminate all the remaining technical obstacles to free trade. It stressed the importance of harmonisation and standardisation of the legal, financial and fiscal framework within which firms have to operate and called for the promotion of transnational mergers, particularly in high technology sectors. It also referred to the problems of industrial adjustment and the need for Community solidarity in external economic relations. It was a list of good intentions which did not lead very far. Ideological differences between member countries still persisted, although one could talk of a slow process of convergence in the industrial policies pursued by different governments. Moreover since industrial policy is rarely a very coherent form of policy, agreement at the Community level was bound to be very difficult indeed. Last but not least, national interests or at least the perception of them also differed.[8]

Industrial policy, together with regional and social policy, became closely linked with the first round of enlargement and the creation of an EMU. At the Paris Summit of 1972 the heads of state or government committed themselves 'to seek to establish a single industrial base for the Community as a whole' and invited the Commission to produce an action programme. But the Spinelli Memorandum which followed was no more successful than its predecessor. Spinelli was more interventionist than Colonna di Paliano; naturally enough, since he was a socialist later to be elected to the Camera dei Deputati as an independent on the communist ticket. He also attached tremendous importance to close co-operation among Community countries in high technology sectors, which was seen as the only way in which European companies could compete with the leading American or Japanese firms. He called for the adoption of common guidelines for industrial restructuring and for an extension of the Commission's powers which would enable the latter to supervise and co-ordinate national aids to industry in accordance with those guidelines. Thus Spinelli was seen by some as trying to lay the foundations of indicative planning at the Community level.[9] Yet again, very little happened in practice.

In the leading industrial sectors governments continued to promote what Raymond Vernon has called the 'national champions'[10] despite the fact that in many cases this did not make much economic sense. Government aids were given to national firms and public procurement policies made sure that foreigners were usually excluded. Until now transnational co-operation in the field of high technology seems to have been little affected by the existence of the Community. To the extent that there has been co-operation, it has usually involved individual European governments and private industry, the Airbus being a good example of this. It is rather ironical that the area in which the Commission later succeeded in acquiring power, albeit of limited scope, and in giving some flesh to industrial policy was not in the field of high technology but in dealing with the lame ducks such as steel, textiles and shipbuilding.

In those aspects of industrial policy which relate to the creation of a single market within the Community, such as the elimination of technical barriers, harmonisation of technical standards and regulations and public procurement, there has been slow but continuous progress.[11] Such activities which now constitute a very large part of the Commission's everyday business, although important for the creation of a single market, have also contributed to the growing bureaucratisation of the Commission.

In addition, the Brussels institution has gradually developed its policy on competition on the basis of a number of test-case decisions and exemptions.[12] The role of the European Court of Justice in interpreting the relevant articles of the treaty and, in most cases, supporting the Commission in its attempt to develop a Community anti-trust policy has been absolutely crucial. At the same time the relatively low political profile of those issues, as compared, for example, with problems of industrial policy, has made the Commission's task much easier. It is characteristic that in its competition policy the Commission has been more successful in dealing with private firms than with national governments. We are referring here to action on state aids and subsidies which has met with very strong resistance from all the governments concerned.

The example of state aids and subsidies illustrates the dilemmas and constraints, both internal and external, with which the Commission has been faced in its attempt to develop a coherent policy.[13] In the Treaty of Rome the emphasis is clearly placed on competition and the need to eliminate various distortions such as aids and subsidies given to private firms. But already during the first decade of the application of the treaty there was an unmistakable trend towards greater government intervention at the micro level. Apart from the need to aid 'national champions' in their 'infant' stage, which sometimes became a permanent state of affairs, government intervention was also a response to the growing sensitivity to distributional problems and especially regional inequalities within member countries, the objective usually being to bring 'work to the workers' in depressed regions. More recently the emphasis has shifted towards declining sectors of industry, although in most cases declining sectors happen to be concentrated in particular areas, thus turning them into depressed regions. It is to this problem that we shall now switch our attention.

Sensitive Sectors and the Problem of Adjustment

When reference is made to declining industries in the European Community three sectors are usually singled out, namely, steel, textiles and clothing, and shipbuilding.[14] The reason is that the problems faced by those sectors are not only a function of the economic cycle and the prolonged recession of the 1970s. On the contrary, they are deemed to be structural problems which necessitate a long-term adjustment. This in turn implies the need for a shift of productive resources away from those sectors as well as rationalisation which can restore their competitiveness in international markets.

Adjustment is certainly not a new phenomenon in the industrial world. However it becomes extremely painful when large shifts of productive resources have to take place over a relatively short period of time and especially when there are very few opportunities for employing them elsewhere. This is exactly what happened during the crisis of the 1970s. Falling world demand and rapidly rising costs in Western Europe, combined with serious structural problems in these three sectors, led to massive over-capacity, big financial losses as well as employment losses. In a period of growing unemployment it was the loss of jobs that became the main preoccupation of all the governments concerned. One theoretical solution, which was immediately rejected at the political level in response to pressure from both industrialists and trade unions, was to leave it to the market forces to bring about the necessary adjustment. But once the pure leave-it-to-the-market approach was rejected, the question immediately arose as to whether state intervention would take the form of national protectionist measures, which would mean the end of the common market in those sectors, or Community measures. The second question was whether Community members would try to avoid the burden of adjustment by resorting to purely protectionist measures directed against non-members of the club.

The response has varied from one sector to the other. In the case of steel, the common market was preserved until 1980 by the setting up of a cartel of producers, the adoption of minimum prices for the most sensitive products, a voluntary agreement on production quotas and the introduction of strong protectionist measures *vis-à-vis* the outside world. The external measures included anti-dumping action and bilateral negotiations with foreign suppliers, which usually led to voluntary restrictions on exports. In all this, the Commission played a leading role. The above measures formed part of the so-called anti-crisis plan which also contained an important medium-term objective, namely, the rationalisation of production and the restructuring of the Community industry. Here the Commission faced a real struggle with national governments and private industry. There was very little agreement either about the size or the sharing of the burden of adjustment. Some rationalisation did, however, take place, the extent of which varied from one member country to the other, although it was clearly not sufficient to allow the Community's steel industry to work at a near-full-capacity level. The Commission also tried to control state aids, especially those not intended to promote the process of adjustment. Its powers in this field were considerably strengthened with the adoption of a new code on state aids in 1979.

A major decline in the global demand for steel which started in the second half of 1979, and which led to a complete breakdown of the voluntary agreement among the major steel producers and a fierce price war, finally forced the Community members to declare the steel industry as being in a state of 'manifest crisis' and thereby invoke Article 58 of the Paris Treaty. This, therefore, gave the Commission the power to impose production quotas on steel producers.

With respect to textiles and clothing, Community policy has been limited mainly to external protectionist measures. After the disastrous experience of the first Multi-Fibre Agreement (MFA) a new, more stringent agreement was signed in 1977, coupled with bilateral agreements with about thirty low-cost exporting countries from the developing world. On the domestic front different restructuring programmes were adopted by member governments. The Commission has succeeded in limiting the abuse of state aids but seems to have achieved very little in terms of actually promoting adjustment.[15]

Finally, as far as the shipbuilding industry is concerned, the Community's role has so far been almost non-existent despite a series of initiatives emanating from Brussels. The latest such initiative is the scrap and build programme which is now on the Council's table and the omens are that it may have to wait there for quite some time.

The problems faced by Community industry in those sectors and the responses made by governments and Community institutions raise some general questions. The increasing openness of national economies, the rapid transfer of technology and the shift of productive resources to many Third World countries have intensified the need for continuous internal adjustment in advanced industrialised countries. At the same time, serious rigidities have developed in product and factor markets which make adjustment increasingly difficult. These are the result of economic changes such as the growth of specialisation, of skill and capital intensity, changes in the attitudes and power of organised labour and the development of popular expectations concerning job security and growing incomes. The social and political changes have been more pronounced in Western Europe where the welfare state has become most firmly established and where organised labour seems to be particularly resistant to change or to a fall in real income. *A propos*, the existence of both a democratic parliamentary system and organised labour clearly distinguish Greece, Portugal and Spain from most of the other so-called NICs and also exclude by definition the adoption of certain models of economic development which are characteristic of other developing countries.

The recession of the 1970s made adjustment even more painful and costly. Thus governments were forced to resort increasingly to measures which were intended to resist adjustment, slow it down or in the best of cases make it easier for the people concerned. Since industrial policy is often a substitute for external protection and even more so since Community governments had been deprived of the instruments of tariff protection, it was to be expected that they would resort to various measures which come under industrial policy and which economists usually lump together under the name of non-tariff barriers. The Commission tried, with some success, to avoid the spreading of uncontrolled state aids and subsidies which would make nonsense of the common market. It also tried to emphasise the need for adjustment and impress the fact that protectionist measures *vis-à-vis* third countries, which had to be negotiated by the Commission itself as the Community's representative, should only be considered as a temporary solution.

Another important consequence of the crisis has been more frequent consultations and negotiations between governments as regards international trade. Unlike the 1930s, the recent crisis did not in general lead to unilateral protectionist measures but to intergovernmental negotiations and jointly agreed solutions. One should certainly not exaggerate the originality of 'voluntary' restraints on exports, since there is usually in the background the threat of unilateral measures. However there has been an important qualitative change in the attitudes of national policy-makers and in most cases the various measures introduced were intended to control the rate of growth of imports as opposed to outright protectionism and autarchical policies. There are some people who now think that we are moving slowly towards a more general acceptance of terms such as 'fair' as opposed to 'free' trade and to changes in the international division of labour which will be the result of a combination of international negotiations and the 'free interplay of market forces'.[16] This could be seen after all as an attempt to solve the contradiction of government industrial policies at home and the liberal international economic order.

This also has very important consequences for intra-Community relations. It implies the need for even closer consultations and co-ordination of policies, both in order to reach a common position *vis-à-vis* the rest of the world and also to agree on internal solutions. The experience with the three sensitive sectors discussed above suggests that this is by no means easy. Until now there has been very limited success both in terms of co-ordinating national restructuring policies and, closely related to it, agreeing about the sharing of the burden of adjustment.

Various peculiar characteristics of each sector help to explain, at least in part, the different responses to the problem of surplus capacity. There is however one general factor which seems to determine to some extent the adoption of common policies at the Community level. It is certainly not a coincidence that most joint measures have been taken in the field of external economic policy. The explanation that it is always easier to pass the burden on to foreigners through protectionist measures is not entirely convincing because protection could have been introduced at the national and not at the Community level. The existence of a common instrument, the external tariff and the common commercial policy, forced member countries to act in unison. The same point seems to be confirmed if one examines the success or failure of common internal measures in the three sectors. The implementation of the anti-crisis plan in the steel industry, and later on the imposition of production quotas, are certainly not unrelated to the legal powers given to the supranational institution by the Treaty of Paris.

In its attempt to engineer an internal consensus and promote adjustment the Commission has been subject to a number of constraints. Sometimes internal co-ordination between competition and regional policy or competition and industrial policy has not been easy. The different attitudes adopted back in the 1960s on the issue of transnational mergers is a well-known example. More recently, in 1978, the conflict between the two Commissioners responsible for competition and industrial affairs over the legalisation of the producers' cartel in man-made fibres is another example.

Moreover the Commission has had a legal stick with which to beat national governments but little political power and no carrot to offer. Its ability to influence national restructuring policies and promote adjustment would have been much greater if it had had more money at its disposal for the creation of new jobs, the retraining of unemployed workers, early retirement and other social and structural measures. In the 1978 Community budget, regional policy accounted for 4·7% and manpower policy for 4·6% of total expenditure, the latter being less than 1% of Community GDP. The Regional Development Fund (RDF) was set up in March 1975 and spending has been based on a strict national quota system which became slightly more flexible in 1979 when 5% of the fund's total resources were taken outside the quota system. Moreover the effect of Community regional policy has been even more marginal because those few resources have been spread too widely and also because in most cases the money has been paid directly into national government coffers. This in turn means that there is no guarantee that RDF expenditure will be in addition to the already existing expenditure undertaken by member governments. As far as state aids for regional development are concerned, there are now ceilings set for different areas of the Community either in terms of project-fixed capital costs or in terms of jobs created. This is the so-called co-ordination solution.[17] Other financial instruments available at Community level are the loans given by the European Investment Bank (EIB) for specific projects amounting to over 3,000 million ECUs a year, the 'Ortoli facility' which was set up in 1978 to provide loans for energy and infrastructural investment in the Community's poorer regions (1,000 million ECUs) and a scheme for interest rate rebates on loans which was linked to the EMS.

The attempts to develop some form of common industrial policy at the Community level have so far met with very limited success. The changing political and economic environment inside as well as outside the Community has made this task much more urgent than it might have appeared to be in the early years of European integration. The obstacles have been too many to enumerate here. Let us mention only a few. Ideological differences have been an important factor, although one sometimes has the impression that they are deliberately exaggerated. For example, the liberal image that the Federal Republic tries to present abroad is not entirely consistent with reality. Even more important is the fact that economic structures differ significantly, which means that uniform solutions are far from feasible. Moreover welfare issues are now the main stuff of modern politics and the re-election of governments in power depends largely on their success in delivering the goods. European integration has not so far brought about the withering away of the nation-state nor has it led to that degree of political and economic convergence which would make the co-ordination of policies and the creation of jointly administered instruments a relatively easy task. Effective co-operation in the field of industrial policy means moving from negative to positive integration. Experience so far suggests that the transition may be both arduous and long.

Enlargement – Adding to the Problem?

We shall discuss here some of the problems which may arise from enlargement with respect to sensitive sectors of Community industry. Industrial trade with the three Mediterranean countries now represents only a very small percentage of total trade for individual member countries and the Community as a whole (Table 4.1). Moreover, in view of the fact that with the exception of a few sensitive products imports from the Three already enter the Community market freely (relatively low tariffs only in the case of Spanish imports), one should not expect that accession will drastically alter the flow of industrial exports from the new members to the Nine. Sensitive products may prove an exception and it is on these that we propose to concentrate our discussion.

Another general point one should bear in mind is that all three countries run big deficits in their industrial trade with the Nine. If we take an average of the 1976 and 1977 data (OECD), we find that the coverage of imports by exports in the Community's trade with Greece was 252%, and 235% and 210% with Portugal and Spain respectively. Moreover, given the limited degree of reciprocity in trade concessions to date, one would expect these deficits to increase after the complete liberalisation of trade. Thus, as regards industrial trade as a whole, the Nine are most likely to gain rather than lose from enlargement. The Spanish market is by far the most attractive, given its present high level of protection, its size and also its potential for growth.

However, much concern has been expressed about the likely effects of enlargement on sensitive sectors suffering from surplus capacity. Table 4.2 contains data on trade between each of the three countries and the Community in steel, textile fibres, yarns and fabrics, clothing and footwear. Greece and Portugal are big net importers of steel products and textile fibres. The exact opposite applies to yarns and fabrics and even more so to clothing and footwear, where both countries have very high positive figures in their normalised trade balances.[10] As regards Spain, the only important difference is in its trade in steel products where for both years the normalised trade balance was very near zero.

The data in Table 4.3 show the relative importance of the three countries as suppliers of the Community for all the above-mentioned sensitive products. With the possible exception of footwear, where Spanish exports alone accounted for 7% of total imports (average of the 1976 and 1977 data) the three countries are relatively marginal suppliers. However this is only the case if we include intra-EC trade in our calculations. As a percentage of imports from third countries alone, imports from the Three represent more than 10% of the total for

Table 4.1 Trade with Greece, Portugal and Spain as a Percentage of Total Exports and Imports in Manufactures (SITC classification 5–8)[1]

	Greece 1976		Greece 1977		Portugal 1976		Portugal 1977		Spain 1976		Spain 1977		Σ 1976		Σ 1977	
	X	M	X	M	X	M	X	M	X	M	X	M	X	M	X	M
EC-9	0·7	0·3	0·7	0·3	0·5	0·2	0·5	0·2	1·5	0·8	1·4	1·0	2·7	1·3	2·6	1·5
France	0·6	0·2	0·7	0·2	0·6	0·1	0·6	0·2	2·1	1·7	2·2	2·1	3·3	2·0	3·5	2·5
Germany	1·0	0·6	0·9	0·6	0·5	0·2	0·5	0·2	1·6	0·8	1·5	0·9	3·1	1·6	2·9	1·7
Italy	1·2	0·3	1·3	0·3	0·5	0·1	0·6	0·1	1·8	0·5	1·7	0·9	3·5	0·9	3·6	1·3
UK	0·5	0·1	0·6	0·1	0·7	0·5	0·7	0·4	1·2	0·6	1·2	0·6	2·4	1·2	2·5	1·1

[1] Figures include intra-Community trade.

Sources: OECD, *Trade by Commodities: Series B* (Paris: OECD, various issues); own calculations.

Table 4.2 **Balance of Trade in Sensitive Products (in millions of US dollars)**

	(SITC No.)	X 1976	X 1977	M 1976	M 1977	X−M 1976	X−M 1977	$\frac{X-M}{X+M}$ 1976	$\frac{X-M}{X+M}$ 1977
Greece – EC–9									
Iron and steel	(67)	73·0	35·3	143·6	194·5	−70·6	−159·2	−0·33	−0·69
Textile fibres	(25)	14·3	12·1	62·4	58·2	−48·1	−46·1	−0·63	−0·66
Yarns and fabrics	(65)	202·3	228·6	147·7	184·9	+54·6	+43·7	+0·16	+0·11
Clothing	(84)	379·2	436·6	24·5	30·9	+354·7	+405·7	+0·88	+0·87
Footwear	(85)	23·6	27·7	0·7	0·9	+22·9	+26·8	+0·94	+0·94
Portugal – EC–9									
Iron and steel	(67)	16·1	13·5	94·1	158·7	−78·0	−145·2	−0·71	−0·84
Textile fibres	(25)	3·5	1·6	37·9	32·2	−34·4	−30·6	−0·83	−0·91
Yarns and fabrics	(65)	153·3	173·9	73·2	80·2	+80·1	+93·7	+0·35	+0·37
Clothing	(84)	112·3	128·5	9·8	6·9	+102·5	+121·6	+0·84	+0·90
Footwear	(85)	13·0	20·1	0·4	0·3	+12·6	+19·8	+0·94	+0·97
Spain – EC–9									
Iron and steel	(67)	339·6	408·7	286·8	439·0	+52·8	−30·3	+0·08	−0·04
Textile fibres	(25)	32·2	38·1	98·6	77·0	−66·4	−38·9	−0·51	−0·34
Yarns and fabrics	(65)	122·2	161·1	145·1	142·0	−22·9	+19·1	−0·09	+0·06
Clothing	(84)	115·4	139·7	34·5	43·3	+80·9	+96·4	+0·54	+0·53
Footwear	(85)	161·0	173·4	5·6	6·3	+155·4	+167·1	+0·93	+0·93

Sources: OECD, *Trade by Commodities: Series B* (Paris: OECD, various issues); own calculations.

Table 4.3 Community Imports of Sensitive Products from Greece, Portugal and Spain (as a percentage of total imports)[1]

(SITC No.)	Greece		Portugal		Spain		Σ		Intra-EC	
	1976	1977	1976	1977	1976	1977	1976	1977	1976	1977
Iron and steel (67)	0·5	0·2	0·1	0·1	2·4	2·9	3·0	3·2	69·9	68·8
Textile fibres (26)	0·3	0·3	0·1	0	0·7	0·8	1·1	1·1	32·6	32·2
Yarns and fabrics (65)	1·7	1·7	1·3	1·3	1·0	1·2	4·0	4·2	65·9	65·3
Clothing (84)	3·9	3·9	1·1	1·2	1·2	1·3	6·2	6·4	48·7	49·3
Footwear (85)	1·0	1·0	0·6	0·8	7·5	6·5	9·2	8·3	67·6	67·7

[1] Including intra-Community trade.

Sources: OECD, *Trade by Commodities: Series B* (Paris: OECD, various issues); own calculations.

all the above-mentioned sensitive products except textile fibres. Thus the argument that the three applicants are only of marginal importance as suppliers of the Community market is no longer valid. This is especially true in the case of clothing and even more so of footwear.

There are a number of factors which have to be taken into consideration before making any predictions concerning the future development of trade in those sensitive sectors. Community restrictions, usually in the form of quotas, apply to exports from the Three. Therefore one should expect the latter to increase their share of the Community market after trade liberalisation. But it is interesting that those sectors are also heavily protected in Greece, Spain and Portugal. One should not therefore take it for granted that there will only be a one-way traffic after their integration into the customs union.

The main comparative advantage of the Three in sectors such as textiles, clothing and footwear is their relatively low wage cost. Table 4.4 gives the average hourly earnings in existing member countries (there are no data for Luxembourg), the three applicants and three representative countries of the Third World, namely, Brazil, South Korea and India. These data refer to the textiles and clothing sectors. Although international comparisons of wages should be treated with much caution, the differences here are so enormous that some general conclusions are permissible. Wage differences between Denmark and Portugal are about six to one but are also three to one between Denmark and Italy. On the other hand, similar differences exist between the three Mediterranean countries and important Third World exporters of textiles and clothing. If we take South Korea, for example, where average wages are at least three times as high as those received by workers in India, and convert monthly into hourly earnings, we find that the average Korean worker receives less than half the wage earned by his Portuguese counterpart who is by far the lowest paid in the context of the enlarged Community,[19] So the comparative advantage which the three Mediterranean countries seem to have *vis-à-vis* Northern European producers disappears when they are compared with some developing countries which have been constantly increasing their share of cheap textiles and clothing in Community markets.

In textile yarns and clothing Portuguese and Greek exporters are likely to expand their exports to the Community. We are however talking about relatively small quantities. The Portuguese have concentrated so far on the British market while the Greeks have done the same with the German one. Moreover it has been suggested that 'Greece specialises in quality textile products which seem to present less serious problems to the existing Community'.[20] The Spanish industry, most of which is concentrated in the Catalan region, has been

Table 4.4 **Wages: Average Hourly Earnings in the Textiles and Clothing Sector (in US dollars)[1]**

Country	Textiles 1973	Textiles 1977	Clothing 1973	Clothing 1977
Belgium	2·11	4·42	1·63	3·58
Denmark	3·26	6·28	3·05	6·06
France	1·61	2·83	1·46	2·53
Germany	2·56	4·42	2·32	3·99
Ireland[c]	1·80/1·13	3·08/1·90	1·78/1·11	2·66/1·80
Italy[b]	1·25	2·28	1·18	1·87
Netherlands	2·73	5·20	2·66	4·68
UK[c]	1·90/1·24	2·80/2·13	1·77/1·18	2·60/1·95
Greece[a]	0·68	1·46	0·58	1·24
Portugal[b]	0·44	1·07	0·34	0·95
Spain[a, b]	0·88	1·61	0·69	1·30
Brazil[a, b, e]	104·70	133·98	85·50	117·60
South Korea[e]	48·06	117·14	37·54	94·50
India[a, e, f]	34·10	32·60	29·73	28·99

[1] Exchange rate conversions based on annual averages.
[a] Footwear is included in the same category as clothing.
[b] 1977 data not available; 1976 used.
[c] Separate figures for men and women. In each case the first number refers to men.
[e] Average monthly earnings.
[f] 1977 data not available; 1975 used.

Sources: ILO, *Yearbook of Labour Statistics 1978* (Geneva: ILO, 1979); IMF, *International Financial Statistics* (Washington, DC: IMF, various issues); own calculations.

hit by the textile crisis and extensive restructuring has already been undertaken. Furthermore there has been a persistent trend of relative decline in all traditional industrial sectors in Spain which is expected to continue in the foreseeable future.

When we turn to footwear and steel, the two smaller applicant countries can be safely ignored because of their small size and the insignificant effect which their exports have on Community industry. However, Spanish footwear production is equal to one-quarter by volume of Community production. Exports are dependent to a large extent on the possibilities of access to the Northern American market which absorbs approximately half Spain's exports.[21] Regarding steel all three countries are net importers in their trade with the Community. Both the Portuguese and the Greeks had big plans for expansion which were not received with much enthusiasm in Community circles, given the serious crisis undergone by the European steel industry in recent years. However, if one takes into account the heavy dependence of those countries on imported steel and the small size of their existing production, arguments against expansion are difficult to sustain unless the Commission can offer suggestions and financial aid for investment in other sectors. As regards Spain, there have been many difficulties in the past. Anti-dumping action has been taken against Spanish exports coupled with the introduction of substantive duty charges. There has also been strong pressure from Brussels to make investment plans which were intended to improve the productivity and competitiveness of the Spanish steel industry, compatible with the process of rationalisation inside the Community. Spain is the tenth largest producer of steel in the world. The size of the industry, the fact that a large part of it is controlled by INI and its high level of competitiveness have led to some concern in Brussels over the incorporation of Spanish steel into the common market.

The situation in shipbuilding, another declining sector with big surplus capacity, is rather different because of the lack of any tariff protection and the existence of flags of convenience, to mention but two factors distinguishing shipbuilding from other industrial sectors. Spanish shipbuilding, which is almost entirely controlled by INI, reached sixth place in the world league table in 1978. It is however faced with the same problems of overmanning and surplus capacity as its counterparts in other Western European countries. For its competitors in the Community Spain's accession should be welcome because it will enable Brussels to have more control over aids and subsidies granted by the Spanish government. In Portugal and Greece, this sector is still relatively small and the main emphasis has so far been on ship-repairing.

Although enlargement is likely to lead to a greater penetration of Community markets in the above-mentioned sectors by exports from the three new members, the main threat to the Community industries does not come from the Three but from other NICs and Japan. The ability of the three countries to increase their exports to the main markets of Western Europe will depend very much on the degree of protection for the Community as a whole from third country imports. The entry of the Three is bound to increase the protectionist tendencies inside the Community. There are at least two other important factors which are also likely to influence decisively future developments in the above-mentioned sectors. The greater the problems that Greek, Portuguese and Spanish industrialists have to face after accession, especially in capital and skill-intensive products, the more they will be forced to concentrate on those sectors where they now seem to have a comparative advantage. The second factor which should be borne in mind concerns the degree of protection in intra-EC trade. This does not necessarily have to be in the form of tariffs or quotas. The greater the freedom in intra-EC trade, the more likely it is that production of labour-intensive goods such as textiles, clothing and footwear will be concentrated in countries on the inner periphery of the Community. This has already been happening with respect to both Italy and Ireland. It is however dangerous to generalise too much about whole sectors. The experience of the German textiles and clothing industry, for example, suggests that intra-sectoral special-isation is also very likely.

Dangers for the New Entrants

The need for adjustment will be much greater for the three prospective members of the Community. They will have to bring down their tariff protection *vis-à-vis* EC producers and adopt the CET which is much lower than their own tariffs against third countries. They will also have to adopt all the association, preferential and other trade agreements signed so far by the Community, which will mean opening their market further to competition from developing countries. One should however add that tariff structures in developing countries are not always rational in the sense of being part of a consistent policy which aims to promote industrialisation. On the contrary, their rationality is very often measured in terms of the political power of particular industrialists.[22]

Community membership also implies some control over govern-ment aids and subsidies as well as the various export incentives which seem to have been used rather liberally by all three applicant countries. The same will also apply to the various types of non-tariff barriers although it could be argued that we can safely rely on the ingenuity of the Mediterraneans to be always ahead of the Brussels bureaucracy in inventing new ways of protecting their domestic industry against foreign competition!

Since governments in the three countries will not be able to use various policy instruments in order to protect their industries inside the Community, it could be maintained that they will want to ensure that they retain full freedom in the use of the exchange rate which can serve as an instrument for preserving the price competitiveness of their internationally traded goods. This is exactly what they have been doing since the beginning of the international recession. One can go even further and argue that the exchange rate might be used as an instrument for protection, which implies some form of undervaluation of the national currency.

The above arguments could lead to the belief that the new members will have no interest in joining the EMS.[23] However, as long as periodic readjustments in exchange rates are an essential part of the whole arrangement, membership of the EMS does not deprive a member government of the use of the exchange rate instrument. It is true, though, that as long as the three countries are inflating much faster than the present members of the EMS, there will be constant need for devaluations and membership of the system might restrict their freedom of movement. One last but very important point is that there are serious objective constraints on the use and the effectiveness of the exchange rate instrument. One could mention, for example, the low price elasticity of demand for many imported goods in the three countries (mainly raw materials and capital equipment) and the inflationary effects of devaluation in a small and open economy.

Accession will also mean changes in the system of indirect taxation. This should lead to some rationalisation which might not have taken place unless it had been imposed from outside. We read, for example, that in Greece VAT will substitute for as many as forty-six actually existing indirect taxes.[24] This should help to alleviate the administrative burden for firms and might lead to greater efficiency.

A number of econometric studies have already been published in which an attempt has been made to predict the possible effects for the industries of the applicant countries of tariff elimination. One is not surprised to find out that in most cases the 'revealed comparative advantage' of the Three lies in traditional industries with a high labour input or those based on domestic resources. Thus Greece's most competitive sectors are textiles and clothing, followed by rubber and leather products, iron and steel, non-ferrous metals and metal manufactures.[25] It is interesting that even with respect to textiles and clothing there has been some anxiety about the likely effects of membership. Producers have expressed concern about competition from developing countries, the removal of export incentives and also the effects of equalisation of wages between men and women in an industry where women account for a large part of the labour force.[26] The least competitive sectors appear to be transport equipment and mechanical and electrical engineering, where most existing firms may find it extremely difficult to survive under free trade conditions.

Similar studies undertaken for Spanish industry suggest that food products, leather and footwear are the sectors most likely to benefit from free trade.[27] They are followed by wood and furniture and, interestingly enough, transport equipment and oil products. At the bottom of the list, that is, the least competitive sectors, we find electrical appliances, industrial and agricultural machinery, office equipment and chemical products. It was rather surprising to find that drinks and tobacco were also included in the list of the most vulnerable sectors, which must indicate a high level of protection.

We have not been able to find a similar study for the Portuguese industry. Silva Lopes[28] has expressed optimism over the likely effects of trade liberalisation with the Community, based mainly on the existing low level of protection in Portugal. He has expressed greater concern about the possible effects of free trade with Spain. It is certainly true that tariff protection in Portugal is relatively low compared with Greece and Spain, and in that respect we should expect that the elimination of tariff barriers will not be felt as much by Portuguese industry. We have not been able, however, to examine other measures of protection which may be used by the Portuguese authorities and which in most other countries seem to be more efficient than tariffs.

Given the strong dualistic nature of the three industries, it probably does not make much sense to talk in terms of sectors or even subsectors. Even in what appear to be the most competitive ones, there will be a large number of small and inefficient firms which are unlikely to withstand foreign competition. In Greece more than 90% of the total number of industrial establishments have fewer than ten employees. Approximately the same percentage is true of Portugal, but only if we take the number of twenty employees as the dividing line. In Spain 72% of all firms have fewer than five employees. These firms account respectively for more than 40% of industrial employment in Greece and 15% in Spain.[29] One should, however, beware of always equating smallness with inefficiency. Many small and medium-sized firms have been among the most dynamic firms in Italy during the recession. Moreover small size is at least partly a function of the structure of industry and the relative importance of some traditional sectors. We read, for example, that the usual size of a Greek textiles firm is not significantly smaller than that found in other Community countries.[30] This statement appears somewhat surprising. Another point which should be borne in mind as regards the effects of free trade is that small enterprises often cater for local markets where the problem of import competition is not likely to arise.

On the basis of the existing structure of trade between the three applicant countries and Community members, as well as the degree of trade liberalisation reached before enlargement, one can say that free industrial trade which is an integral part of EC membership would be expected to have a negative effect on the balance of payments and the manufacturing sector of the three countries. This is certainly based on a *ceteris paribus* assumption but there is little else one can do at this stage.

If we think in dynamic terms there is a much bigger danger, namely, that enlargement may lead to the freezing of the existing vertical division of labour between the Three and the industrial core of Western Europe. In free trade conditions the Three may be forced to specialise even more in those sectors where their present comparative advantage lies. This would exacerbate the tensions inside the Community with respect to the so-called sensitive sectors, would strengthen the protectionist tendencies *vis-à-vis* the rest of the world and would compromise the future prospects for growth in the three new members. Specialisation in a relatively small number of products for which the income elasticity of demand is low and price competition very strong is not a good investment for the future. Moreover there is no possibility that European countries with an organised labour force can compete with Third World countries in labour-intensive goods such as textiles and clothing. The three Mediterranean countries need a more diversified and vertically integrated industrial structure in order to place future economic growth on a more self-sustained basis. Diversification and vertical integration are certainly related to the size of the domestic economy. There is therefore an important difference in the potential that exists for a country like Spain on the one hand and Greece and Portugal on the other. The three countries need to climb up the ladder of international division of labour. After all, in most cases comparative advantage does not exist, it is created.

Let us now examine whether the adoption of Community rules as regards the free movement of labour and capital is likely to have an important effect on the industrial sector of the three countries. Free labour movement has been a major concern for Community members and especially countries such as Germany and France. The existence of high rates of unemployment in the whole of Western Europe, coupled with the continuous shift of German industry, for example, towards more technology and skill-intensive industries make it highly unlikely that there will be any massive migration of unemployed workers from the new members in the foreseeable future. The above-mentioned economic reasons are further strengthened by the social and political conditions which apply at either end of the migration flow. If the above argument is correct then labour migration will no longer constitute the safety valve for countries with high rates of unemployment which already applies to the two Iberian countries, even if, as is likely, unemployment becomes worse on accession to the Community owing to the disappearance of many inefficient firms in the new members and the consequent laying-off of workers.

Ceteris paribus, Community membership should not be expected to have a significant influence on foreign investment flows to the three Mediterranean countries.[31] First of all, membership will not bring about any significant change in the regime covering foreign direct investment although, for example, repatriation of profits will become easier in the case of Greece. All three countries are already operating an 'open door' policy towards foreign investment, with some qualifications in the case of specific sectors, chiefly in the two Iberian countries. Thus membership of the Community will not signify any radical departure from the status quo. Moreover to the extent that import substitution has been the single most important factor which has hitherto appealed to foreign investors, membership of the Community should have a very small, and, if anything, negative effect since domestic markets will no longer be protected. It is however possible that there will be an increase in investment in those sectors where the labour input is very high and restrictions exist at present on trade between the Three and the Nine. The obvious examples are textiles and clothing. However, assuming that wage costs are a major consideration determining the location of a particular investment, why should German investors prefer one of the three Southern European countries to the Third World countries where wage costs are substantially lower? In this connection, another relevant factor will be the degree of protection of Community markets from the rest of the world. Last but not least, it could be argued that as long as membership of the Community increases the confidence of foreign investors in the preservation of the political and economic status quo in the countries concerned, then this again may lead to a larger capital inflow than would otherwise have taken place.

Government policies and economic developments at home and abroad are likely to play a much more important role in influencing investment decisions of transnational enterprises than Community membership as such. At times of recession and rising unemployment there is likely to be a scramble among member governments for the few internationally mobile capital projects available. Should the Community not attempt to work out some jointly agreed rules or a list of priorities? Or were the authors of a recent publication on regional policy right when they argued that such a goal flies in the face of the realities of the situation?[32]

Let us now add a few words about compensatory payments and sources of financing which will become available to the new members after accession. All three countries are expected to be net beneficiaries from the Regional and Social Fund but the amounts involved are very small indeed. The EIB and the 'Ortoli facility' should also provide them with extra sources of financing for industrial investment. No prediction can be made as to the likely amounts involved. The only thing one can say is that so far there has been a clear preference shown towards the less developed countries and regions of the Community.

All in all one can conclude that accession presents a real challenge and threat to the industrial sector of the three Mediterranean countries. We have already seen in Part One that the rapid industrialisation of the 1960s and early 1970s took place behind a shield of protection which in many cases still remains relatively strong. The industrialisation process was also facilitated by a host of government measures and, last but not least, a very favourable international economic environment. As regards the latter, the picture has already changed drastically following the recession. Membership of the Community will mean that much of the protection will disappear while at the same time governments will be more constrained in the use of other policy instruments. The three countries enter a liberal economic environment where the main emphasis is on free trade and where there is very little in terms of internal transfers of resources such as take place on a massive scale inside each member country. Will the fresh wind of competition that will result from their integration into the common market help to invigorate their infant industries? Or is there a big danger that the infant will catch pneumonia?

Suggestions for the Future

How far its members can get in handling industrial policy as a Community issue instead of a national one (as it largely still is) is one of the tests of how much integration will develop in Western Europe.[33]

So Diebold argued in his pioneering study on *Industrial Policy as an International Issue*. In a world of slow rates of growth and high unemployment the problems of industrial adjustment in Western Europe will become increasingly acute. A shortage of energy in the near future is also likely to add to the already existing pressure for structural change. Faced with such a situation, Community member governments will be forced to resort more and more to industrial policies since macroeconomic measures are clearly inadequate for dealing with structural problems. If nothing is done at the Community level, there is a real danger of uncontrolled protectionism in intra-EC trade while at the same time the Community's ability to act as a unit in negotiations with third countries, which may increasingly involve bargaining about market shares and possibly also investment decisions, will be seriously impaired.

If the above analysis is correct the Community will need a new approach to trade and industrial problems as well as new policy measures going far beyond the field of negative integration. The Community may have to take measures to control the rate of expansion of imports from third countries in order to avoid the adoption of unilateral measures by member governments acting under strong domestic pressure. Such measures may have to be taken before a crisis situation is actually reached. What was thought yesterday to be appropriate for steel, textiles and clothing applies today to motor cars and may tomorrow also apply to various branches of electronics and electrical engineering. The Community should also be prepared to become involved in intricate negotiations with third parties which may involve a difficult discussion over internal policies. At the same time the Community should share, together with member governments, the burden of adjustment resulting from growing import penetration in particular industrial sectors and also try to facilitate change. The Community is very much dependent on international trade and no member country can afford to cut itself off from the international division of labour. Thus if the Nine, and tomorrow the Twelve, want to retain their competitiveness in foreign markets continuous adjustment will be necessary. The above also implies the need for closer consultations and co-ordination of national policies inside the Community. The higher the degree of economic interdependence reached, the stronger will be the need for management.

We believe that enlargement adds to the already existing pressure for change in such a direction. The three prospective members have specialised in what are now declining sectors in the industrial core of Western Europe. Their accession will therefore strengthen the pressure for adjustment. At the same time it will also highlight the lack of any specific policy designed to cope with the problems of less developed areas inside the Community. If nothing happens in this field the danger is that intra-EC income disparities may remain, or even worsen, and this in turn could lead to growing protectionism both inside the Community and *vis-à-vis* third countries.

In a very heterogeneous economic unit such as the Community it makes little sense to talk of a single industrial policy. Moreover in such a Community centralisation of decision-making, especially when it involves intervention at the micro level, would be counterproductive. However, Community institutions can still play a very useful role. One needs more clearly defined structural policies which would operate in parallel with member government policies, greater expenditure through the Regional and Social Funds, more resources for the EIB in order to promote new investment and a wider use of financial instruments such as the 'Ortoli facility'. Transfers or loans could be linked to specific projects and would thus enable the Community to exercise some influence over investment decisions. This would also reassure potential donors that their money will be spent in a good cause. A more selective use of financial resources could have a major impact on particular areas or sectors without immediately necessitating large and politically difficult increases in the Community budget. Agreement might also be easier to reach if the emphasis were placed on loans linked to specific projects and the raising of funds in the international capital market under Community guarantee.

We believe that more clearly defined policies, based on what Pinder called 'parallel instruments'[34] at the EC level, and more resources would enable Community institutions to play an active role in promoting adjustment in the industrial sector. The Commission and the Community in general could also play a valuable role in collecting and disseminating information to national and regional administrations as well as to private enterprises. Textiles is an example where a decision has already been taken to set up a better information system in Brussels in order to provide manufacturers with data on output, stocks and demand inside the Community as well as with relevant developments in the rest of the world.[35]

Previous experience suggests that it is not at all easy for the Commission to play an active role in the field of high technology. The record of many governments at 'picking the winners' has not been very good and it is unlikely that a supranational institution with limited political powers could perform better in this field. The Commission could however perform a useful function in raising issues of common interest, encouraging member governments to co-ordinate their sectoral policies, promoting mergers, and so on. The existence of national industrial policies has virtually prevented EC industrialists from exploiting the large size of the Community market in some high technology sectors where this would in fact constitute an important advantage.

Various proposals have been put forward with reference to the problems arising from the second enlargement. Commissioner Natali has spoken of a special fund for all Mediterranean regions, the aim being to narrow the economic gap between the North and the South inside the Community and make the transition towards full membership easier for the three new members. The availability of funds for new investment in the Mediterranean regions would also provide the Commission with some leverage which could be used to avoid further specialisation in sensitive industrial sectors.

In its fresco, the Commission talked in terms of structural measures in the new members being part of multi-annual action programmes agreed upon at the Community level. This implied some form of planning, or programming, to use a more inoffensive term. The experts of the German Development Institute in West Berlin which published a series of studies on enlargement went much further. They spoke of an agreed specialisation which would involve both governments and enterprises in different member countries.[36] Their argument was that industrial expansion within the Community should be controlled by comprehensive consultation and negotiation procedures to supplement the market as an allocation mechanism. This could ensure balanced growth inside the Community while also facilitating economic relations with third countries. The idea of agreed special-isation is not very different from the analysis and conclusions reached by people like Pinder, Hager and Diebold[37] or from what the French usually refer to as 'organised trade'. The analysis we have made in previous sections of this chapter points in a similar direction. We believe however that this can only come about very slowly. In order to assist such a development the Community will first of all have to develop new policy instruments, backed up by increased financial resources.

The new members will need additional finance if they are to achieve structural reforms which will enable them to adapt to Community membership and gradually close the economic gap separating them from the other member countries. The first years of the transitional periods will be crucial and therefore urgent action will be needed. In this respect it is encouraging that the Community has been discussing the possibility of transferring funds to Portugal through the Com-munity budget and the EIB before accession. The provision of Community finance tied to specific projects is the type of stick and carrot policy which could help to calm the fears expressed by the Commission and many industrialists in the existing members about the likely effects of enlargement on declining sectors. However, with the entry of the three countries which are still in the process of industrialisation, some special provisions would have to be made for their particular needs. For example, small and medium industry is of vital importance for the Three and will have to bear the brunt of competition after accession. Hummen has made the obvious point that since in the Community all enterprises with up to 500 employees are counted as small and medium industry, a transfer of this definition to Greek conditions would be meaningless since it would encompass Greek large-scale industry as well.[38] Provision should be made to facilitate the financing of small and medium firms. A special instru-ment, the 'global loan', has been developed within the framework of the EIB for financing such firms but the results so far have been limited.

In the foreseeable future industrial policy is likely to remain mainly the preserve of national governments. It may be useful here to add a few words about the role of governments in facilitating the transition of the three applicant countries to full membership and promoting their industrial development in the future. The experts of the German Development Institute have argued that the three countries need to protect their industries after accession in order to avoid both the closure of many firms with the concomitant disastrous implications for employment and growth and the freezing of the existing division of labour with the advanced industrialised countries. They have advocated the use of educational tariffs for infant industries and have asked for flexibility and tolerance on behalf of Community institutions.

It is almost certain that large parts, if not the whole, of the three countries will be considered as development areas following the example of Protocol 30 of the Irish Treaty of Accession. This recorded an understanding that in applying its competition policy the Community would deal leniently with Ireland's incentive schemes. The new members will need special incentives in order to attract new investment. Given the high unemployment rates, especially in the two Iberian countries, employment premiums appear to be highly desirable. Instead of devoting all its efforts to a 'witchhunt against any distortion of competitive conditions',[39] as Pinder has so aptly described it, the Commission should show some flexibility and tolerance towards countries or regions which are still in the process of industrialisation. Close consultations with the governments concerned would however be essential in order to avoid overinvestment in sectors where there is not much scope for expansion.

The Irish have relied much on foreign direct investment for their recent industrialisation.[40] Political stability, low wages, a generous set of incentives and free access to the British and later the Community market have attracted more and more transnational enterprises into the country. As we have seen in Part One, foreign investment has also played a major role in the industrialisation process of the three Mediterranean countries and is likely to continue to do so in the future, especially if the host country has a carefully designed industrial strategy with a clear list of priorities. We have however argued that accession alone will not radically change the relative attraction of the three countries to foreign investors. Moreover the political balance of power in Greece, Portugal and Spain, which is substantially different from that found in the Republic of Ireland, makes it rather unlikely that these countries will base their industrialisation strategy on foreign investment.[41]

It is therefore inevitable that a substantial amount of investment will have to be domestically financed. This will require, among other things, an improvement of their financial systems and capital markets in order to channel national savings to productive investments more effectively. Will the necessary rationalisation take place? This question is also very relevant with regard to the three national administrations which have hitherto been characterised by many and gross inefficiencies. After all, under- or semi-development is not only manifest in terms of low levels of income. It may be true that the greatest challenge of Community membership is addressed towards the state bureaucracies which will have to undergo major reorganisation if they are to survive in the new political environment. This applies particularly to the two Iberian countries where a large and strategic part of the industrial sector is directly controlled by the state.

If the Community continues to develop its own structural policies and financial instruments slowly, then it should at least show some flexibility *vis-à-vis* the new members in the application of Community rules. The Commission itself views recourses to safeguard clauses as an undesirable but necessary alternative if the appropriate measures are not taken at an early stage. This is of course only a second- or third-best solution but in a Community consisting of members with mixed economies and with large differences in income levels and economic structures free industrial trade with very little in terms of joint management and compensatory payments can hardly achieve an equilibrium.

5

Mediterranean Agriculture

For many people the CAP has been the greatest achievement of the European Community. The adoption of a common policy and the liberalisation of trade in an economic sector with a long tradition of heavy government intervention is undoubtedly a big success for European integration. For others however the CAP seems to be a totally irrational policy which acts as a factor of disintegration in Western Europe and causes serious problems in relations with third countries. Different views usually reflect divergent interests.

Still, very few would be prepared to argue that free trade could provide a feasible alternative to the existing CAP. There are some peculiarities of the agricultural sector which have forced governments, not only in Western Europe, to interfere with the 'free interplay of market forces'. The interaction of a fluctuating and seasonal supply with a rigid and inelastic demand causes short-term instability in agricultural markets. On the other hand increases in production due to productivity growth are not usually matched by similar increases in demand because of the low income elasticity of demand for food in developed countries. Thus in the long term there is a tendency for agricultural prices to decline in real terms. Internal imbalances between supply and demand, coupled with severe international competition, have made agriculture a declining sector in Western Europe.

The above factors, among others, bring about a strong pressure from the farming population for protection and government intervention. For social, political and economic reasons this pressure has been very difficult to resist. Moreover most governments have been extremely sensitive to the risks involved in a high degree of dependence on food imports from abroad. Thus security of supply has been another major consideration which led to government intervention in favour of domestic agriculture. In a world where most governments play an active role in agricultural markets and in guaranteeing a certain level of income for their farmers and where international trade is usually trade in residuals, with dumping as a common phenomenon, 'world prices' have little economic meaning.

The Treaty of Rome outlined the concept of a CAP in the broadest of terms (Articles 38–47). The common agricultural market was to be created gradually during the transitional period but there was nothing like the detailed timetables envisaged with respect to the customs union. The main objectives were set out in Article 39 as follows:

(a) to increase agricultural production by promoting technical progress and by ensuring the rational development of agricultural production and the optimum utilisation of the factors of production, in particular labour;
(b) thus to ensure a fair standard of living for the agricultural community, in particular by increasing the individual earnings of persons engaged in agriculture;
(c) to stabilise markets;
(d) to ensure the availability of supplies;
(e) to ensure that supplies reach consumers at reasonable prices.

The above objectives were sufficiently general to enable the authors of the Treaty to enlist the agreement of all six member governments. On the other hand some inherent contradictions were not avoided; these became more obvious as the general objectives were translated into concrete action.

The period between 1962 and 1967 has been characterised as the transitional period when the basic principles of the marketing and pricing policy were agreed. These were the unity of the market, Community preference and financial solidarity. In 1967 the first common prices were adopted and since then common market organisations have been set up for most product categories. At the present moment the only important product which is still not covered is potatoes.[1]

This chapter starts with an examination of the structure of agricultural production and the policies followed until now in the three prospective members. This is intended to fill the gap left in Part One where we concentrated entirely on industrial developments in the Three. It is then followed by a brief survey of the CAP, especially as it applies to the Mediterranean regions of the Community. The first two sections provide the groundwork for what constitutes the main objective of this chapter, namely, to explore the likely effects of enlargement on the farming populations in the Nine and the Three and also to examine the broader economic effects of integrating the three agricultural sectors into the CAP and the pressures which may arise for reform.

It may be objected that disproportionately great attention is paid to agriculture which after all will account for a relatively small percentage of GDP in the Community of Twelve. Moreover it has often been argued that the best form of agricultural policy in the three Mediterranean countries is the development of industry and infrastructure. Our justification for this long chapter is that the agricultural sector is certainly not small in the three applicant countries and it is also unlikely that its economic size will shrink rapidly in the foreseeable future. Although we share the view that further economic development in the Three will crucially depend on a sustained effort in the industrial sector, it is however true that the adoption of the Community's agricultural policy will have an important effect not only on Greek, Portuguese and Spanish farmers but also the three economies as a whole. Moreover the CAP is by far the most developed common policy and the subject of much controversy. For many people enlargement is seen as an opportunity for reform. And this is what we propose to discuss here.

The Agricultural Sector in the Three Prospective Members

In countries with high rates of unemployment or underemployment the agricultural sector has traditionally played a very important role in terms of social stability. It provided an extensive system of social security long before the state took over this responsibility in modern welfare societies. At the same time the agricultural sector has constituted a source of surplus human resources always ready to be tapped. Thus the rate of exodus from the land has always depended on the availability of economic opportunities in other sectors at home or abroad. During the first stages of a country's industrialisation the agricultural sector did not only provide the economy with cheap labour. It also offered raw materials and food at very low prices, much needed foreign exchange and accumulated savings which were channelled to industrial investment. These observations are not purely theoretical. On the contrary, they are very relevant to the recent experience of the three applicant countries, at least for a good part of the postwar period.

Recent economic growth in Western Europe has been characterised as industry-induced. The three Mediterranean countries, together with all member countries of the Community, have experienced a sharp decline in the relative economic importance of their agricultural sectors. This is clearly manifest in terms of the latter's share of the total labour force, GDP, or external trade (Chapter 1). However it is also true that agriculture occupies a more important position in the three economies than in any of the nine members, with the exception of Ireland. If we take the percentage of the labour force engaged in agriculture, it varies from 31·3% in Portugal to 20·2% in Spain and from 22·2% in Ireland to 2·7% in the United Kingdom, with an average of 8·0% for the Community of Nine.[2] As regards agriculture there are also other important characteristics which the three countries have in common. One is their relatively small livestock production and their specialisation in the so-called Mediterranean products. This is not only a function of natural and climatic conditions. It is also closely related to farming structures and other social and economic factors. Thus, with many small family farms and an ample supply of labour, it makes economic sense to specialise in intensive crops. Productivity per hectare or per worker is considerably lower than the Community average for the same products, but not very different from what we find in other Mediterranean regions of the Community of Nine. Furthermore governments in the three countries have played and continue to play a very important role in production and investment, while they also provide their farmers with heavy protection against foreign competition. But this is not a peculiar feature of Greece, Portugal and Spain.

Despite the continuous exodus from the land, total agricultural production in Greece has been rising very fast (Table 5.1). Productivity growth compares very favourably with that experienced by

Table 5.1 **Indices of Agricultural Production and Agricultural Productivity Per Capita 1976 (1961–65 = 100)**

	Total agricultural production	Per capita agricultural productivity
Belgium and Luxembourg	120	118
Denmark	99	88
France	122	108
Germany	120	112
Ireland	131	118
Italy	124	114
Netherlands	162	141
UK	118	112
Greece	159	153
Portugal	99	103
Spain	145	127

Source: John Marsh, 'The impact of enlargement on the Common Agricultural Policy', in Wallace and Herreman (eds), op. cit., p. 188, table 5.

Community members (Table 5.1), although yields per hectare are still relatively low (Table 5.2). The difference is particularly noticeable with respect to wheat and dairy products. The data in Table 5.3 show that big increases in production have been registered with respect to most fruit and vegetables, while for traditional products such as tobacco production has remained almost stagnant. Greece is more than self-sufficient in almost all fruit and vegetables.[3] The same also applies to wheat, rice, sugar beet, tobacco and olive oil (Table 5.4). On the other hand, despite the fast increases in production with respect to maize and most meat and dairy products, the rates of self-sufficiency have declined because of even faster increases in consumption. There has been a constant rise in the demand for feedstuffs, while at the same time the improvement in living standards has brought about a switch in consumption in favour of meat products.

Greece remains a net exporter of agricultural products in contrast to both Spain and Portugal. In 1978 the coverage of agricultural imports by exports was of the order of 163·4% (Table 5.5). In relative terms Greece's surplus with the Community was much larger. Most of Greece's imports of meat came from non-Community sources and so, naturally enough, did its imports of tropical products (SITC classification 07) which was the second most important item on the import side. As for dairy products and eggs, it appears that the Community countries have already captured the biggest share of the market left for

Table 5.2 **Yields of the Main Agricultural Productions (average 1975, 1976, 1977)**

Product	Unit	Greece	Portugal	Spain	EC–9
Wheat	100kg/ha	22·6	11·7	15·8	40·66
Rice	100kg/ha	46	39·7	61·3	42·7
Maize	100kg/ha	41·4	12·1	38·0	48·4
Potatoes	100kg/ha	155·8	89·4	141·3	247·8
Sunflower seed	100kg/ha	13·3	6·1	6·2	16·6
Cauliflower	100kg/ha	114·4	—	237·5	237·2
Tomatoes	100kg/ha	316	337·4	171·5	336·8
Onions	100kg/ha	127·3	179·2	278·0	278·5
Melons	100kg/ha	208·5	64·4	189·5	230·6
Grapes	100kg/ha	75·4	34·5	26·8	79·0
Tobacco	100kg/ha	11·3	15·5	17·2	20·2
Cow's milk	kg/cow	1,431	2,252	2,918	3,517·7

Sources: FAO, *Production Yearbook 1977*, Vol. 31 (Rome: FAO, 1978); Eurostat, *Yearbook of Agricultural Statistics 1974–77*. (Luxembourg and Brussels, various issues); own calculations.

imports. Fruit and vegetables accounted for more than half of Greece's agricultural exports to the Community and the rest of the world. The second most important item was tobacco and this was followed by exports of cereals. In both cases the bulk of Greek exports went to non-Community countries.

Table 5.3 **Indices of Agricultural Production (average 1975, 1976, 1977; 1965–7 = 100)**

Products	Greece	Portugal	Spain	EC–9
Cereals (total)	118	87	142	117
wheat	104	94	84	114
rice	100	78	107	125
maize	185	77	150	179
Potatoes	159	104	127	68
Sunflower seed	150	—	1,762	657
Sugar	319	90	416	139
Vegetables and melons				
cauliflower	103	—	74	89
tomatoes	233	104	179	101
onions	98	87	111	165
melons	261	111	171	114
Wine	113	71	98	104
Fruit				
apples	129	141	303	82
pears	137	92	250	107
peaches	263	142	214	94
apricots	262	100	85	116
oranges/tangerines	157	84	122	157
lemons	140	154	275	130
Olive oil	137	73	122	115
Tobacco	112	—	87	130
Cattle	111	120	119	110
Pigs	144	112	180	125
Sheep	101	67	82	100
Beef and veal	169	151	n.a.	186
Sheep and lamb meat	94	76	n.a.	140
Pigmeat	240	164	n.a.	130
All fresh milk	143	163	187	104
Condensed and evaporated milk	—	—	333	89
Dried milk and buttermilk	—	267	325	193
All cheeses	137	123	148	151
Butter	75	200	320	115

Sources: FAO, *Production Yearbook*, op. cit., various issues; own calculations.

Table 5.4 **Rates of Self-Sufficiency for the Main Agricultural Products (in percentage terms)**

Products	Greece 1965–7	Greece 1975–7	Portugal 1965–7	Portugal 1975–7	Spain 1965–7	Spain 1975–7
Cereals (total)	101	89	72	41	78	88
wheat	115	111	61	53	96	98
rice	112	121	32	60	97	113
maize	54	43	72	27	35	31
Potatoes	99	107	110	94	96	98
Sugar	65	95	7	5	59	83
Tomatoes	100	100	100	100	119	110
Onions	100	102	102	99	122	120
Melons	100	—	103	100	111	105
Wine	115	126	131	131	110	126
Apples	100	105	100	100	100	101
Pears	100	112	100	100	108	101
Oranges/tangerines	131	156	100	100	240	168
Lemons	149	174	100	100	192	198
Peaches	164	—	100	100	102	105
Apricots	138	—	100	100	115	108
Olive oil	107	107	110	100	122	123
Tobacco	343	176	—	50	42	28
Cattle	98	98	100	99	100	100
Pigmeat	98	96	95	93	—	95
Sheep and lamb meat	71	87	100	99	—	99
Beef and veal	68	63	79	70	—	92
Fresh milk	100	100	100	99	99	99
Evaporated and condensed milk	0	0	0	87	87	65
Dried milk	0	0	71	75	19	26
All cheeses	96	99	105	96	91	90
Butter	82	79	62	87	77	89
Sheep	92	100	101	100	100	100

Sources: FAO, *Production Yearbook*, op. cit.; FAO, *Trade Yearbook* (Rome: FAO, various issues); own calculations.

Table 5.5 Greece: Trade in Agricultural Products (US dollars m., 1978)

Groups of products (SITC No.)	Imports			Exports		
	EC-9	World	EC-9/world (in percentage terms)	EC-9	World	EC-9/world (in percentage terms)
Live animals (00)	1.5	9.0	16.7	2.3	2.3	100.0
Meat and meat preparations (01)	23.0	255.0	9.0	0.0	2.0	0.0
Dairy products and eggs (02)	75.0	86.4	86.8	0.0	5.8	0.0
Cereals and cereal preparations (04)	19.0	67.5	28.1	2.3	81.0	2.8
Fruit and vegetables (05)	11.3	31.0	36.5	340.9	614.0	55.5
Sugar, sugar preparations and honey (06)	3.0	3.0	100.0	4.0	10.0	40.0
Coffee, tea, cocoa, spices and manufactures (07)	14.0	92.0	15.2	3.0	7.0	42.9
Feedingstuff for animals (08)	19.8	12.7	64.1	2.6	21.2	12.3
Miscellaneous food preparations (09)	14.0	11.0	78.6	2.0	1.0	50.0
Beverages (11)	12.4	13.0	95.4	25.0	44.0	56.8
Tobacco, unmanufactured (121)	7.4	6.8	91.9	73.5	212.6	34.6
Hides, skins and furskins (21)	10.0	33.0	30.3	7.0	55.0	12.7
Oilseeds, oil nuts and oil kernels (22)	0.0	37.0	0.0	0.0	2.0	0.0
Cotton (263)	0.0	36.4	0.0	3.4	42.6	8.0
Crude animal and vegetable materials (29)	11.0	17.0	64.7	5.0	12.0	41.7
Animal and vegetable oils and fats (4)	11.3	13.4	84.3	54.6	70.6	77.3
Total	232.7	724.2	32.1	525.6	1,183.1	44.4

Trade balance, Greece – EC-9: +292.9.
Trade balance, Greece – world: +458.9.

Source: OECD, Statistics of Foreign Trade – Annual: Tables by Reporting Countries, Series B, Vol. 3 (Paris: OECD, 1978).

Greece is a mountainous country which suffers from lack of water. Therefore its agricultural potential is relatively limited. Irrigation is a very important factor indeed. According to figures quoted by Pepelasis,[4] irrigated areas in Greece account for 21·6% of cultivated land. This should be compared with 29·0% in the case of Italy and 14·6% and 11·8% in the case of Portugal and Spain respectively. It is believed that given water availability, accessibility and soil morphology, a further 20% can be irrigated in Greece. The agricultural sector suffers from the preponderance of small farms which cannot operate as economically efficient units of production (Table 5.6). Almost half the agricultural area is divided into farms smaller than five hectares. On the other hand big farms (fifty hectares and over), which in the Community account for 42% of the agricultural area, are virtually non-existent in Greece. In recent years, as a result of massive internal and external migration, there have been shortages of manpower in many areas, particularly in peak periods. Part-time farming is also a very widespread phenomenon.

The Greek government guarantees minimum prices for the main agricultural products. Intervention is undertaken by several state or co-operative agencies. Price stabilisation is coupled in many cases with direct and indirect income aids which are intended to keep consumption prices relatively low, and with export subsidies. Fertilisers, pesticides and feedstuffs are distributed at subsidised prices. In addition almost all farmers are totally exempt from direct taxation. As regards imports there is a very strict system of controls usually operating through the granting of licences or quotas. The association agreement with the EEC made provisions for the harmonisation of agricultural policies between the two sides. However the only progress achieved was in terms of a reduction, or elimination mostly in the case of the Community, of customs duties. Other forms of trade protection remained.[5]

It has been argued that 'measures aiming to protect the level of farmers' incomes tend by their very nature to maintain a given social structure and a structurally deficient economic environment'.[6] A compromise between the two types of objectives has not been easy to find. This is certainly true of the recent experience of the three applicant countries as well as the Community. In Greece governments have often been criticised for paying insufficient attention to structural measures and investment. There has certainly been no comprehensive agricultural policy. However the role played by the state in these areas has been far from negligible. The cost of surface irrigation has been borne entirely by the state. Large amounts of credit have also been offered to farmers through the Agricultural Bank at subsidised interest rates. During the period 1965–76 almost 40% of agricultural invest-

Table 5.6　**Size of Farms in Greece, Portugal, Spain and EC–9 (hectares)**

Country	0–4.9	5–49	50 and over	Total
Greece				
A average size of a farm for each size group	1·96	8·75	101	3·45
B %⌈distribution of the number of farms per size group	79	20·5	0·5	100
C % distribution of the agricultural area per size group	45	52·5	2·5	100
Portugal[1]				
A average size of a farm for each size group	1·18	9·86	276	6·16
B % distribution of the number of farms per size group	78	21	1	100
C % distribution of the agricultural area per size group	15	34	51	100
Spain				
A average size of a farm for each size group	1·65	14·20	259·9	15·1
B % distribution of the number of farms per size group	62·5	33	4·5	100
C % distribution of the agricultural area per size group	6	26	68	100
EC–9				
A average size of a farm for each size group	2·52	17·22	113·73	17·18
B % distribution of the number of farms per size group	42	52	6	100
C % distribution of the agricultural area per size group	6	52	42	100

[1] Size groups 1–4 and 4–50.

Sources: NSSG, *Greek Statistical Yearbook 1976* (Athens, 1977), data for 1971. Instituto Nacional de Estatística (INE), *Estatísticas agrícolas 1969* (Lisbon, 1970), data for 1968. Ministerio de Agricultura, Secretaría General Técnica, *Anuario de estadística agraria 1977* (Madrid, 1978), data for 1972. Eurostat, *Yearbook of Agricultural Statistics* (Luxembourg and Brussels, 1978), data for 1975.

ment was financed by public funds.[7] The proportion of total agricultural budgetary support to agricultural value added in Greece is comparable to that of the Community (the ratio in 1977 was 33% in Greece and 39% in the EC, including national aids in member countries).[8] Little however seems to have been done to improve distribution and marketing or to increase the share of the final price of an agricultural good received by the producers themselves and thereby reduce the profits of the various middlemen who intervene at successive stages. Co-operatives could play a very important role here, but although they are many and large in number they have not as yet succeeded in liberating themselves from governmental tutelage. It is actually the hope of many people, including members of PASEGES (Panhellenic Confederation of Agricultural Co-operatives), that changes in this direction will be forced upon the Greek government by accession and economic necessity.[9]

The government has been trying to control the production of certain goods which are in surplus and for which foreign markets are difficult to secure. Such agricultural goods are sugar, tobacco, currants and rice. It usually relies on quotas or licences to producers. At the same time various incentives have been offered to encourage the production – and consequently reduce Greece's import dependence – of feedstuffs (for example, maize) and meat. Nevertheless the price policy on livestock products seems to have been inconsistent with this objective and was therefore changed in January 1979. The production of early varieties of certain fruit and vegetables has also been strongly encouraged.

Since 1975–6 the main objective of the annual agricultural programmes has been to bring about a progressive harmonisation of institutions, policy, instruments and prices with those of the CAP. During the accession negotiations agriculture proved for both sides, the most difficult subject to tackle. It is therefore rather surprising, from a health point of view, that such a heavy dish was left for the last course.

The experience of Portuguese agriculture in the last two decades has been quite different. Production and productivity have stagnated (see Table 5.1). As a matter of fact the very slow increases in total production during the 1960s were reversed in the first years following the 1974 revolution. With respect to most products included in Table 5.2, yields per hectare in Portugal are substantially lower than those registered in Greece. The picture which emerges from Table 5.4 is even more depressing. Self-sufficiency with respect to many products, especially cereals, has declined considerably between the mid-1960s and mid-1970s. A word of caution is necessary at this point. The figure for tomatoes, one of the main agricultural exports of Portugal, is rather misleading. It refers solely to raw tomatoes, while almost all exports are in a processed form and therefore not taken into account in this table. Production of most meat and dairy products has risen fast (Table 5.3) but consumption has increased even faster.

Portugal has been for many years a net importer of food. Trade deficits have risen dramatically since 1974 because of the serious cutback in domestic production and the addition of about half a million *retornados* to the consuming population. In 1978 Portuguese agricultural exports accounted for 30·6% of imports (Table 5.7). None the less Portugal ran a small surplus in its trade with the Community for the very simple reason that imports from the Nine represented only 11·3% of total imports while its exports to the Community were almost one-half of total exports. Cereals, cotton and oilseeds were the main import items. The only significant exports were beverages, more than 50% going to Community markets, and fruit and vegetables.

Natural conditions over a large part of the country are hardly favourable for farming. In addition the economic policy pursued by the Salazar–Caetano regime was almost entirely geared towards industrial development, and investment in agriculture has been extremely low. In 1972, for example, the ratio of gross fixed asset formation to total agricultural output was only 7·2% in Portugal, as compared with 12% in Spain and 17% in Greece.[10] There has been a lack of credit facilities and extension services offered to farmers. Prices were fixed for most agricultural products at each of the three different stages, namely, production, processing and consumption. The aim was to keep consumer prices down and the difference was made up by a complicated system of subsidies and aids granted at each successive stage. Price guarantees and intervention measures were undertaken by specialised commodity boards, the national *Juntas*. But prices were only raised sporadically and often remained stable for several years. The situation changed drastically after the revolution when there was a big jump in prices to levels surpassing those found in most Community countries. As regards tomatoes, one of the few success stories, the Junta Nacional de Frutas made advance cash payments to producers, which seems to have acted as an important incentive. In the case of many products, for example, wheat, the state commodity boards enjoyed a power of monopsony over products. This was sometimes matched by an exclusive right to purchase from abroad.

Until the revolution Portugal was divided between very small farms in the north and latifundia in the south. According to the data in Table 5.6, 78% of the farms were smaller than four hectares. At the same time 1% of the farms accounted for 51% of the total agricultural area. This was an extreme form of a dualistic structure. According to a survey made in 1968, 45% of the farmers were over 55 years of age and 44% were illiterate.[11] This, combined with the existing farm structure and government policy, could hardly be expected to make a dynamic sector out of Portuguese agriculture.

Table 5.7 Portugal: Trade in Agricultural Products (US dollars m., 1978)

Groups of Products (SITC No.)	Imports			Exports		
	EC-9	World	EC-9/world (in percentage terms)	EC-9	World	EC-9/world (in percentage terms)
Live animals (00)	3·2	4·9	65·3	0·1	0·5	20·0
Meat and meat preparations (01)	2·0	24·0	8·3	0·0	0·0	—
Dairy products and eggs (02)	7·0	8·4	83·3	1·4	5·3	26·4
Cereals and cereal preparations (04)	25·9	358·0	7·2	0·0	5·0	0·0
Fruit and vegetables (05)	8·5	15·6	54·5	23·2	82·6	28·1
Sugar, sugar preparations and honey (06)	10·0	56·0	17·9	0·0	2·0	0·0
Coffee, tea, cocoa, spices and manufactures (07)	1·0	41·0	2·4	1·0	2·0	50·0
Feedingstuff for animals (08)	14·0	75·3	18·6	0·8	1·7	47·1
Miscellaneous food preparations (09)	3·0	5·0	60·0	0·0	2·0	0·0
Beverages (11)	15·9	16·0	99·4	99·0	163·0	60·8
Tobacco, unmanufactured (121)	1·5	16·2	9·3	0·0	0·0	—
Hides, skins and furskins (21)	4·0	20·0	20·0	3·0	5·0	60·0
Oilseeds, oil nuts and oil kernels (22)	0·0	144·0	0·0	0·0	0·0	—
Cotton (263)	0·1	155·0	0·1	0·5	0·6	83·3
Crude animal and vegetable materials (29)	10·0	19·0	52·6	10·0	18·0	55·6
Animal and vegetable oils and fats (4)	3·6	26·4	13·6	2·1	13·2	15·9
Total	109·7	984·8	11·3	141·1	300·9	46·9

Trade balance, Portugal – EC-9: +31·4.
Trade balance, Portugal – world: −683·9.

Source: OECD, *Statistics of Foreign Trade – Annual: Tables by Reporting Countries, Series B*, Vol. 3 (Paris: OECD, 1978).

After the revolution agricultural workers occupied the big estates in the south. Then, two main forms of organisation were established. One was the 'collective units of production' (UCP) favoured and essentially run by the Portuguese communist party and the other was agricultural co-operatives which had the support of the socialist party. The law on agrarian reform has been one of the most controversial issues in post-1974 Portugal. The socialist party which initiated this law was attacked from both left and right and in the process lost some of its members and even ministers. Although the law was finally approved by the National Assembly it has not yet been fully implemented because of the strong resistance put up by some of those occupying lands which are supposed to be returned to their former owners. Thus the situation is not yet very clear. Confusion is compounded by the fact that there is no statistical information on farm structures after 1974, although one should add that the pattern in the north has hardly changed at all and thus the average size of farms there continues to be around three hectares.

Because of the unsettled situation in Alentejo and the long period of political instability in the country, one can hardly talk as yet of a comprehensive agricultural policy in Portugal. Democratic governments inherited the institutions and policies from the pre-1974 period. The first reaction was to redistribute the land and raise prices in order to improve the living standard of farmers. But at the same time the need to increase production and reduce the country's dependence on imports remains a primary objective which becomes even more urgent in view of Portugal's accession to the Community.

Despite the rapid exodus from the land, total agricultural production in Spain has risen fast, owing to productivity growth (see Table 5.1). In this respect the Spanish experience is similar to that of Greece, although increases in productivity rates per capita have been considerably faster in the latter. Here again we find that average yields for most agricultural products are much lower than those found in the Community of Nine (see Table 5.2). The only exceptions are certain vegetables like cauliflower and onions, as well as rice. The most remarkable increases in production during the ten-year period covered in Table 5.3 have been with respect to dairy products, fruit and sunflower seed. As regards meat products, there has been a noticeable switch in production away from mutton and lamb to beef and veal. During this period Spain increased its rate of self-sufficiency in cereals although it still remains heavily dependent on imports of maize. Spain continues to be a net exporter of various kinds of fruit and has also increased its wine surplus from 10% to 26% of domestic production. As regards meat and dairy products Spain remains a net importer and in some cases dependence on imports has actually increased. This is the same phenomenon we have observed in the other two countries. Owing to a high income elasticity of demand for those products increases in domestic supply have not been sufficient to satisfy the growing demand (Table 5.4).

Although an important exporter of agricultural goods, Spain has had a food deficit every year since 1965 with the sole exception of 1970. As we see from Table 5.8 the main import items in 1978 were cereals, oilseeds and tropical products. The Community was only a marginal supplier of the Spanish market, accounting for only 12·6% of total imports. On the export side fruit and vegetables were by far the most important items, representing more than half of Spanish agricultural exports. Other significant items were beverages, oils and fats. The Community provided the main export outlet for Spanish agricultural exports. Thus Spain had a sizeable surplus in its agricultural trade with the Nine which was however overcompensated by its deficit with the rest of the world.

It is much more difficult to generalise about Spanish agriculture than it has been for smaller countries like Greece and Portugal, which are also more homogeneous in agricultural terms. In the northern and north-western part of the country, from the central Pyrenees to the Portuguese border, we have an area with relatively heavy rainfall which presents many common points with the dairy belt of the Western part of the Community. It is mostly devoted to livestock production. Average incomes here are very low, mainly because of the small size of farms and the consequent lack of economically efficient units. We then have the central plateau area (la Meseta). This is a group of regions which represent the biggest part of Spanish territory. The average rainfall is small and climatic conditions are basically continental. The type of agriculture practised is mostly centred on extensive cereal production and livestock production, the latter based on rough grazing. The pattern of farm structures in those areas is a combination of large traditional estates and small-scale peasant farming, especially in the south in Andalusia. Some areas of small farms specialising in fruit and vegetables can be found in the valleys of Ebro in the Saragossa basin, around Seville and in the Tagus valley. Finally, we have the Mediterranean coast which is limited in size but benefits from the most favourable natural conditions for intensive agricultural production. Most of this area is under irrigation and it is mainly here that the so-called Mediterranean products are grown. Thus it would be a serious mistake to consider the whole of Spain as a Mediterranean region. The definition of what constitutes such a region will be discussed in the following section.

The farming structure in Spain is similar to that found in Portugal before the revolution. A very large number of small farms coexist with

Table 5.8 Spain: Trade in Agricultural Products (US dollars m., 1978)

Groups of Products (SITC No.)	Imports			Exports		
	EC-9	World	EC-9/world (in percentage terms)	EC-9	World	EC-9/world (in percentage terms)
Live animals (00)	7.4	12.9	57.4	1.5	12.0	12.5
Meat and meat preparations (01)	47.0	184.0	25.5	12.0	26.0	46.2
Dairy products and eggs (02)	66.2	81.2	81.5	0.3	24.1	1.2
Cereals and cereal preparations (04)	7.4	610.5	1.2	7.0	53.1	13.2
Fruit and vegetables (05)	35.2	160.8	21.9	1,025.9	1,381.3	74.3
Sugar, sugar preparations and honey (06)	10.0	38.0	26.3	9.0	31.0	29.0
Coffee, tea, cocoa, spices and manufactures (07)	11.0	521.0	2.1	33.0	98.0	33.7
Feedingstuff for animals (08)	12.0	133.7	9.0	22.2	40.5	54.8
Miscellaneous food preparations (09)	21.0	26.0	80.8	5.0	28.0	17.9
Beverages (11)	55.0	60.0	91.7	175.0	303.0	57.8
Tobacco, unmanufactured (121)	0.7	157.4	0.4	0.0	1.4	0.0
Hides, skins and furskins (21)	55.0	205.0	26.8	3.0	4.0	75.0
Oilseeds, oil nuts and oil kernels (22)	1.0	593.0	0.2	3.0	4.0	75.0
Cotton (263)	1.5	91.3	1.6	0.3	1.1	27.3
Crude animal and vegetable materials (29)	40.0	83.0	48.2	8.0	75.0	10.7
Animal and vegetable oils and fats (4)	19.0	129.2	14.7	68.4	288.7	23.7
Total	389.4	3,087.0	12.6	1,373.6	2,371.2	57.9

Trade balance, Spain – EC-9: +984.2.
Trade balance, Spain – world: −715.8.

Source: OECD, Statistics of Foreign Trade – Annual: Tables by Reporting Countries, Series B, Vol. 3 (Paris: OECD, 1978).

latifundia. Farms of fifty hectares and above represent 68% of the total agricultural area (Table 5.6). The concentration of land ownership is thus more pronounced than the average of the Community of Nine.

Minimum guaranteed prices by the state cover about 60% of the total agricultural production.[12] As with other countries, fruit and vegetables are not included. For the latter there are various kinds of subsidies which are offered to farmers for storage, processing and marketing. The price system for cereals is exactly similar to that practised by the Community. To a large extent the same observation applies to wine and livestock production. In fact Spanish governments have tried to harmonise their agricultural policies with those of the Community, presumably in preparation for full membership. Olive oil receives no official aids. It is however indirectly supported through restrictions on imports of competing vegetable oils. Many olive oil producers are among the poorest farmers in Spain.

With the Decree No. 3221 which was introduced in 1972 Spain adopted a new system for regulating external trade which at least in principle is very similar to the Community system. It was based on variable regulating levies which were intended to cover the difference between world and domestic prices. It applies mainly to cereals, vegetables and oilseeds. In addition to the Spanish version of variable levies there are also other forms of protection. Customs duties still apply to most agricultural imports. Moreover there is the so-called global regime with respect to canned meat, canned fruit, hops and other products which implies the fixing of annual quotas by the state. As regards wheat and tobacco, the relevant state agencies have a monopsony power *vis-à-vis* both domestic and foreign producers. In the 1970 Agreement signed with the Community almost all agricultural products were excluded from the list of trade concessions offered by Spain.

It has been estimated that in Spain public expenditure per unit of agricultural value added is about half of the Community average and only one-fifth if we take the ratio between total public expenditure and hectares of agricultural land.[13] Apart from price support measures, state subsidies are also offered to farmers for the purchase of seed, for mechanisation and for the improvement of farms. The cost of irrigation has been borne partly by the state. However, as we have seen, in this respect Spain lags behind both Greece and Portugal. IRYDA, the state agency responsible for structural policy, has been active in creating new, economically viable farms and also consolidating existing ones. As an answer to the small size of many farms, group farming has been extended, particularly in wheat-growing areas in the Meseta. On the other hand, as regards marketing the role of agricultural co-operatives is still very small.

Spanish governments have been trying to encourage the production of feedstuffs and the rearing of cattle through various incentives offered to farmers. Various measures have also been taken to control total production and at the same time improve the quality of wine and olive oil produced in the country. These measures include the restructuring of the olive sector, the elimination of marginal plantations, limits on new planting, the prohibition of irrigation in vineyards, and so on. None the less those who fear the creation of wine and olive oil lakes in the Community of Twelve can argue that even if the total area devoted to vines and olive trees is frozen, total production can still increase very substantially in the future, given the incentive of higher Community prices and the present low rates of productivity.

In Greece and Spain the farming population has shared the fruits of postwar economic development and rising living standards although the same cannot really be said of Portugal. It is however still true that farmers' incomes remain substantially lower than those enjoyed by people engaged in other economic activities; but this is equally true of every existing member of the Community. For reasons related to climate and natural conditions, reinforced by the kind of farming structures prevailing in the three countries, they have specialised more in the so-called Mediterranean products. Their main agricultural exports consist of fruit, vegetables and wine, while they are all net importers of cereals (maize in the case of Greece and Spain), meat and dairy products. Although Greece is the only net exporter of agricultural goods all three have a food surplus in their trade relations with the Community. Western European markets have provided them with the most important outlet for their agricultural exports while they have preferred for obvious economic reasons to import from cheaper sources. In their trade with the Community they have taken advantage of the complementarity that exists between the two sides and the fact that as far as most of their main exports are concerned, the Community of Nine is far from being self-sufficient. The main competition usually comes from other Mediterranean countries. As regards trade with the Community, Greece received the most favourable treatment as a result of its association agreement.

The potential for further expansion of their agricultural production seems to be rather limited. The farming population has been declining rapidly and this trend is likely to continue in the future, albeit at a slower rate, if the economic recession persists. Moreover, natural conditions are usually not very favourable. In countries with typical Mediterranean weather, irrigation will be a determining factor for future production possibilities. Average yields for most products are much lower than those registered in Community countries. This may suggest that the potential for productivity growth is enormous.

However, for many kinds of agricultural production, such as cereals and livestock, there is no possibility that they can attain the same levels of productivity as farmers in north-western Europe. Whether we like it or not, productivity in agriculture is in general closely related to factors which are outside man's control.

The agricultural sectors in the three applicant countries suffer from serious structural problems. This is actually one of the main reasons, if not the main reason, why so much money has to be spent on short-term measures which may be considered by some as only palliatives but no real cure for the problem. However, structural policies are sometimes difficult to implement and the effects take a long time to materialise, which makes them somewhat unattractive to politicians. Nor should one ignore the existence of vested interests and the general resistance to change. Thus restructuring can only take place very slowly.

Mediterranean Agriculture in the Community – A Poor Relation?

While Britain and Germany usually complain about the heavy cost of the CAP and high prices for consumers, the southerners are very critical of the allegedly unfair treatment accorded to Mediterranean producers inside the Community. Europe's North–South problem is well known. Many people also argue that Community policies and the CAP in particular tend to aggravate existing disparities instead of helping to narrow the economic gap.

From an agricultural point of view the Mediterranean regions are defined in a somewhat tautological way as the areas where Mediterranean products are grown, the latter being identified as such by the place where they are mostly grown.[14] The Commission considers as Mediterranean all regions where such products as durum wheat, rice, fruit and vegetables (including citrus fruit), flowers, wine, tobacco, olive oil and sheepmeat represent 40% or more of the total agricultural production. The only products which are grown exclusively in the Mediterranean regions of the Community are durum wheat, rice, olive oil and some fruit. The rest can also be found in other areas as, for example, most fruit, vegetables and wine, the use of energy to heat the greenhouses serving as a substitute for the Mediterranean sun. This is why the French often refer to Dutch tomatoes as 'petrotomates'!

According to the above definition, the Mediterranean regions in the Community of Nine are Provence, the Côte d'Azur, Languedoc-Rousillon, the southern part of Rhône-Alpes and also Aquitaine in France, and most of Italy with the exception of the Po Valley and the Northern Alps. This is a larger area than that encompassed by the application of a strictly geographical definition.

The Mediterranean regions have a number of characteristics in common. They rely rather heavily on agriculture which is a corollary of their low level of industrialisation. Incomes are much lower than in other parts of the Community. Most of the Mediterranean regions also suffer from relatively high rates of unemployment which is combined with underemployment, the latter particularly evident in the agricultural sector. Thus during the postwar economic boom those regions provided the industrialised North with surplus labour. The economic and social characteristics of those regions, in addition to climatic conditions, are very similar to those encountered in Greece, Portugal and Spain.

The Mediterranean regions of the Community represent an agricultural area of 15·6 million hectares (17% of the EC total), with 1·8 million farms (30% of the EC total). They supply about 18% of the Community agricultural production.[15] Labour productivity is considerably lower than in northern regions although productivity per hectare is very similar. There is a sharp contrast between infertile hilly and mountainous areas suitable only for extensive agricultural productions and coastal or fluvial plains of more limited size with fertile alluvial soils cultivated under irrigation. It is in the latter areas that intensive, relatively profitable horticultural and wine production takes place.

The proportion of the labour force engaged in agriculture varies from 5·5% in Provence–Côte d'Azur, where the tertiary sector is extremely important, to 27% in the Mezzogiorno. As regards the share of Mediterranean products the Mezzogiorno comes first again with about 75% of total agricultural output. This percentage falls to approximately 50% in the case of central and northern Italy. In the French Mediterranean regions such products represent 60% of the total output, with wine alone accounting for two-thirds of this figure.[16]

Since the problem of the Community's Mediterranean regions is not confined to agriculture, we should examine the effects of economic integration and Community policies in general rather than restrict ourselves to the CAP. But this would be an enormous task which goes much beyond the scope of this chapter. Moreover the Community has very limited financial instruments and no overall development policy for its backward regions. We will therefore have to concentrate on the effects of the CAP which is not only the most developed policy of the Community but the one which accounts for more than 70% (75·7% of the appropriations for the 1979 budget) of Community expenditure.

The CAP consists of a number of different market organisations applying to groups of products. The standard scheme which regulates production and trade and which applies to cereals, beef, dairy products, sugar and olive oil is intended to insulate Community farmers from world market influences and provide them internally with a system which underpins the market prices for their products. Imports are allowed inside the Community at the threshold price which protects European farmers against the usually lower prices prevailing in world markets. A variable levy is charged on imports which corresponds to the difference between the threshold price and the lowest representative offer price (c.i.f. Rotterdam). In the case of exports, refunds, also known as 'restitutions', are paid to farmers in order to compensate them for the difference between the market price in the Community and the average world price. The internal support system is based on 'target' and 'intervention' prices, the latter being the level at which the appropriate agencies intervene in order to prevent the price from falling any further. The products bought into intervention are stored until they can be sold on the Community or world markets when the economic conditions are favourable.

A brief examination of the provisions made with respect to the main Mediterranean products is appropriate at this point, beginning with those enjoying a strong system of intervention and external protection. The production of durum wheat is covered by the common organisation of the market in cereals. Some farmers in Italy also receive additional special aid in the form of flat-rate payments per hectare harvested. An analogous regime also exists for rice. The two regimes have always tended to be treated as a pair because of French and Italian demands that rice producers are accorded the same treatment as other cereal producers. In the case of tobacco there is a combination of intervention and direct payments to producers. The aim is both to ensure that producers receive a 'fair income' and that manufacturers continue to purchase raw tobacco at world prices. Given the Community's very low degree of self-sufficiency, the system of external protection has been abolished and intervention relies basically on deficiency payments to producers and premiums to purchasers. The regime for olive oil has been subject to changes in recent years in order to reverse the declining trend in consumption. In the Community of Nine more than 99% of the total production of olive oil comes from Italy, which in fact also consumes most of its output. However, demand for olive oil has been declining steadily with a concomitant gain in demand for cheaper competing vegetable oils which are mostly imported. One alternative solution would be to strengthen the system of external protection by levying taxes on imported substitutes which entered Community markets duty-free. But this was strongly resisted by consumers' organisations, importers and, last but not least, the main exporting countries such as the United States. As a result the Commission has adopted the alternative policy of making the price of olive oil more competitive by increasing subsidies to producers and consumers. Thus, in addition to the usual system of target and intervention prices for internal regulation of the market and threshold prices for controlling imports, the Community also pays a production aid – a flat-rate payment per tree to producers – and a consumption aid to refiners in order to bridge the gap between the price paid to producers and the target price. The result is a very expensive system which is still politically tolerable because of the small share of olive oil in total agricultural production.

The regime for wine is extremely complex mainly because of the high degree of heterogeneity of the product, market fluctuations in production and the wide range in quality between years. The support system is intended to deal with problems arising in the market for table wines. It is based on 'guide' prices for different types of wine and intervention measures take the form of aids for storage and distillation. Much of the detail of the wine regime is concerned with improving the quality of wines. There is also control over any new planting in order to avoid a long-term imbalance between supply and demand. As regards imports, protection is based on a system of 'reference' prices and countervailing duties.

With respect to fruit and vegetables the system of internal intervention and external protection is very weak when compared with other product categories covered by the CAP. The only form of intervention that exists applies to nine products (cauliflowers, tomatoes, apples, table grapes, pears, peaches, lemons, oranges and mandarins). 'Withdrawal' prices are fixed as a percentage of basic prices, at which producer groups may buy from their members and thus withhold supplies from the market. If prices fall even further then intervention agencies may take measures to arrest the decline in prices. However withdrawal prices are very low (around 45% of the basic price) and therefore do not provide producers with the same guarantee as intervention prices for most other products which are usually around 90–5% of the target price. In the agricultural year 1977–8 the quantities of the above nine products which were withdrawn from the market represented 0·45% of total production.[17] Those products, with the exception of cauliflower, as well as plums, cherries and cucumbers, also enjoy protection against external competition in the form of customs duties and 'reference' prices which ensure that no imported goods can be sold in Community markets below a certain minimum level of prices. For the remaining fruit and vegetables there is no intervention system whatsoever, and only a weak system of external protection in the form of low tariff rates.

This brief description of Community market organisations for the different Mediterranean products suggests that generalisations can be very misleading. Marketing schemes differ considerably from one group of products to the other. However, in terms of both internal market regulations and external protection, we can distinguish between durum wheat, rice, olive oil and tobacco on the one hand and wine, fruit and vegetables on the other. In the case of the former group of products the Community plays an active role in securing stable prices and fair incomes for farmers. This does not apply to wine and even less to fruit and vegetables. Big fluctuations in production, which are a regular phenomenon, lead to fluctuations in prices and incomes, although one should add that the price elasticity of demand is usually greater than for most cereals and dairy products. The system of external protection is also rather weak. Farmers in Italy and the south of France complain about the agricultural concessions offered to other Mediterranean countries as part of the various bilateral agreements signed prior to 1972 and those which followed the adoption of the so-called global policy. Agriculture has always been a thorny issue in the Community's negotiations with other countries in the Mediterranean littoral. All concessions made, usually in the form of a reduction of customs duties, were strongly resisted by Mediterranean farmers in the Community because they felt threatened by outside competition. However, one should add that concessions for most products were only limited to certain periods of the year during which there was no Community production.[18] This provision, coupled with the existence of reference prices and quotas as, for example, in the case of wine, was intended to allay the farmers' fears. Nevertheless the Commission interservice group which studied the problems of the Community's Mediterranean regions under the direction of Adolfo Pizzuti, found serious weaknesses in the system of external protection, particularly with respect to fruit and vegetables, both fresh and processed.

The various market schemes have so far been discussed mainly in terms of internal regulation and external protection. It is also important to examine the distribution of Community expenditure on each group of products. This is presented in Table 5.9, while in Table 5.10 we find the relative contribution of the same groups of products to total agricultural production. From those two tables it becomes clear that Community expenditure on Mediterranean products has been substantially and consistently below the contribution of the latter to the Community's agricultural output. Tables 5.9 and 5.10 also confirm the fact, much vaunted by the press, that the dairy sector receives the lion's share of total expenditure. Sugar is another product with a disproportionately high share of FEOGA's (European Agricultural Guidance and Guarantee Fund) expenditure. Dairy products and sugar are of course mostly produced in northern regions of the Community.

These two tables suggest once again that we cannot generalise about

Mediterranean products. In relative terms both olive oil and tobacco are heavily subsidised. Yet in view of the market organisation for fruit, vegetables and wine we should not be surprised that expenditure for those products is very small relative to their share in the total farm produce. In fact it seems that the picture is even worse than would appear from these statistics. The breakdown in Table 5.10 of the Community's agricultural production by product or group of products is inevitably based on registered prices which are a function of market forces and Community intervention. Since the prices of many 'Northern' products are kept artificially high, their share of agricultural output is also inflated.

We have mentioned before various factors which seem to determine the kind of market organisation adopted for different groups of products. Expenditure is very much a function of that. For relatively weak marketing schemes, such as the one applied to fruit and vegetables, the usual argument presented is that these goods are not only subject to big seasonal fluctuations but are perishable and there are, moreover, many different varieties of each product. Therefore it is

Table 5.9 **Expenditure by Sector of FEOGA's Guarantee Section (in percentage terms)[1]**

Products	1976	1977	1978	1979[2]
Cereals	13·8	11·2	14·3	16·5
Milk products	48·0	51·8	51·7	46·3
Sugar	4·8	10·6	11·3	10·5
Beef and veal	13·0	8·3	8·2	7·2
Mediterranean products[3]	15·1	12·6	7·4	12·1
Rice	0·4	0·2	0·2	0·4
Olive oil	4·1	4·0	2·3	4·1
Fruit and vegetables	3·9	3·2	1·3	4·4
Wine	2·8	1·6	0·8	1·0
Tobacco	3·9	3·6	2·8	2·2
Sheepmeat and goatmeat	0·0	0·0	0·0	0·0

[1] Excluding monetary compensatory amounts (MCAs).
[2] Provisional.
[3] The only important Mediterranean product which is not included in this table is durum wheat. As for sheepmeat and goatmeat, there was no Community expenditure before 1980.

Sources: Commission of the EC, *The Agricultural Situation in the Community*, op. cit., various annual reports; own calculations.

Table 5.10 **Products as a Percentage of Final Agricultural Production in the Community**

Products	1976	1977	1978
Cereals	10·1	11·0	12·3
Milk products	18·9	19·5	19·7
Sugar	2·6	2·6	2·6
Beef and veal	15·8	15·5	15·8
Mediterranean products[1]	18·4	18·9	19·8
Rice	0·2	0·2	0·3
Olive oil	0·7	1·0	0·8
Fruit and vegetables	11·0	11·5	11·9
Wine	4·8	4·6	5·0
Tobacco	0·4	0·3	0·4
Sheepmeat and goatmeat	1·3	1·3	1·4

[1] The only important Mediterranean product which is not included in this table is durum wheat.

Sources: Commission of the EC, *The Agricultural Situation in the Community*, op. cit., various annual reports; own calculations.

practically impossible to adopt the same kind of intervention measures as those applying to most cereals, meat and dairy products. Furthermore the Community is far from being self-sufficient and therefore imports are needed in order to satisfy domestic demand. Denis Bergmann[19] has pointed to additional factors which help to explain why most countries have traditionally supported the domestic production of cereals, meat and dairy products, while the same is rarely true of fruit, vegetables and wine. In fact the policies pursued by the three applicant countries provide the best illustration of this argument. Such factors are the nutritional value of the so-called Northern products and the price inelasticity of demand which would lead to big fluctuations in farmers' incomes if market forces were left on their own.

Although one cannot easily question the validity of these arguments, it does not necessarily follow that about half of the total expenditure of FEOGA's Guarantee Section should go to dairy farmers alone or that Mediterranean farmers should receive only a very small share. Mediterranean regions are probably more in need of structural measures than price guarantees. Thus there would be little cause for complaint if the imbalance found in the expenditure incurred by the Guarantee Section of FEOGA were compensated by action taken by the Guidance Section. Table 5.11 gives a breakdown by country of the total expenditure between 1973 and 1978 incurred by the Guidance Section of FEOGA as a result of the Community's structural policy in agriculture. It appears that about 30% of total expenditure went to Italy, which may be taken to imply that Mediterranean regions had a relatively large share of the cake. But the size of the cake is extremely small. On the basis of the appropriations made for the 1979 budget the Guidance Section was allotted only 4·6% of the total amount of funds set aside for the CAP. The rest was to be spent on various intervention measures and for the payment of MCAs. Therefore the amount of money spent by the Community on structural policy is so small that it can hardly compensate for the imbalance created by the different kinds of market organisation.

It is therefore possible to reach the conclusion that the Mediterranean regions, although among the poorest in the Community of Nine, do not even receive their 'fair' share of agricultural expenditure, which after all constitutes the bulk of Community expenditure. If Community agricultural expenditure by country is examined, one finds that subsidies to Danish, Dutch, Belgian and Irish farmers are well above the average, while exactly the opposite applies to Italian farmers.[20] Coda Nunziante[21] has found a positive correlation between public subsidies and value added per head of the farming population. In other words this means that the Community spends more money per unit of output produced for the relatively more productive (and consequently better-off) farmers than for the less productive ones. This is an amazing example of an economically regressive policy. As a matter of fact the picture deteriorates further if account is taken of

Table 5.11 **Expenditure of FEOGA's Guidance Section, by Country (in percentage terms, 1973–8)**

Belgium	5·36
Denmark	3·83
France	17·90
Germany	20·05
Ireland	6·18
Italy	30·06
Luxembourg	0·12
Netherlands	5·38
UK	11·12

Sources: Commission of the EC, *The Agricultural Situation of the Community, 1979 Report,* op. cit., own calculations.

national aids to farmers since relatively rich countries of the Community seem to spend more money on their farmers than, for example, a country like Italy.

By concentrating almost entirely on short-term measures, the CAP can be described as a highly conservative policy which does very little to remove the real causes for expensive intervention measures. The lack of a common structural policy for agriculture has to be considered in conjunction with the absence of development or regional policies at the Community level. What exists at present can hardly qualify as Community regional policy.

Effects of Integration

The integration of the three agricultural sectors into the CAP has been the most controversial issue in the enlargement negotiations. It has brought forth strong reactions from farmers' organisations in some member countries which now threaten to delay the accession of the two Iberian applicants. In view of the importance of the CAP in the process of European integration, it is understandable that agriculture should take pride of place in any negotiation with a prospective new member. Moreover, since government intervention and protection are widely accepted rules of the game as regards agriculture but not necessarily industry, negotiations which lead to liberalisation of trade and the adoption of common rules are bound to be complex and protracted. With respect to the second round of enlargement one should also bear in mind that the size of the problem as regards agriculture is totally different from that encountered in industry. The Commission has estimated that in approximate terms enlargement will mean an increase of 55% in the number of people working in agriculture in the Community; a 49% increase in arable land; a 57% increase in the total number of farms and a 24% increase in agricultural production.[aa] The latter is a clear indication of the low agricultural productivity in the three applicant countries.

Table 5.12 gives a more detailed account of the relative importance of agriculture by category of products as compared with Community production. With respect to cereals, meat and dairy products, the three countries are marginal producers. An extreme case is butter production which in the Three accounts for as much as 1·4% of Community production. The only two exceptions are rice and sheepmeat, both being typical Mediterranean products. The picture is very different with respect to most fruit and vegetables, sunflower seed, olive oil and tobacco. In most cases only the entry of Spain will in fact seriously affect the balance between supply and demand inside the Community. With virtually no exception Portugal is a marginal producer. As for

Table 5.12 **Agricultural Production in Greece, Portugal and Spain as a Percentage of Total EC Production (average 1975, 1976, 1977)**

Products	Greece	Portugal	Spain	Greece-Portugal-Spain
Cereals (total)	3·7	1·4	13·8	18·9
wheat	5·4	1·3	11·0	17·7
rice	10·0	12·5	42·7	65·2
maize	3·7	3·2	12·7	19·6
Potatoes	2·8	3·2	16·4	22·4
Sunflower seed	2·2	5·1	268·1	275·4
Sugar	2·8	0·1	10·9	13·8
Vegetables and melons (total)	11·5	6·5	28·8	46·8
cauliflower	2·3	—	13·1	15·4
tomatoes (fresh)	29·5	16·2	49·5	95·2
onions	17·8	10·1	136·7	164·6
melons	123·5	1·7	105·3	230·5
Wine	3·1	5·5	18·3	26·9
Fruit (total)	8·5	4·8	24·7	38·1
apples	3·4	1·7	12·6	17·7
pears	5·1	2·4	16·0	23·5
peaches	22·0	3·6	20·0	45·6
apricots	41·5	4·3	75·4	121·2
oranges/tangerines	27·5	5·9	120·5	153·9
lemons	22·6	2·3	31·9	56·8
Olive oil	48·8	8·7	80·8	138·3
Tobacco	69·5	5·1	14·7	89·3
Cattle	1·5	1·4	5·6	8·5
Pigs	1·1	2·7	12·2	16·0
Sheep	15·6	7·2	30·0	52·8
Beef and veal	1·8	1·4	6·7	9·8
Sheep and lamb meat	14·9	4·3	25·9	45·1
Pigmeat	1·4	1·6	8·1	11·1
All fresh milk	1·8	0·9	6·0	8·7
Condensed and evaporated milk	—	0·1	10·0	10·1
Dried milk	—	0·3	1·1	1·4
All cheeses	5·5	0·9	3·9	10·3
Butter	0·3	0·2	0·9	1·4

Sources: FAO, *Production Yearbook 1977*, op. cit.; own calculations.

Greece, its entry will have a considerable impact in the case of some fruit and vegetables and an even greater effect on olive oil and tobacco.

This complementarity in production between the Three and the Nine is also demonstrated in their present trade relations (Tables 5.5, 5.6, 5.7 and 5.13). In somewhat simplified terms, it is an exchange between fruit, vegetables and beverages on the one hand and animal products (meat, milk, as well as hides and skins) on the other. We have already discussed the importance of the Community as an export outlet for the three countries. Table 5.13 contains data on the Community's trade with third countries, including a column on trade with the Three. As we should expect, the Three are important suppliers with respect to beverages, fruit and vegetables. As for their total exports to the Community, they are only a small fraction of imports to the Nine. Exactly the same applies to the Community's exports to the three countries. The only exceptions are raw tobacco, which is an almost insignificant export item for the Community of Nine, and hides, skins and furskins. As a result of the association agreement of 1961, the Greek market appears to be more open to imports from Community countries than either the Spanish or the Portuguese markets.

Predictions about the likely effects of enlargement on producers and consumers as well as the other general economic effects of integrating the three agricultural sectors into the CAP are extremely hazardous.[23] One has to make assumptions about the future relationship between world and Community prices, production levels in the Nine, the effect of the application of the CAP on production and consumption in the three applicants, exchange rates and MCAs, to mention but a few. Furthermore it should not be forgotten that developments in the agricultural sector depend very much on general trends in the economy and the availability of opportunities in other sectors of economic activity.

Transitional periods for agricultural products have been a hot issue in the Community's negotiations with the three applicant countries. Greece was finally given five years, with the exception of peaches and tomatoes for which the transitional period was extended to seven years. One can safely assume that transitional periods will be even longer in the case of Spain and Portugal, with the added possibility that these will incorporate 'flexibility' clauses.[24] Therefore all forecasts should be treated with great caution and taken merely as an indication of the general direction of likely effects.

In discussing the agricultural aspects of enlargement a distinction can be made between trade and budgetary effects. The incorporation of the three agricultural sectors into the CAP will increase trade between the two sides. This is more likely to strengthen the existing

Table 5.13 **EC-9: Trade in Agricultural Products with Greece, Portugal and Spain (Million US dollars, 1978)**

Groups of products (SITC No.)	Imports			Exports		
	GPS[1]	World[2]	GPS/world%	GPS[1]	World[2]	GPS/world%
Live animals (00)	3·9	505·5	0·8	12·1	212·0	5·7
Meat and meat preparations (01)	12·0	2,179·0	0·6	72·0	1,033·0	7·0
Dairy products and eggs (02)	1·7	561·0	0·3	148·2	2,284·0	6·5
Cereals and cereal preparations (04)	9·3	3,286·0	0·3	52·3	2,284·0	2·3
Fruit and vegetables (05)	1,390·0	7,146·0	19·5	55·0	1,143·0	4·8
Sugar, sugar preparations and honey (06)	13·0	1,050·6	1·2	23·0	1,201·0	1·9
Coffee, tea, cocoa, spices and manufactures (07)	37·0	7,577·0	0·5	26·0	1,065·0	2·4
Feedingstuff for animals (08)	25·6	3,097·0	0·8	45·8	626·6	7·3
Miscellaneous food preparations (09)	7·0	159·0	3·8	38·0	660·0	5·8
Beverages (11)	299·4	620·0	48·3	83·3	3,156·0	2·6
Tobacco, unmanufactured (121)	73·5	1,732·6	4·2	9·6	58·0	16·7
Hides, skins and furskins (21)	13·0	1,542·0	0·8	69·0	418·0	16·5
Oilseeds, oil nuts and oil kernels (22)	3·0	3,805·0	0·1	1·0	28·0	3·6
Cotton (263)	4·2	1,292·9	0·3	1·6	34·5	4·6
Crude animal and vegetable materials (29)	23·0	1,176·0	2·0	61·0	761·0	8·0
Animal and vegetable oils and fats (4)	125·1	1,818·0	6·9	33·9	777·0	4·4
Total	2,040·3	37,547·6	5·4	731·8	15,741·1	4·6

[1] Greece, Portugal and Spain.
[2] Excluding intra-Community trade.

Source: OECD, *Statistics of Foreign Trade – Annual: Tables by Reporting Countries*, Series B, Vol. 3 (Paris: OECD, 1978).

pattern of trade rather than reverse it. As a result of Community preference the three new members will increase their imports of meat, dairy products and sugar from other Community countries. The same should also be expected to apply to Portuguese imports of cereals. Since Community prices are usually much higher than prices prevailing in world markets, this will imply a serious economic loss for the new members. This will also be true even if they continue to import from third countries since the variable levy will be added to the price paid to foreign producers. Silva Lopes[25] has estimated that the cost to Portugal of its imports of agricultural products in 1978–9 would have increased by approximately 350 million US dollars if the country had had to apply the CAP rules. As long as production in the three countries lags behind the fast-growing domestic demand for those products this loss will continue to be incurred. Moreover the increase in prices paid for feedstuffs will have negative repercussions on livestock production in the three Mediterranean countries.

The other side of the coin is that enlargement will provide producers of Northern-type products with new export outlets. The Community's rate of self-sufficiency with respect to sugar, beef and milk products will be reduced but enlargement will not by itself solve the problem of structural surpluses (see Table 5.14).[26]

Another problem for the new members arising from enlargement will be the liberalisation of imports for vegetable oils which will intensify the competition with domestically produced olive oil. This may bring about a serious drop in the consumption of olive oil with negative repercussions for domestic producers, the balance of payments of the Three and the Community budget.

Liberalisation of trade will also lead to increased exports from the Three of fruit, vegetables and wine. However, given the different type of market organisation for these products, producers in the three countries will not have the same price guarantees as cereal and dairy farmers. Mediterranean producers in the south of France and the Mezzogiorno are likely to suffer from low-price competition from the three new members and especially Spain. Enlargement will lead to a substantial increase in the Community's self-sufficiency in most fruit and vegetables (especially citrus fruit) and olive oil (Table 5.14). Although the figure for olive oil is only slightly above 100% there is the danger of growing surpluses in the future because of possible increases in production in the Three, coupled with a decline in consumption levels resulting from the adoption of higher Community prices. The effect of enlargement on the Community's self-sufficiency ratio appears to be small, although a further increase in production, especially in a country like Spain, cannot be excluded. The increase in the Community's self-sufficiency in all Mediterranean products will

Table 5.14 **Production, Trade Balance and Rate of Self-Sufficiency for EC–9 and EC–12**

	EC–9			EC–12		
	Produc-tion	Trade balance	Rate of self-suffi-ciency	Produc-tion	Trade balance	Rate of self-suffi-ciency
	1,000 metric tonnes		%	*1,000 metric tonnes*		%
Wheat	47,518	− 3,046·0	94·0	54,912·9	− 2,146·5	96·2
Barley	39,488	+ 2,897·9	107·9	48,359·9	+ 2,888·3	106·4
Maize	16,402	− 12,659·2	56·4	19,076·4	− 19,769·3	49·1
Rice	793	− 520·6	60·4	1,635·9	− 532·5	75·4
Potatoes	37,630	+ 151·2	100·4	45,166·8	+ 162·0	100·4
Sunflower seed[2]	129	− 881·0	12·8	613·0	− 1,011·8	37·7
Tomatoes[1]	5,092	− 327·7	94·0	9,675·0	− 167·3	98·3
Onions	1,491	− 199·9	88·1	2,617·5	− 171·4	93·9
Melons[2]	492	− 120·6	80·4	3,199·0	− 10·6	96·8
Apples	6,100	− 229·5	96·4	9,061·0	− 287·3	96·9
Pears	2,110	− 36·1	98·3	2,219·0	− 36·1	98·4
Peaches and nectarines[3]	1,686	− 38·2	97·8	2,517·0	− 12·8	99·5
Apricots	172	− 45·0	79·3	471·0	− 30·6	93·9
Oranges and similar	1,935	− 2,388·0	44·8	4,990·0	− 2,040·3	71·0
Lemons	780	− 138·9	84·9	1,072·0	− 27·0	97·5
Sugar	11,812	+ 1,463·3	114·1	13,058·0	+ 1,210·7	110·2
Tobacco[1]	173	− 536·6	24·4	328·5	− 525·0	38·5
Olive oil	497	− 85·5	85·3	2,801·0	+ 6·2	100·2
Wine	13,218	+ 162·9	101·2	17,114·0	+ 406·7	102·4
Beef and veal	6,425	− 49·8	99·2	7,000·5	− 224·0	96·9
Sheep and lamb meat	527	− 254·8	67·5	756·0	− 270·8	73·6
Pigmeat	9,329	− 43·7	99·5	9,825·0	− 95·6	99·0
Condensed milk	1,462	+ 543·3	159·1	1,570·7	+ 522·5	149·9
Dried milk	2,657	+ 731·3	137·9	3,595·5	+ 722·7	125·2
Butter	1,896	+ 121·0	106·8	1,953·4	+ 117·6	106·4
Cheese	3,082	+ 101·2	103·4	3,537·4	+ 84·5	102·4
Eggs (in shell)	3,933	+ 24·5	100·6	4,564·1	+ 7·3	99·9

[1] Excluding processed goods.
[2] The Greek export figure was derived by assuming that 80% of total Greek exports went to EC–9.
[3] The Greek export figure was derived by assuming that 75% of total Greek exports went to EC–9.

Sources: FAO, *Production Yearbook 1978*, Vol. 32 (Rome: FAO, 1979); Eurostat, *Analytical Tables of Foreign Trade NIMEXE – 1978* (Luxembourg and Brussels, 1979); Eurostat, *Yearbook of Agricultural Statistics* (Luxembourg and Brussels, 1978); NSSG, *Monthly Statistical Bulletin* (Athens, 1978); INE, *Estatisticas agricolas 1978* (Lisbon, 1979); Ministerio de Agricultura, *Anuario de estadistica agraria 1978* (Madrid, 1979).

reduce the export possibilities of other Mediterranean countries for which Western Europe has traditionally been an extremely important market outlet. The three applicant countries already account for more than half of all agricultural imports to the Community from the Mediterranean area.[27] Their share is bound to increase with accession. What will then happen to Moroccan and Israeli oranges, Tunisian olive oil and Algerian wine?[28] Various countries which have signed co-operation agreements with the Community in the context of the latter's global policy have already raised the issue of compensation payments arising from enlargement. It is therefore almost inevitable that relations with Mediterranean non-member countries will become even more difficult in the future. Trade diversion will also adversely affect other third countries which are presently exporting sugar, meat and dairy products to the three prospective members. They include the United States, Yugoslavia, and Latin American countries such as Argentina.

We have compared guaranteed prices for various products in the three applicant countries with existing CAP prices. Such comparisons are however extremely difficult and potentially misleading. National statistics are often inadequate and the prices given are not always comparable. As already pointed out, the three countries use various kinds of income subsidies and aids to producers which in most cases will have to be abolished after accession or at the end of the transitional period. Ideally these should be incorporated in the guaranteed prices offered to producers before any comparison is made with CAP prices. But this is an almost impossible operation to undertake. Moreover comparisons between national (and/or CAP) prices are not particularly useful when exchange rates vary substantially from one year to the other and governments can also decide to make use of MCAs. For all these reasons, we have abandoned our original plan of reproducing here a table comparing prices in the Three and the Nine.

The continuous depreciation of national currencies in Greece, Portugal and Spain *vis-à-vis* the currencies participating in the old snake arrangement has made the prospect of Community membership much brighter for all farmers in the three countries. The prices they now expect to receive in national currency terms from the CAP are much higher than they would have been otherwise. In the case of Portugal the rapid devaluation of the escudo in recent years has made guaranteed prices for most cereals, meat and dairy products comparable or slightly lower than those prevailing in most Community countries. For the agricultural year 1976–7 Portuguese prices were still higher for maize, milk and beef.[29] Greek producer prices in 1979 were with very few exceptions lower than Community guaranteed prices. The Agricultural Bank of Greece has estimated the effect of various subsidies on the producers' final income and reached the conclusion that Greek farmers would be worse off with respect to some cereals and tobacco.[30] Comparisons for fruit and vegetables are of little use since Community guaranteed prices are nothing else than withdrawal prices which usually apply to a very small fraction of total production. The biggest gain is likely to accrue to olive oil producers since the Greek price is substantially lower than the Community one. The same also applies to olive oil and wine in Spain. These are, in fact, the two products for which the price differential between Spain and the Community (about one to two) is simply enormous.[31] This also justifies to some extent the fears expressed by French and Italian farmers and the nightmares which some Community officials have about the creation of wine and olive oil lakes after Spain's accession. From the Spanish side the adoption of Community prices is likely to present very serious problems to dairy farmers as well as producers of sugar beet and maize. Serious concern has been expressed in Spain for all three cases.

Thus it appears that with respect to most products farmers will become better off after the accession of their countries to the Community. This will be the result of higher guaranteed prices and more export opportunities. Everything, however, will depend on the future trend in Community prices as well as exchange rates. Judging from the experience of recent years when agricultural prices expressed in units of account have not kept up with inflation and in view of the persistence of surpluses and the growing criticism of the CAP heard even in some French quarters, Greek, Portuguese and Spanish farmers should not expect very much in terms of price increases coming from Brussels. They should however expect some compensation in national currency terms as long as the drachma, the escudo and the peseta continue to depreciate and their governments take no measures, such as the introduction of MCAs, to arrest the increase in agricultural prices. Assuming that the exchange rate depreciation continues, the three governments will be faced with the serious dilemma of having to choose between their consumers and their farmers, the latter representing a large section of the population. The choice will be even more difficult for the Spaniards and the Portuguese since both countries are net importers of agricultural products and thus, *ceteris paribus*, import subsidies in the form of MCAs would make more economic sense.

The other side of the coin is that food prices will go up in the three countries as a result of accession. This will contribute further to the existing inflationary spiral. The Greeks had estimated in 1978 that an immediate adoption of CAP prices would have led to an increase in the cost of living index of about 4·5%. The effect is expected to be more serious in the case of Portugal because of the present gap between producer and consumer prices. In that country which already has galloping inflation, serious income inequalities and falling real wages, a big increase in food prices could have a disastrous effect. Consumers in the Nine are likely to benefit from lower prices and better qualities for most Mediterranean products.

As regards the effects of enlargement on agricultural expenditure and levies going through the Community budget, one can make two very general observations. The first is that the bulk of Community expenditure results from the storing and disposing of surpluses. Only relatively small amounts are spent on products for which the rate of Community self-sufficiency is much below 100%. On the other hand the amount of levies collected from each country is a function of its import dependence on food products. In 1978 agricultural levies, including sugar contributions, covered 26·28% of total expenditure incurred by the Guarantee Section of FEOGA.[32] Various estimates have been made of the likely budgetary effects of enlargement. They are all based on a static analysis assuming existing policies and prices together with current production and consumption levels. Moreover those estimates are intended to provide some indication of the budgetary effects assuming that the three applicant countries were full members without any transitional period in the year for which the estimate has been made. On the basis of the 1978 budget the Commission estimated[33] that enlargement would result in additional expenditure for the FEOGA of about 1,500 million u.a., or about 16% of FEOGA expenditure for the Community of Nine, minus about 450 million u.a. likely to be collected from import levies and sugar contributions. Therefore the three countries' net receipts from FEOGA were expected to be much less than the percentage of their contribution to the Community's agricultural product, not to mention their share of the total farm population. Greece was expected to gain the most, mainly because of the relative importance of tobacco and olive oil in its total agricultural production. On the other hand Portugal's net gain would be marginal. Jim Rollo's estimates were very similar.[34] As for the estimates presented in the House of Lords Report,[35] the net figure was found to be smaller but the calculation was based on 1977 prices. More recently there have been reports about revised estimates based on current data and also horror stories about the exorbitant amounts likely to be spent on olive oil when Spain becomes a full member. In a revised estimate the Commission now expected that after enlargement expenditure on oils and fats, of which olive oil constitutes the major item, would rise from about 800 to 1,500 million ECUs.[36] However, according to internal French sources which did not contradict this particular estimate, the additional expenditure for FEOGA, assuming that the three countries were full members in 1980, would not exceed about 20% of current expenditure. One would then have to subtract agricultural levies which in the case of the three new members would amount to about one-third of current receipts from the CAP. Here again Greece appeared to be the main beneficiary in budgetary terms, while Portugal was expected to end up with a net loss.

Enlargement will also present a serious problem for both sides in terms of agricultural policies and institutions. The CAP will have to accommodate the interests of three new members with large farming sectors which, moreover, have very different characteristics from those prevailing in the Community of Nine. An even wider divergence of structures and interests combined with the need for unanimous decisions may test the limits of well-established Community methods of decision-making such as the marathons and the package deals. New market organisations will have to be set up for products of special interest to the new members. In Greece's Treaty of Accession provision has been made to include cotton under the CAP and to consider production aids for dried figs and raisins. On the other hand the three new members will have to dismantle their armoury of policy instruments applying to the agricultural sector and adjust to CAP rules. The latter will necessitate important institutional changes which in turn imply a serious economic cost. From the bird's eye view of the three agricultural policies presented earlier it appears that both Spain and Greece have already travelled some way towards harmonising their policies with the CAP. For Portugal the problem of adjustment will be quite formidable.

It is usually taken for granted that the three countries will be net beneficiaries following the incorporation of their agricultural sectors into the CAP. From the above analysis this conclusion does not seem to be at all evident. Spain and Portugal have a food deficit and therefore their integration into a highly protectionist group where prices are much higher than world prices cannot easily be turned to their advantage. Moreover the fact that they specialise in Mediterranean products for which guaranteed prices are usually not very high exacerbates the problem for them. In the foreseeable future Portugal is bound to be a net loser, certainly in trade terms and possibly also in budgetary terms. As for Spain, it seems rather unlikely that higher prices for its agricultural exports will be sufficient to compensate for higher import prices. On the budgetary side Spain is expected to make a small net gain. For Greece, the prospects are certainly much better. Participation in the CAP will lead to a substantial net transfer of resources from FEOGA. As regards trade the Greeks rely on the dynamism of their fruit and vegetables sector in order to compensate for losses resulting from more expensive imports of feedstuffs, meat and dairy products.

For the Nine, enlargement is likely to lead to an improvement of their trade balance with the new members. At the same time, assuming that existing policies remain unchanged, the budgetary cost will not be exorbitant although it will be more than just another straw on the camel's back. This cost may increase substantially if enlargement leads to a significant increase in the rate of self-sufficiency for sensitive products such as wine and olive oil which may result from the adoption of CAP rules by the three new members. However the most serious problem arises with respect to Mediterranean regions in France and Italy which already constitute problem areas for the Community of Nine. The strong reaction of farmers in the affected regions has clouded the atmosphere of the enlargement negotiations and threatens to prolong them unduly.

The Crisis of the CAP

The crisis of the CAP can be summarised under three different headings: (a) structural surpluses in some sectors, mainly milk and sugar, which have become very costly because the Community finds it extremely difficult to dispose of extra quantities in international markets, (b) divergence in inflation rates and exchange rate changes which have led to the introduction of MCAs and thus put an end to the unity of the market and (c) growing regional disparities coupled with the lack of any integrated programmes for less developed areas and only a fledgling structural policy for the agricultural sector.

Since 1976 price increases in agricultural units of account (or ECUs since 1979) have been very small indeed. Even when we take the devaluations of 'green' rates into account, agricultural prices in national currency terms have been lagging behind inflation rates in most member countries. However, the total expenditure incurred by FEOGA has been rising fast in real terms. From 5·6% of the final agricultural product in 1975, it had already reached 9% by 1978.[37] Growing expenditure has been mainly the result of the persistent, not to say swelling, butter and sugar mountains. The Community of Nine now has high self-sufficiency ratios for most products, with maize, tropical goods and oilseeds being the main exceptions. The real problem however arises with respect to milk products and sugar where the Community is faced with what is usually referred to as structural surpluses. The latter term should imply some form of long-term disequilibrium between supply and demand which cannot be easily corrected through price changes, or at least price changes which are politically and socially feasible. We think, though, that a distinction should be drawn between the dairy sector and sugar, since production of the latter is more sensitive to price changes and it is also easier for producers to switch into alternative cultivations.

A co-responsibility levy of 1·5% was introduced in the milk sector in 1977. However this has not been sufficient to check the growth in production and the surpluses have continued. Repeated attempts by the Commission to freeze prices and raise the co-responsibility levy paid by producers have so far failed because of the unpopularity of such proposals with most agricultural ministers and the farmers' lobbies. A similar fate has met the Commission's attempts to reduce production quotas for sugar. Thus while domestic consumption remains almost stagnant production goes on increasing because of productivity growth. Unless more drastic measures are taken at the Community level, the problem is expected to continue and indeed worsen as production grows faster than demand.

Surpluses do not only entail a financial cost for the Community's taxpayer. They also present serious problems in the Community's relations with third countries since the former tries to dump large quantities in international markets with the effect of depressing world prices even further. This is obviously resented by traditional agricultural exporters such as Australia and New Zealand. Surpluses in cereals, which do occasionally occur, present a less serious problem because of the world shortage and the growing needs of the developing countries. But it is very difficult to justify or tolerate for long surpluses in butter and sugar which are almost impossible to unload on foreign markets. With enlargement there will be an increased danger of wine and olive oil lakes being formed inside the Community, with surplus quantities of some fruit and vegetables also floating on the surface. This would make the Community's trade relations with other Mediterranean countries even more difficult than they are at present, while it would also add to the existing heavy burden of CAP expenditure on the EC budget.

One important reason why the financial crisis related to the CAP is likely to come to a head soon is that the Community budget is expected to hit the ceiling of 'own resources' by 1981 or 1982 at the latest. The new negotiations over the system of 'own resources' are bound to strengthen the bargaining power of those countries which are dissatisfied with the status quo. After Margaret Thatcher's renegotiation of the British budgetary contribution, one result of which was that Germany has become once again the Community's paymaster, Schmidt's resolution to control Community expenditure seems to have been much strengthened. At the same time there are various rumours emanating from Paris that even the French are seriously considering a reform of the CAP.[38] They are reputed to want to cut down on price support expenditure and to raise the productivity of their farmers. However, even though such reports may be correct, this thinking is not yet reflected in all official pronouncements. Short-term political calculations, such as preparations for the presidential election in 1981, tend to interfere with long-term policy objectives. Another factor which has to be borne in mind is that France has now become a net contributor to the budget which should certainly make it more concerned with growing expenditure.

The amounts of money spent on agriculture represent about 70% or more of total Community èxpenditure. But this can imply two different things: either that the Community is wildly overspending on agriculture or that there is very little spent on anything else. Although it is difficult to deny that there is a waste of resources resulting from the persistence of surpluses, a problem however which is not very easy to solve, it is also true that member governments spend large amounts of money for their agriculture in addition to what is spent at the Community level.[39] One could in fact argue that the major problem is one of distribution of costs among member countries rather than the absolute amounts involved.

The collapse of the Bretton-Woods system, together with fixed parities, put an end to what we have called elsewhere 'the agricultural mythology'.[40] When governments had to choose between fixed exchange rates and common agricultural prices, the latter were in the end abandoned. Thus MCAs were invented in order to cover the difference between fictitious 'green' rates and the actual exchange rate. The invention saved governments from having to take extremely unpopular or economically difficult decisions, such as lowering the prices offered to farmers after a revaluation or raising food prices and thus adding further to the inflationary spiral after a devaluation of the national currency. But MCAs did not provide an easy solution to the awkward dilemma of having to reconcile a continuing divergence in inflation and exchange rates with common agricultural prices expressed in the European unit of account. This led to a serious misallocation of resources and political tension inside the Community. Thus German farmers, for example, increased their heavily subsidised (through MCAs) exports of dairy products to Italy, much to the annoyance of local farmers, while they continued to purchase their feedstuffs and other inputs at a much more favourable exchange rate. It is also worth pointing out that the bulk of butter surpluses are to be found in the Federal Republic. The abolition of MCAs became a major issue again with the introduction of the EMS whose entry into force was delayed by France for a few months for this very reason. Since then, MCAs have been substantially reduced. The task was certainly made easier by the exchange rate stability which may be at least partly attributable to the successful operation of the EMS during its first year of life. However, in June 1980, after the resolution of the budgetary crisis, Helmut Schmidt openly questioned the viability of the system of common prices as long as the divergence in inflation rates continued.[41] Nobody could offer a serious reply to this argument.

The treatment of Mediterranean agriculture in the context of the CAP provides a very good illustration of the Community's inability to deal with growing regional disparities and the inadequacy of structural measures for the agricultural sector. The French Socialist Party has accused French governments of leaving Italy on its own to fight for the protection of Mediterranean farmers.[42] In the first years of the CAP this was certainly not far from the truth. Thus the balance of power inside the Council of Ministers was as important a factor as the very nature of Mediterranean products in explaining the relatively little attention received by them. Mediterranean agriculture became an important issue in the Community's negotiations with third countries. But it was only in the 1970s that the real discussion started inside the Community. The main spark came from the preparation of the global Mediterranean policy. It was reinforced by a growing sensitivity to regional disparities. Then the prospect of the second round of enlargement brought it to the top of the Community's agenda.

Enlargement and Pressures for Reform

We have already referred to the different kinds of criticism levelled against the CAP by consumer countries such as Britain and, with less consistency and fervour, the Federal Republic as well as Mediterranean countries such as Italy and more recently France. The former countries worry about high prices and financial costs while the latter complain about the unfair treatment accorded to their own products. The objectives pursued by the two sides often appear to be incompatible although this should not necessarily be the case. While the pressures for change have been mounting, the forthcoming accession of the three Mediterranean countries has given both sides more reasons and new weapons with which to fight. The second round of enlargement brings existing problems into sharper relief and thus strengthens the need for change.

Some changes have already been implemented on the Mediterranean front largely in anticipation of enlargement. After the submission of the Pizzuti Report in November 1976 the Commission followed with concrete proposals which were submitted to the Council of Ministers. France and Italy presented their own memoranda in July 1977.[43] They both wanted a better market organisation for Mediterranean products which meant in most cases increased price support and protection from third countries. The French also came up with a very controversial proposal for minimum prices applying to intra-Community trade in fruit, vegetables and especially wine, which was directed as much against Italian exports to France as against future Spanish exports. This was where the two countries parted company on the Mediterranean dossier. The French proposal for minimum prices for intra-Community trade followed relatively shortly after the Franco–Italian wine war of 1975–6. It was also seen as part of the famous *préalables* set by the French before enlargement would be allowed to take place. For their part the Italians laid more emphasis on structural reforms in the Mediterranean regions. The two memoranda had been preceded by various reports in both France and Italy and strong reactions from farmers which were also expressed by COPA, the Community farmers' lobby, in a special meeting in June 1977.

The measures which have been taken so far relate to different market organisations for Mediterranean products as well as structural policy at the Community level. They went some way towards meeting the demands made by the two governments and also helped to defuse the issue. However, the more recent reactions of French farmers against Spanish agricultural exports in the summer of 1980 is indicative that more trouble is yet to come.

As regards the wine regime measures have been taken to prevent a further growth in production of low-quality table wines. There is strict control over new planting and premiums are offered to producers as an incentive to switch to other products. Moreover, in order to avoid serious market disturbances such as the ones which followed the record crop of 1974–5, there are new provisions for massive distillations and also a reinforced system of external protection. The new measures seem to be fairly successful; another record crop in 1979 was put under control and a new crisis was averted. The Commission tries to improve the quality of wine produced and increase consumption by, for example, forcing various governments, like the British and the Irish, to reduce their excise duties. We cannot help but agree with Adrien Ries who wrote: 'Il ne faut ni gérer ni surtout taxer le vin; il faut le boire'.[44]

We have already referred to measures which were taken in 1978 to encourage the consumption of olive oil. Meanwhile the Commission has tried to discourage new planting by limiting the payment of production aids to olive groves planted before October 1978. The problem remains, however, in that the price of this product is too high when compared with that of close substitutes such as vegetable oils. The Community has a rather peculiar policy with respect to oils and fats which is almost self-defeating. While it runs an expensive policy of price support, coupled with strong external protection for butter and olive oil, it allows imports of vegetable oils and oilseeds, which are close substitutes, at very low or zero customs duties. This creates a price relationship which is highly unfavourable to butter and olive oil and therefore the consumption of those products remains stagnant or even declines. With the prospect of Spain's accession to the Community and the consequent increase in the Community's self-sufficiency in olive oil, which may lead to surpluses, the Commission has discussed the imposition of a tax on all vegetable oils. An internal tax on consumption which would also hit domestic producers would thus avoid the problem of having to conduct an extremely difficult negotiation within the framework of the General Agreement on Tariffs and Trade (GATT). It would also add extra money to the coffers of national or possibly Community authorities. If nothing is done on this front then the cost of price support, coupled with a system of direct aids, will increase substantially.

New measures have also been taken with respect to fruit and vegetables. The use of 'penetration premiums' which had been introduced in 1975 as a form of sales subsidy for Italian oranges was extended to other types of citrus fruit. The problem of Italian citrus products however is a much more fundamental one which cannot be solved simply by Community financial aid. More important is the aid given to producers' groups, which may lead to more efficient marketing, and the system of processing premiums intended to encourage processors to use Community products as their raw materials. Processed fruit and vegetables had been singled out in the Pizzuti Report as a sector where concrete measures and Community aid were imperative. The extra expenditure entailed appears for the first time in the 1979 figures (Table 5.9).

In 1980 a new market organisation was also adopted for sheepmeat. This was the result of the Anglo–French lamb war and part of an overall package deal. It is characteristic that although Italy had long since expressed a strong interest in a Community regime for sheepmeat, nothing happened until the Anglo–French war erupted. Goatmeat was left out despite Italian protestations and to the disappointment of the Greeks who were likely to be the main beneficiaries.

Some of the above-mentioned measures formed part of the so-called Mediterranean package which was adopted in May 1978, and additional ones were also introduced in February 1979. The Council agreed to spend a total of 3,600 million u.a. from 1980–4 on structural measures. This meant almost a doubling of the annual expenditure incurred by the Guidance Section of FEOGA. The new structural measures included special provisions for processing and marketing as well as aid for the formation of producer groups in Italy, the south of France and Belgium, irrigation in the Mezzogiorno and Corsica, flood protection in the Hérault valley and infrastructural investment in less developed Mediterranean areas. The Commission has also put forward new proposals for structural measures in other Community areas such as Greenland, the west of Ireland and the Western Isles of Scotland. The Commission now recognises the need for integrated development programmes and a close co-ordination between FEOGA and the Regional and Social Funds.

For a variety of reasons, already pointed out, the CAP now finds itself at a crucial turning point in its relatively short yet chequered history. The entry of three new members with a big farming population, serious structural problems in the agricultural sector and low productivities resulting in low incomes for farmers, will add to the existing pressures for change. It is interesting that some changes affecting Mediterranean farmers have already occurred. In this respect the prospect of enlargement seems to have acted as an important catalyst. However this has been only one step in the right direction. The CAP has so far relied almost entirely on price support which becomes extremely expensive when Community production exceeds internal demand, while at the same time it contributes very little to the raising of poor farmers' incomes. Moreover structural reform which should seek to make European agriculture more efficient and eradicate the causes which bring about the need for financial support has been given insufficient attention. We believe that the Community should move towards a more incomes-oriented policy which differentiates between large, highly productive farm units, which do not usually need subsidies, and small family holdings which cannot rely only on the price they can fetch for their products in the free market. Such an incomes-oriented policy would have to be coupled with a more active policy in the structural field and the encouragement of co-operation among small producers.

The enlarged Community will need to tackle the problem of structural surpluses in products such as milk and sugar. Finn Olav Gundelach, the late Commissioner responsible for agriculture, had suggested that 'the deterrent measures have to be borne by the more efficient producers, for the simple reason that this milk surplus is not predominantly produced by the small farmers with precious few alternatives to agriculture'.[43] This would mean, for example, that the co-responsibility levy could increase progressively with the total amount of production of each farm unit. There is no obvious reason why the Community should, through artificially high prices, subsidise the so-called milk factories which go on raising their productivity and thus the total output. It should be noted in passing that the big increases in productivity are partly attributable to an intensive use of imported agricultural inputs, including oil. A similar proposal has been made by Edgar Pisani, a leading member of the French Socialist Party, who suggested that above a certain level of production per farm unit there should be a progressive reduction in guaranteed prices, restitutions, premiums, and so on, paid by the Community.[46] Thus the market organisation system would remain but some discrimination would be introduced against large producers. The Community will need to develop new instruments in order to tackle the problem of structural surpluses. It will need, for example, to establish some control over new investment in crisis sectors as well as over national aids to producers. It is rather absurd that governments should complain about Community surpluses while at the same time they try to encourage the growth of domestic production. New measures will also have to be introduced at an early stage before new surpluses arise. In this respect olive oil appears to be a strong candidate. One should however add that quick solutions are not politically and economically feasible and thus surpluses are likely to continue for some time.

Although it would be naïve to advocate a *laissez-faire* policy for agriculture, one should however note that the Community which is heavily dependent on international trade for industrial goods cannot preach self-sufficiency for agriculture – or even worse continue dumping its surpluses in world markets – irrespective of any economic criteria of efficiency. The 'fortress Europe' approach usually associated with French policy is not easily tenable.[47] At the very least, the Community's international obligations and its dependence on external trade add one more strong reason for eliminating structural surpluses in milk and sugar. Another serious problem which appears to be almost insoluble in the near future concerns the enlarged Community's trade relations with other Mediterranean countries. These are the countries which will be most affected by trade diversion resulting from enlargement. People have referred to different ideas such as joint planning, diversification of production and also long-term supply contracts with Mediterranean countries for the export of Community agricultural products. Apart from the simple fact that these ideas cannot easily be translated into practice, none of them can in the foreseeable future solve the problem of much-needed export outlets for Mediterranean products coming from the Maghreb, Israel or Turkey.

Without a growing convergence in national inflation rates, the EMS cannot bring about the exchange rate stability which is needed for the preservation of, or to be more exact the return to, common agricultural prices. The divergence in national economic trends cannot be explained away as being the result of a lack of political will nor can it be stopped simply because the CAP is based on a system of common prices. When it comes to the crunch, it will always be the latter which has to give way. Thus if the divergence continues it is likely to act as a centrifugal force inside the CAP. Even the myth of common prices would then become untenable.

During the 1960s it was almost commonplace to argue that the main problem of European agriculture was a structural one which could be solved, at least in part, by a more rapid exodus from land. For many years there was in fact a steady decline in the agricultural labour force in all Western European countries. The Mansholt Plan of 1968, which was issued at a time of prosperity and growth, was intended to accelerate this trend. However, many farms are still economically unviable today, the age structure of the labour force is poor and many farmers are only part-time.

All these problems will be aggravated by enlargement. But in the 1980s a rapid reduction in the farm labour force is neither the panacea it was seen to be in the 1960s nor is it a sustainable proposition in a period of prolonged recession and growing unemployment. It makes little sense to encourage farmers to leave the land in order to join the dole queues in the cities. Since 1973 the rate of exodus has fallen sharply and there is little that governments could or should do about it. If the same economic situation continues into the 1980s, then the constraints imposed on agricultural policy will become even more stringent.

At the same time, for political, social and environmental reasons, most governments will want to keep farmers in areas where agriculture cannot be a very profitable activity. It is a serious mistake always to equate private with social costs and benefits. Thus various forms of income support will continue to be needed in conjunction with measures for price stabilisation and external protection.

The enlargement of the Community will strengthen the need for an active structural policy in the agricultural sector, closely co-ordinated with regional and social policies, and the creation of new financial instruments. Community structural policy should be pursued in parallel with policies at the national level. This does not differ at all from the conclusion reached in our discussion on industry. Structural measures are the best way to tackle the problems faced by Mediterranean regions, as a policy which relies on higher price guarantees might lead to more unwanted surpluses.

There is only one member country calling, or at least hoping, for a radical reform of the CAP. With the smallest percentage of the labour force engaged in agriculture, with relatively few small farms and a heavy dependence on imported food, Britain naturally has little interest in the existing policy. But it is very much isolated in this respect inside the Community and therefore has little hope of succeeding unless the objectives are more modest. John Marsh[48] has come up with an ingenious proposal which is intended to provide an alternative to the existing form of the CAP. He suggested the adoption of 'trading prices' as opposed to common prices which then become uncommon through the introduction of MCAs. Trading prices would operate in the same way as existing prices but member governments could also allow internal prices to deviate in order to subsidise farmers or consumers. The main condition would be that the financial cost of deviations from the trading price would fall entirely on national treasuries instead of the Community. Thus Marsh would legalise the existing system of MCAs and possibly make it less untidy. He might also provide the Council of Ministers with a more flexible price instrument that could be more effective against surpluses. But in the process he would take a further big step towards the renationalisation of agricultural policies. The adoption of Marsh's system would put an end once and for all to the unity of the market and would also considerably affect another principle of the CAP, namely, Community financial solidarity. Moreover it would legalise, as he himself points out, 'long-run and potentially growing distortions in the use of agricultural resources throughout the Community as a result of varying levels of government support'.[49]

There can be no simple or ideal reform of the CAP which takes into account the political and economic realities of Western Europe. Agriculture is a declining sector of economic activity but with great political and social importance. For the Community the CAP still constitutes, despite its many weaknesses, the most developed policy and is also an important element in a delicate balance of interests which is very difficult to upset. The forces of inertia are extremely strong and the pressure groups involved politically vocal. However, the preservation of the status quo no longer seems feasible. The growing cost of surpluses, the complicated system of border taxes and the widening gap between different regions have already created a crisis situation. Enlargement may provide the incentive or the need for various changes and the introduction of new policy instruments. In a Community of Twelve, there will be pressure for a more incomes-oriented policy and structural measures. However it will be politically impossible to raise more funds for structural policy unless there is a substantial reduction in the cost incurred by adding every year to unwanted stocks of surplus commodities. As regards common prices it seems unlikely that the Community will be able to return in the foreseeable future to the good old days of the 1960s when people thought that a *de facto* monetary union had already been achieved. Thus once the unity of the market has been broken it may be extremely difficult to stick all the pieces together again.

6

Conclusions

The interest of the three Mediterranean countries in Western European integration is certainly not a recent one. Since the formation of the EEC, and of EFTA, the three countries have shown great concern over European integration efforts. This was, after all, inevitable since developments in the industrial core of Western Europe were bound to have direct and significant repercussions for the peripheral countries. Political as well as economic constraints, however, prevented them from participating in the integration process. The rapid transform-ation of their economies and the eventual fall of the three dictatorial regimes, changed the picture. For the first time, full membership of the European Community – EFTA no longer presented a real alternative – appeared as a political option and indeed, it might be added, a necessity. The Community as a major trade bloc and an emerging political unit on the international scene was a reality which could simply not be ignored. Its mere existence had already forced many third countries to conclude special agreements in order to minimise the negative effects, including trade diversion effects, for their economies. For the new democratic governments in the three Mediterranean countries economic and political factors combined to make the application for membership an almost inevitable next step in their relations with the Nine. The existing degree of economic interdependence between the Three and the Nine, the stage of development of the former as well as the size of the domestic market, which made 'autonomous economic models' no longer feasible, all combined to make access to Western European markets an imperative for further economic growth. The protectionist trends in the world economy and the moves towards 'organised trade' have meant at least one thing for the three applicant countries, namely, that nothing short of membership can guarantee free access to Community markets for their exports. Even that can no longer be an absolute guarantee. Moreover in a world economy where international negotiations have gained an increasing importance, being on the outer periphery of a big trade bloc could mean that a country leads a very lonely and dangerous existence. If the Community moves beyond negative integration, which may be necessary for free trade to survive in the adverse economic conditions likely to prevail in the 1980s, then membership of the Community and direct participation in the decision-making system will become even more important for the three Mediterranean countries.

One cannot simply draw a clear line of distinction between economic and political factors. Therefore, close co-operation in trade and industrial affairs will inevitably be reflected at the political level. We believe, however, that for the three Mediterranean countries recent developments have strengthened the purely political reasons militating in favour of membership. The fall of the three dictatorships has also marked the end of the undisputed American hegemony in the area, which was soon followed by an increasing role of Western European countries and especially the Federal Republic of Germany. Meanwhile there have been signs of a growing divergence of interests in different areas of policy between the two sides of the Atlantic. If this eventually leads to a more assertive and independent role for European countries in international affairs, and further assuming that this is expressed through Community institutions, then the three applicant countries have a strong interest in acquiring the status of a full member. The alternative for them may be the role of a satellite.

To say that membership of the Community is a political and economic necessity for Greece, Portugal and Spain should not be taken to imply that there are no risks involved for them. First of all, the above analysis is based on a series of assumptions about international as well as internal Community developments which might prove to be wrong. Some have already been mentioned such as the spread of protectionist trends and the Community's role in international negotiations. Much of our discussion has also been based on an implicit assumption about the real influence which small countries can exercise in the Community decision-making system. This therefore excludes such developments as the institutionalisation of different tiers or the formation of a directorate, which will be discussed in more detail below. The integration of the three countries into the Community can be seen as a challenge but also a calculated risk for their economies and institutions. If it fails then this failure will have serious repercussions for their future political and economic development. It seems to us that Spain is best prepared to take the leap forward, and Portugal least so. This conclusion is not only based on the economic structure of the three applicant countries but also on the apparent ability of institutions, especially the state bureaucracy, to adjust to the requirements of membership and the endless series of negotiations over a wide range of subjects with the other partners. It is true that some people in the Three believe, or seem to believe, that Community membership offers the key to paradise and that the solutions to all problems will be found in Brussels. They have great expectations especially as regards the flow of resources which is supposed to follow accession. Although on the basis of existing policies the three countries should benefit from a net inflow of resources, such hopes or expectations seem to be totally out of proportion with reality. The main responsibility for economic development will still lie at home.

Although the political forces which favour membership in the three countries represent the large majority of the electorate, there is no unanimity of opinion except in Spain. A critical approach to European integration, which in some cases amounts to outright opposition, is to be found exclusively on the left wing of the political spectrum. This should certainly signify something about the nature of the integration process in Europe. Another general conclusion one can reach from the internal debate in the three countries, which is also corroborated by the available evidence in the existing members, is that European integration can no longer generate any real enthusiasm among the general public. The technical nature of most Community issues limits the discussion only to the initiated few. The inability of political parties to stimulate a genuine debate on the wider, political issues which should concern the European citizen was amply illustrated during the campaign for the direct elections to the European Parliament of June 1979. For most Greeks and Spaniards, though, membership of the Community means something more than the adoption of the *acquis communautaire*. The term 'Europe' has a real meaning in these two countries and the general attitude is different from that found in the countries which joined the Community in 1973. The Greeks and the Spaniards, unlike the British and the Danes, for example, do not seem to face the 'existential' problem of whether they belong to Europe or not. In this respect it appears that the Portuguese have been, and still feel, isolated from the European continent.

In the existing members the prospect of enlarging the Community from Nine to Twelve has generated no enthusiasm whatsoever, either among the political leadership or the general public. There was very little in terms of concrete economic benefits that they expected to derive from it. On the contrary, enlargement is seen as an economic burden and an addition to the abundance of problems already faced by the Community countries. The fact that it has coincided with an international economic recession and various internal difficulties, which were at least partly due to the Community's need to adjust to the first enlargement, made things much worse. Although all member countries now seem to consider enlargement a necessary evil, probably because they realise that the Community cannot remain an exclusive club, some of them have tried to delay enlargement and may continue to do so in the near future. In view of the present crisis of the CAP and also the political strength of the farmers' lobby, particularly in France, there is a real danger that the accession of the two Iberian countries may be unduly prolonged. It could be argued that such a delay will be worthwhile if it allows the Nine and, from 1981 the Ten, to implement reforms with respect to Community policies and institutions which are by common consent overdue. We remain sceptical about the validity of such an argument. First of all we believe that the two Iberian countries are not likely to be the main stumbling block to reform. Secondly, any reform would be counterproductive if it were meant to face the new members with a *fait accompli*. One should have learned something from the experience of the first enlargement. Thus it would make little sense to reform the CAP against the interests of the Spaniards.

Changing Environment

The second enlargement is taking place against the background of a rapidly changing international environment which presents Community members with a major challenge. The first two decades of European integration, starting with the formation of the ECSC in 1953, were characterised by rapid and uninterrupted economic growth. This has now given way to stagflation which is likely to continue into the early 1980s. In periods of recession and high unemployment, issues related to income distribution and transfers of resources at the national or international level become extremely difficult to tackle. The same applies to international trade. Growing import penetration in specific sectors can raise serious problems and lead to strong protectionist pressures. In the 1950s and the 1960s, the entry of the NICs on the international economic scene would not have caused so much alarm in Western industrialised countries. After all, the system was able to accommodate Japan, to mention but one important example. Moreover international trade negotiations have become very intricate since tariff barriers have ceased to be the main issue. Countries often find themselves negotiating about the use of domestic policy instruments which have direct repercussions on foreign competitors. It takes some time for policy-makers to reconcile themselves to the necessity of discussing with foreigners issues which not long ago were considered to lie in the sacrosanct area of national sovereignty.

The abrupt change in the terms of trade between the oil producing countries and the rest of the world has brought about a large shift of resources towards the former countries, which has also been accompanied by a shift of economic and political power. At the same time

North–South relations have acquired a new dimension, at least partly because of a rather uneasy alliance between oil producers and less fortunate Third World countries. Thus the Community, together with the rest of the industrialised world, has been faced with pressing demands for a new international economic order. This is taking place at a time when the threat of an imminent energy shortage is hanging like the sword of Damocles over each country.

The 1970s has also been a period of monetary disorder which followed the breakdown of the Bretton-Woods system. Exchange rate instability and large balance of payments deficits for most member countries created a very different environment from the one which had existed during the previous decade. The collapse of the dollar standard and the inability of Western countries to agree on the reform of the international system provided the driving force behind the moves towards European monetary integration and the creation of a regional currency bloc.

Many of the economic changes which have occurred in the international system during the 1970s are at least indirectly associated with the decline of American power. It is not always easy to distinguish cause from effect. The postwar economic system was essentially a Western system effectively run by the Americans. Some lesser mortals such as big oil producers have, in the meantime, presented rather impressive credentials to back the pressing demand to join the group of leading actors. At the same time there has been a redistribution of the main roles, with the Americans losing to both the Japanese and the Western Europeans. We believe that the tension in Euro-American relations, which has reached unprecedented peaks in recent years, cannot be explained simply in terms of the *faux pas* made by the American administration or the well-known lack of understanding between Carter and Schmidt. There is a genuine divergence of interests between the two sides of the Atlantic, in trade and monetary affairs among others, which can no longer be resolved as family squabbles by relying in the last resort on the intervention of the pater-familias who can effectively force all sides to accept his final verdict. In the Western alliance the paterfamilias (read United States) no longer has the undisputed power he used to enjoy in the past. Relations with the Eastern bloc and the value that each attaches to détente has appeared as yet another dividing factor between the United States and Western Europe. One may also refer to the gradual shift of the centre of gravity inside the United States away from the East coast and towards the South and the West. It may not be a pure coincidence that the two finalists at the 1980 presidential election were a Georgian and a Californian. The loss of power by politicians from the East coast may lead to a more isolationist policy or at least a policy in which Western

Europe does not necessarily figure as the privileged partner.

In the next few years Community countries will be engaged, not always willingly, in many negotiations with third countries. A wide range of subjects will come under discussion, such as Japanese cars and US chemical fibres, commodity agreements with primary producing countries, the law of the sea and international shipping. Treaty regulations and, even more important, the degree of interdependence among EC countries, as well as the realisation that in most cases individual members can have only a marginal influence in international negotiations if they act alone, are factors which can constitute a strong integrating force inside the Community. The new international environment may also provide a strong impetus for closer co-operation in the traditional areas of foreign policy, as the recent discussions on an EC initiative in the Middle East suggest. However, external pressures can also cause serious strain inside the Community and act as a disintegrating factor. The first energy crisis of 1973–4 and the inability of the Nine to adopt a common stand is the first example that comes to mind. Moreover the economic crisis has not only created a much more difficult environment for co-operation among member countries but has also strengthened the divergent trends among national economies. This in turn has reduced the possibilities for the adoption of common policies.

Community Adaptability, Institutions and Bilateralism

After the end of the twelve-year transitional period, the European integration process entered into a new phase. In addition the Community was enlarged to include Great Britain, Ireland and Denmark. This happened in a very unstable and unfavourable environment. The Community's process of adaptation has been extremely slow and arduous. During the 1960s the customs union and the CAP had provided the two main driving forces behind European integration. EMU was then seen as the new *force motrice* of the 1970s. However, the Werner Plan was too rigid and unrealistic. Some years later it was replaced by the EMS which constitutes a new form of co-operation inside the Community and may prove to be one of the most important achievements of recent years. On the industrial front, it is in itself a remarkable achievement that intra-EC free trade has survived in the midst of recession and growing unemployment, although some allowance should be made for the growth of the so-called non-tariff barriers. However, with the possible exception of the steel plan, very little has happened in terms of positive, common measures to cope with the economic crisis. Nor have the Nine succeeded in bringing the CAP expenditure under control. The Community structure is still lopsided, with too much time and money spent on agriculture. As regards the EC policy on energy, it still remains a *tabula rasa.*

Can the Community's relative inability to adapt to internal as well as external changes be attributed to objective political and economic constraints? Or is it related to the institutional machinery available? However efficient the institutional set-up, it cannot overcome differences in economic structures or geopolitical interests among member countries. Institutional inefficiency can, though, add considerably to difficulties which may arise from factors such as those mentioned above. Over the course of years the Community has expanded in both number and functions, while at the same time it has become more intergovernmental in its decision-making. The Commission as the embodiment of supranationality has gradually lost ground in relation to the Council of Ministers and more recently the European Council. This was probably inevitable in view of the Community's constant expansion of tasks which in some cases impinged more directly on sensitive areas of national sovereignty. It was probably too much to expect the Commission to combine the activities of an efficient bureaucracy with those of an initiator of legislation and a representative of the 'European' interest fighting against recalcitrant governments. In the end the Commission has become more bureaucratic in nature and its political role has diminished. Nowadays member governments are often heard complaining about the inefficiency of the Brussels institution. But they themselves are largely to blame. The Germans, for example, cannot level such criticisms against the Commission when they are directly responsible for a series of bad appointments to the latter at the top level. This chapter is being written before the appointment of the new college of Commissioners who will take office in January 1981. With the exception of the new President, Gaston Thorn, there are very few eminent political figures among the names currently under discussion as likely candidates. The appointment of civil servants, however high-ranking they may be, and relatively unknown politicians cannot do much to strengthen the Commission in the intra-Community power game. If this happens it will only confirm a trend which goes back many years.

An increasingly intergovernmental organisation which relies heavily on representatives of national governments, who in turn operate on the basis of unanimity, and which continues expanding in terms of both numbers and functions should not be expected to constitute a model of efficiency. The Community decision-making system is extremely slow and is rarely able to produce initiatives seeking to shape the external environment instead of merely responding to outside changes and pressures. Co-ordination is often lacking as is a clear set of priorities which would make the most efficient use of the time of national ministers and officials, an important scarce resource. Institutional reforms are extremely difficult to implement in the Community. The forces of inertia which have developed in the course of time are very strong indeed and reforms which can command the support or at least the acquiescence of nine different governments are not easy to devise. It may sound self-contradictory if we then hasten to add that some important developments have in fact taken place in the institutional field in recent years. The most important is the creation of the European Council, the institutionalisation of summitry, which may confirm the trend towards intergovernmentalism but at the same time involves heads of state or government directly in the Community decision-making process. The European Council has so far acted as the last court of appeal for highly sensitive and divisive issues, such as the two rounds of Britain's renegotiation, and as an initiator of policy, with the EMS being the most obvious example. A much more unorthodox development, in the eyes of a federalist or a Community lawyer, has been the creation of a new machinery for political co-operation. Entirely intergovernmental and strictly speaking outside the framework of Community institutions, although the Commission has been closely involved, it is seen by some people as a model for European co-operation in the future. Many British 'pragmatists' share this view. It remains to be seen whether such a loose framework is capable of producing many concrete results. For some cynics the EPC or Poco counts for what the latter term means in Italian, namely, 'little'. Many expectations had been built up in connection with the direct elections to the European Parliament. The electoral campaign leading to these elections and the low turnout of European voters have given the first cause for disappointment. It is still too early to draw any conclusions from the short experience of this new directly elected Parliament. It would not however be too rash to say that direct elections are unlikely to affect decisively the institutional balance within the Community in the foreseeable future.

Bilateral relations have remained extremely important inside the Community. Many initiatives which were later taken up by Community institutions had originated in bilateral meetings. A more recent phenomenon is that of issues pertaining to Community affairs being discussed in international summits where only the Big Four are represented. It has been a great success for Roy Jenkins himself and the smaller member countries that invitations are now being issued to the President of the Commission as well. Will this development persist in the future, especially when both the President of the Commission and the President-in-office of the Council happen to come from the smaller countries?

The weaker the Community institutions, the more likely it is that big countries will take it upon themselves to provide the initiative and the leadership. It is no coincidence that concern over the increasing trend towards intergovernmentalism and over the efforts to set up new forms of co-operation outside the framework of the treaties has been largely confined to the smaller members. What is interesting to observe is that Franco-German leadership has been preserved, and indeed strengthened, in the second half of the 1970s, despite the first enlargement and Britain's entry in particular. Again, without trying to minimise the role of personalities such as Giscard and Schmidt in politics, we believe that there are several less ephemeral factors which are at least equally important in explaining what some observers refer to as the Franco–German axis in the Community. After all European integration was begun in order to strengthen Franco–German co-operation and make another war between those two countries virtually impossible. In this respect it has been a remarkable success. These countries constitute the two most important powers of the European continent and co-operation between them will continue to be a determining factor for further progress in European integration. This is like stating the obvious. Political and economic developments during the 1970s have made co-operation easier and at the same time increasingly necessary for both sides. The growing economic strength of the Federal Republic combined with a wider margin of manoeuvre in foreign policy, which is partly a function of Brandt's Ostpolitik as well as détente, have turned the West Germans into the single most important power in Europe. This of course discounts the Soviet Union which is, at least in part, an outsider. The West Germans are perfectly aware of the fact that any efforts to exercise assertive leadership inside the Community will be strongly resisted by their partners. Memories of the last war have still not died out completely. Moreover co-operation with the French is much easier nowadays for at least one reason, namely, that relations with the United States are no longer the divisive factor they used to be in the 1960s. Both countries have covered a large part of the distance which used to separate them. The French are clearly the privileged partner for many historical, economic, political and geographical reasons which should be all too obvious. Despite its relative decline *vis-à-vis* the Federal Republic, France still constitutes a major power in Europe, particularly within the context of the European Community which is after all its own creation. One can add another and probably less obvious point. The presidential system together with what is widely considered to be the most efficient machinery for the co-ordination of a member country's EC policy account in large part for the fact that so many initiatives on Community affairs still emanate from Paris.

Why not Britain and Italy, which are the other two likely contenders for joining the big boys' club inside the Community? The explanation for Italy is much the simpler of the two. Since the end of the Second World War this country has been unwilling or unable to either pursue an active foreign policy or play a major role in European integration. Political instability and economic weakness are two explanatory factors. As far as Britain is concerned many people on the continent were very surprised that it has not as yet played a more assertive role in Community affairs. With the benefit of hindsight, however, it becomes less surprising that such a thing has not happened yet and may not happen in the near future. The economic decline of Britain is certainly one important factor. In addition the existence of a strong anti-European minority, strengthened by a widespread feeling that the country has been on the losing side inside the Community, has acted as a serious constraint on all governments and especially Labour governments. We would also add another factor which is more intangible and impressionistic. The inability or unwillingness of many British politicians and officials to think in European terms does not help any government to come up with major initiatives inside the Community.

Is the Community of Twelve a Contradiction in Terms?

The Community is a *sui generis* form of association among sovereign countries which defies the classifications made by political scientists. It is neither an international organisation nor an emerging federation in the traditional sense of the term. The kind of co-operation established between member countries has no parallel elsewhere in the world. This co-operation also varies from one policy area to the other. Although it is true that the Community is basically an economic organisation its aims are clearly political. Moreover it is inevitable that economic co-operation spills over into the area of politics. Sometimes the political role is thrust upon the Community by the rest of the world. Indeed the second enlargement is another illustration of the EC's growing political importance. Here again we find an interesting combination of economic means and political objectives. Both sides seem to agree on this point.

Although the Community has been very slow in adapting its policies and institutions to an ever-changing environment it has nevertheless shown remarkable resilience even in the midst of serious crises which might have been expected to lead to its breakdown. It has survived de Gaulle and Kissinger, the international recession and the energy crisis. Shared political values, strong economic ties and the pressures from third countries which usually expect the EC to act as a political unit in the international system have all combined to keep the Community together even at times when the centrifugal forces appeared to be overwhelming. It is most likely that this will continue to be true in the future. On the other hand the second enlargement will impose new strains on Community policies and institutions and intensify the already existing need for adjustment. However the effects of enlargement should be relatively marginal when compared with those resulting from the economic crisis, developments in the international trade and monetary system or political developments in the Middle East. Among the three applicant countries only Spain's accession is likely to have a real effect on the development of the Community.

As regards industrial trade the problem for the Three is a major one and centres on their ability to adapt their industrial structure to the new, extremely competitive environment. For the Nine the problem is much more limited and relates to specific sectors where Community industrialists already face fierce competition from third countries, particularly Japan and the NICs. With respect to agriculture, which has attracted a disproportionately large share of public attention in relation to enlargement, the entry of the three new members may add more surpluses to the existing ones while, by accentuating the structural problem, it will expose even further the weakness of a policy which relies too much on the price instrument. Contrary to widespread belief the CAP will not necessarily prove to be a godsend for the three Mediterranean countries and their farmers. What appears to be more certain is that farmers in the southern regions of France and Italy will be negatively affected by enlargement. This is consistent with the general principle that the weak (and relatively uncompetitive) lose from economic integration.

We have discussed some of the likely effects of enlargement, concentrating chiefly on the industrial and agricultural sectors. It has certainly not been a comprehensive analysis. Many areas which are directly affected by EC membership have been left out or only dealt with indirectly. For example, the common fisheries policy has been completely ignored although it will most definitely constitute an important item in the Community's negotiations with Spain. Labour and capital movements have been dealt with in a rather cursory manner. The EMS has only been touched upon, and the same goes for Community institutions and external relations.

One very general point that can be made is that enlargement will increase the economic and political divergence inside the Community. Among the Nine there are large differences in the structure and the performance of national economies. These differences have persisted in spite of the growth in interdependence. In fact if we take the rates of inflation and economic growth, economic divergence has widened during the 1970s. If we turn to economic structures and the long-term adjustments which have taken place during the same period in response to the economic crisis, we again find a very sharp contrast between the Federal Republic on the one hand and Britain or Italy on the other. Large differences in terms of political institutions, ideologies or geopolitical interests have also persisted. Moreover it is natural that the short-term interests of governments each facing elections at different times do not always coincide. If only the timing of national elections could be subjected to the harmonisation obsession that is supposed to characterise many EC officials! The above factors impose a serious constraint on intra-EC co-operation and the adoption of common policies. The accession of the three Mediterranean countries will increase economic divergence and thus make co-operation even more difficult. In the same way the Community's margin of manoeuvre will be reduced because it will not only have to accommodate the interests of more countries but, even more important, the interests of three economically weak new members. The already cumbersome decision-making system will be further burdened by the sheer addition of three new members, the adoption of three more official languages and the integration of officials with no experience in Community procedures and from countries where national bureaucracies are not exactly the most efficient in the world.

One serious danger is that in the Community of Twelve derogations and exceptions from commonly agreed policies will become increasingly the rule. Such a development would inevitably weaken the Community and reduce its importance both for its members and the rest of the world. Some of the economically stronger countries may also be tempted to enter into arrangements from which the other members are excluded because they feel unable to accept the obligations involved. In this respect the EMS is the obvious example. Will the new members be able to join the EMS even in its present, rather loose form? And will there be other arrangements like the EMS from which some member countries have constantly to exclude themselves? This could gradually lead to the creation of a Community of two or more tiers, with an inner core of countries clustered around Germany. However, this would be a very dangerous development. Similarly the institutionalisation of two tiers in decision-making by the creation of a directorate, an idea close to the heart of some French policy-makers, would lead to a breakdown of the Community. On the other hand it would be unrealistic to believe that the real influence which a member country can exercise in decision-making is not at least partly a function of its political and economic power. There is however an enormous difference between the latter situation and the creation of a formal directorate consisting of the largest and/or economically strongest countries. Experience to date suggests that the small countries have increased their bargaining power and influence in international affairs by becoming members of the Community rather than the converse. If this ceased to be true then one of the main arguments in favour of membership as regards the three Mediterranean countries would also disappear.

Will enlargement cause the Community to turn more towards parts of the Third World such as Latin America, the other Mediterranean countries and the Middle East? It is true that the new members have a strong interest in and a tradition of close relations with these areas. Their accession is however likely to accentuate the existing contradiction inside the Community, particularly in French and Italian attitudes towards other Mediterranean countries, namely, the contradiction between means and ends. Any trade concessions to Latin American or North African countries, for example, is likely to hit the new members more than it does a country like Germany or Holland. Moreover the larger the transfer of resources to the poor regions of the enlarged Community, the less money will be available for economic aid to third countries.

Will enlargement lead to a shift in the internal balance of power towards the South? Posing the question immediately implies the existence, or at least the future creation, of a Southern lobby inside the Community. It remains to be seen whether common cause will prevail over divergent interests in relations among the Mediterranean members of the Community. At present, political and economic relations are minimal and the flow of goods and ideas takes place along the North–South axis. It may take a long time before this situation is reversed.

In view of the divergence of interests, which is very pronounced even among the Nine, one may wonder whether the Community of Twelve can make any sense. In fact the applications from Greece, Portugal and Spain may not be the last to arrive on the Community's doorstep. The greater the importance of the EC as a political and economic unit, the more difficult it will be for other Western European countries to remain outside, although in most cases there are important obstacles to Community membership such as political neutrality (Austria, Sweden, Switzerland) or domestic political and economic conditions (Turkey). How long will it then be before Sweden or Norway start reconsidering their relations with the Community, or before Turkey, assuming that democracy is restored, insists on membership accompanied by special provisions? But then there is another question which immediately follows, namely, how long can the Community continue to expand in numbers before it ceases to have any internal cohesion? It is certainly not an easy question to answer.

The EC needs to remain open although each application, if and when it comes, should be examined on its own merits. We have already argued that the applications for membership from the three Mediterranean countries were an inevitable step after the fall of the three dictatorships and that Community members had no other choice than to accept them. Once it is recognised that the second enlargement is a political necessity then what we need to concern ourselves with is the measures which could contribute to its success and thus avoid the development of situations, such as those referred to above, which might jeopardise the future of the Community as a political and economic unit.

On a number of occasions the possibility has been evoked that the accession of the three Mediterranean countries may act as a catalyst for internal Community reforms, which seem to be necessary irrespective of any increase in membership. Up to the present there has been too much emphasis on accession talks, which are largely irrelevant to the long-term development of the enlarged Community. One cannot argue that the really vital issue at stake is the kind and length of transitional measures leading to the adoption of the *acquis communautaire* by the new members. This assumes that Community policies and institutions can remain unaltered after enlargement. A similar view prevailed at the time of the 1973 enlargement and the outcome has not proved to be very encouraging. It would make even less sense to adopt the same attitude again.

In the present political and economic climate member countries do not seem to be ready to undertake major new initiatives or accept far-reaching reforms. Even the relatively modest proposals put forward by the Commission in its fresco as well as those made by the Three Wise Men and the Spierenburg Committee have so far met with little success. We do not however believe that this is an adequate reason for not facing squarely some of the problems likely to arise from enlargement and discussing alternative solutions. This is the approach adopted in the two preceding chapters. There is no point in disguising the fact that there is a strong normative element in our analysis. This should after all be taken for granted in such a policy-oriented work. We shall at least try to make it explicit.

We have argued in favour of the creation of parallel Community instruments which should aim at encouraging growth, promoting adjustment and compensating those who suffer from the working of market forces and the application of common policies. The emphasis has been on common instruments rather than the co-ordination of national policies, the serious limitations of the latter being already manifest. We have proposed the adoption of compensatory measures which should complement free trade and strengthen solidarity among member countries. This may be necessary if regressive measures are to be avoided in the near future, especially if the economic recession continues. The recycling of petrodollars and the extension of foreign exchange loans to countries with weak balance of payments is, for example, an area in which the Community could play a very useful role.

Compensatory measures undertaken through the Community budget imply a transfer of resources with an explicit redistributive bias. An intercountry transfer of resources already takes place but is mainly a function of the CAP and operates in a totally haphazard manner. Since it is highly unlikely that all member countries will agree in the near future on a substantial increase in the total amount of EC expenditure, the successful tackling of the problem of agricultural surpluses and a consequent reduction in CAP expenditure will be a determining factor. One should also add that if structural, regional and social policies at the Community level are to have any impact at all, there should be both a selective use of resources and a substantial increase in the amounts involved.

The above should not be taken to imply that national governments will no longer bear the main responsibility in these areas of policy. Far from it. For many years to come the Community's role can only be complementary to that played by national governments. Equally there is no suggestion that such changes can come about from one day to the other. Change can only be very gradual but there should at an early stage be agreement on the general direction of Community policy, or at least a debate on the general principles involved. Moreover this is a debate which should concern the European voter.

We have stressed growth, adjustment and relief from economic hardship as the main principles which should guide Community policies and the use of scarce resources. The approach is not novel. This is simply an attempt to translate some of the principles which characterise the functioning of modern, Western European societies to the Community level. The creation of a more dynamic economic environment and the easing of the adjustment process should be in the interest of all members in view of the high level of economic and political interdependence which exists among them. This would also facilitate intra-Community co-operation and the adoption of common policies internally as well as *vis-à-vis* the rest of the world. It might be argued that although the above may not amount to a real federation it none the less implies the creation of a minimum welfare state at the EC level. But then the criticism levelled against us would be that we have taken the word 'Community' in its literal sense.

Notes and References

Chapter 1

1 See OECD, *The Impact of the Newly Industrialising Countries* (Paris: OECD, 1979).

2 Commission of the European Communities, 'Opinion on Spain's application for membership', *Bulletin of the European Communities*, Supplement 9/78, table 1, p. 43.

3 George Katsos, 'An evaluation of the structure of protection in Greece during the post-war years', PhD thesis, University of Lancaster, 1975, pp. 162–77.

4 See S. G. Triantis, *Common Market and Economic Development: Greece and the EEC* (Athens: KEPE – Centre of Planning and Economic Research, 1967). This is the only major work on the association agreement published in Greece in the 1960s. The author took a strong stand against it, mainly on economic grounds. See also George Yannopoulos, *Greece and the European Communities: The First Decade of a Troubled Association* (Beverly Hills, Calif., and London: Sage, 1975), pp. 13–17; Stanley Henig, *External Relations of the European Community* (London: Chatham House/PEP, 1971), pp. 72–90; M. Syrianos, 'Political forces and the Association Agreement of 1962', in *Our Accession to the EEC* (in Greek) (Athens: Themelio, 1978).

5 See also Henig, op. cit., pp. 39–71; Loukas Tsoukalis, 'The EEC and the Mediterranean: is "global" policy a misnomer?', *International Affairs*, July 1977.

6 Joseph Loeff, 'La Communauté élargie et l'espace Méditerranéen', in H. Brugmans *et al.*, *La politique économique extérieure de la Communauté Européenne élargie* (Bruges: De Tempel/College of Europe, 1973).

7 Syrianos, op. cit., pp. 79–100.

8 One example is Triantis, op. cit.

9 Syrianos, op. cit., pp. 72–8.

10 op. cit., pp. 118–19 (Greek text).

11 John Pesmazoglou, 'Critical choices of economic policy', *Bank of Greece* (Athens, 1967).

12 op. cit., p. 31.

13 Van Coufoudakis, 'The European Economic Community and the "freezing" of the Greek Association, 1967–1974', *Journal of Common Market Studies*, December 1977, p. 121.

14 Stephanos Stathatos, 'From association to full membership', and Inger Nielsen, 'A view from inside', in Loukas Tsoukalis (ed.), *Greece and the European Community* (Farnborough: Saxon House, 1979).

15 Yannopoulos, op. cit., pp. 28–31.

16 Quoted in Coufoudakis, op. cit., p. 129.

17 See Wilhelm Hummen, *Greek Industry in the European Community. Prospects and Problems* (Berlin: German Development Institute, 1977), table A4, p. 72; George Yannopoulos, 'The effects of full membership on the manufacturing industries', in Tsoukalis, op. cit.

18 See also Achilles Mitsos, 'The new role for the Greek Government after accession', in *The Mediterranean Challenge: IV The Tenth Member – Economic Aspects*, Sussex European Papers No. 7 (1980), pp. 130–9.

19 Achilles Mitsos and Efstathios Papageorgiou, 'Implications for the balance of payments', in Tsoukalis, op. cit., pp. 96–7.

20 A. K. Giannitsis, 'Problems of Greek development' (in Greek), *Oikonomia Kai Koinonia*, May 1979, p. 29.

21 Panayiotis Roumeliotis, *Multinational Enterprises and Transfer Pricing in Greece* (in Greek) (Athens: Papazissis, 1978), pp. 99–102. We have serious doubts about the usefulness, not to mention accuracy, of such estimates.

22 Zolotas, Governor of the Bank of Greece, quoted in John Papantoniou, 'Foreign trade and industrial development: Greece and the EEC', *Cambridge Journal of Economics*, March 1979, p. 35.

23 The average rate of real wage increases in the manufacturing sector was 3·9% per annum, compared with an average growth rate of GDP of 7·6%. This trend was completely reversed after 1973 when the corresponding figures for the period 1973–7 became 7·7% and 2·9% respectively. (Calculations based on data found in OECD, *National Accounts*, OECD, *Main Economic Indicators*, ILO, *Yearbook of Labour Statistics*, various issues.)

24 According to Greek statistics the net number of migrants between 1961 and 1971 was 543,000 (Papantoniou, op. cit., p. 34). In 1977 the number of Greeks employed in Community countries was 221,000, compared with 435,000 Spaniards and 566,000 Portuguese. While about 70% of Greek migrant workers were employed in West Germany, the majority of both the Spaniards and Portuguese were to be found in France (Commission of the EC, 'Opinion on Spain's application for membership', op. cit., table 27c, p. 69).

25 OECD, *The Impact of the Newly Industrialising Countries* (Paris: OECD, 1979), table 29, p. 53.

26 See also Loukas Tsoukalis, 'Impact on the European monetary system (EMS)', in D. Seers and C. Vaitsos (eds), *The Second Enlargement of the EEC, Integration of Unequal Partners*, Vol. 2 (London: Macmillan, forthcoming).

27 Papantoniou, op. cit.; Katsos, pp. 162–212.

28 A. K. Giannitsis, 'Economic integration of Greece into the EEC and foreign direct investments', in M. Nikolinakos (ed.), *EEC, Greece and the Mediterranean* (in Greek) (Athens: Nea Synora, 1978). See also Constantine Vaitsos, 'EEC's second enlargement and strategies of transnational enterprises', paper presented at the Second Conference on Integration and Unequal Development, Madrid, October 1979.

29 Quoted in Papantoniou, op. cit., p. 39.

30 Commission of the European Communities, 'Enlargement of the Community – economic and sectoral aspects', *Bulletin of the EC*, Supplement 3/78, p. 16.

31 See Eric Baklanoff, *The Economic Transformation of Spain and Portugal* (New York: Praeger, 1978), pp. 103–13; Xavier Pintado, *Growth and Structure of the Portuguese Economy* (Geneva: EFTA, 1964); João Cravinho, 'Motives and problems of the second enlargement: the case of Portugal', paper presented at the Madrid Conference, October 1979. See also Klaus Esser et al., *Portugal: Industrie und Industriepolitik vor dem Beitritt zur Europäischen Gemeinschaft* (Berlin: Deutsche Institut für Entwicklungspolitik 1977), Michael Noelke und Eduardo Maia Cadete, *Recherche sur l'économie portugaise*, Vol. 1 (Lisbon, November 1977).

32 See also Andrew Shonfield (ed.), *International Economic Relations of the Western World 1959–1971*, Vol. 1 (London: OUP/RIIA, 1976), pp. 9–18.

33 Correia de Oliveira (Salazar's minister), quoted in I. Cândido de Azevedo, *Portugal Europa face ao Mercado Comum* (Lisbon: Bertrand, 1978), pp. 20–1.

34 On the other hand Stuart Holland seems to argue that the decision was a political one when he wrote that 'Salazar had joined EFTA under a hangover from the old time "special alliance" with the British'. See S. Holland, 'Dependent development: Portugal as periphery', in D. Seers, B. Schaffer and M. L. Kiljunen (eds), *Underdeveloped Europe* (Hassocks, Sussex: Harvester Press/IDS, 1979), p. 139.

35 Cravinho, op. cit.

36 Baklanoff, op. cit., p. 106.

37 João Martins Pereira, *Pensar Portugal hoje* (Lisbon: Don Quixote, 1979), ch. 1, pp. 17–38; see also Cândido de Azevedo, op. cit., p. 13–35.

38 António de Siqueira Freire, 'Portugal and the European Community: past, present and future', in *Spain, Portugal and the European Community* (London: University Association for Contemporary European Studies/St Antony's College, 1979), p. 14; António da Silva Ferreira, 'Une évaluation des échanges entre le Portugal et la CEE', *Economia* (Lisbon), October 1979.

39 Cravinho, op. cit.; Ferreira, op. cit.

40 J. Silva Lopes, 'Portugal and the EEC: the application for membership', paper presented at the workshop on Southern Europe and the Enlargement of the EEC organised by *Economia* in Lisbon, June 1980.

41 R. Sadove and S. A. Chaudhry, 'Portugal: priorities for public sector investment', paper presented at the Second International Conference on Portuguese Economy, Lisbon, September 1979.

42 OECD, *Economic Surveys – Portugal* (Paris: OECD, November 1976), table 1, p. 6.

43 After the elections of December 1979 the new Sa Carneiro government expressed the intention of allowing the creation of private banks. It remains to be seen how this will be reconciled with the provisions made in the constitution of 1975.

44 Because of large-scale illegal immigration all figures used are only estimates. See Heinz-Michael Stahl, 'Portuguese migration and regional development', paper presented at the Lisbon Conference, September 1979.

45 EFTA, *The Trade Effects of EFTA and the EEC 1959–1967* (Geneva: EFTA, 1972), pp. 94–102.

46 op. cit.

47 Cited in Cravinho, op. cit.

48 This seems to have been even more pronounced in the early 1960s. See EFTA, *The Effects of EFTA on the Economies of Member States* (Geneva: EFTA, 1969), pp. 93–105.

49 Baklanoff, op. cit., p. 137.

50 Vaitsos, op. cit.; Jürgen Donges, 'Foreign investment in Portugal', paper presented at the Lisbon Conference, September 1979.

51 op. cit.

52 Presidência do Conselho, *IV Plano de Fomento, 1974–1979*, Vol. 1 (Lisbon, 1974), table VIII, p. 75.

53 Jürgen Donges, 'From autarchic towards a cautiously outward-looking industrialization policy: the case of Spain', *Weltwirtschaftliches Archiv*, Vol. 107, no. 1 (1971), pp. 48–50.

54 See Charles Anderson, *The Political Economy of Modern Spain* (Madison, Wis.: University of Wisconsin Press, 1976), pp. 103–56; Joan Esteban, 'The economic policy of Francoism: an interpretation', in Paul Preston (ed.), *Spain in Crisis* (Hassocks, Sussex: Harvester, 1976), pp. 93–7.

55 In an unprecedented move, Franco's government solicited the opinion of the main economic institutions and universities in January 1959. The response was both unanimous and enthusiastic in favour of economic liberalisation and participation in the European integration process. See Anderson, op. cit., pp. 120–1.

56 For a history of Spain's negotiations with the Six during the 1960s see Antonio Alonso and Camilo Barcia, *El acuerdo España-mercado común* (Madrid: Asociación para el Progreso de la Dirección, 1970); Anderson, op. cit., pp. 190–4. See also Maaike Onkenhout, 'Spain and the European Communities: a question of politics (1957–1980)', M.Phil. thesis, Oxford University, 1980.

57 See Paul Preston, 'The anti-Francoist opposition: the long march to unity', in Preston, op. cit., p. 143; Anderson, op. cit., pp. 103–28.

58 Henig, op. cit., pp. 37–9.

59 Stanley Henig, 'Mediterranean policy in the context of the external relations of the European Community: 1958–73', in Avi Shlaim and George Yannopoulos (eds), *The EEC and the Mediterranean Countries* (Cambridge: CUP, 1976), pp. 316–20.

60 Luis Gamir, 'Política de integración europea', in L. Gamir (ed.), *Política económica de España* (Madrid: Guadiana, 1975), p. 214; see also L. Gamir, *Las preferencias efectivas del Mercado Común a España* (Madrid: Moneda y Crédito, 1972).

61 Ramón Temames, *Estructura económica de España* (Madrid: Guadiana, 1973), p. 772.

62 For a comparative analysis see R. Tamames, *Acuerdo preferencial CEE/España y preferencias generalizadas* (Barcelona: Dopesa, 1972).

62 Commission, 'Opinion on Spain's application', op. cit., p. 15.

64 See also Tsoukalis, 'The EEC and the Mediterranean: is "global" policy a misnomer?', op. cit.; Stefan Musto, *Spaniens Beitritt zur Europäischen Gemeinschaft: Folgen und Probleme* (Berlin: DIE, 1977), pp. 30–4. For a Spanish point of view see Subdirección General de Politica Comercial con la CEE, 'Visión retrospectiva del Acuerdo del 1970: problemas de la adhesión', *Información Comercial Española*, no. 550–1, June–July 1979.

65 See also Baklanoff, op. cit., pp. 11–24; Alison Wright, *The Spanish Economy 1959–1976* (London: Macmillan, 1977), pp. 26–48.

66 Raymond Carr and Juan Pablo Fusi, *Spain: Dictatorship to Democracy* (London: Allen & Unwin, 1979), p. 54.

67 Wright, op. cit., p. 157.

68 For estimates of the effective rates of protection in Spanish industry, see Jürgen Donges, 'The economic integration of Spain with the EEC: problems and prospects', in Shlaim and Yannopoulos, op. cit. For a thorough analysis of Spain's industrial protection see ESADE, *La industria española ante la CEE* (Madrid: Instituto de Estudios Económicos, 1979), pp. 241–96.

69 Wright, op. cit., pp. 38–46.

70 See also Wright, op. cit., chs 3–6; Anderson, op. cit., ch. 6.

71 Quoted in Carr and Fusi, op. cit., p. 67.

72 *La empresa publica en España. Anales del CEEP*, 1978, table 21.

73 *Las grandes empresas industriales españolas en 1975* (Madrid: Ministerio de Industria y Energía, 1978), pp. 52–3.

74 Baklanoff, op. cit., pp. 35–7.

75 ibid., table 5.1, p. 57.

76 Baklanoff, op. cit., pp. 62–3.

77 OECD, *Balance of Payments of OECD Countries, 1960–1977* (Paris: OECD, 1979). Between 1960 and 1975, 76·4% of total foreign investment in enterprises with foreign majority participation was undertaken in the manufacturing sector. See Juan Muñoz, Santiago Roldán and Angel Serrano, *La internacionalización del capital en España* (Madrid: Cuadernos para el Diálogo, 1978), table 12, p. 121.

78 ibid., table 9, p. 109.

79 ibid., table 19, p. 139. Data apply to the period 1963–1971.

80 See, for example, Munoz, Roldan and Serrano, op. cit., pp. 67–113; Wright, op. cit., pp. 35–7; Javier Braña, Mikel Buesa and José Molero, 'The years 60–70: the increase of dependent growth in Spain' (mimeo.), Madrid, June 1977.

81 *Las grandes empresas industriales*, tables 13 and 14, p. 64.

82 ibid., table 15, p. 65.

83 Data provided by the Dirección General de Transacciones Exteriores.

84 The articles written by Spanish economists about the effects of Spain's accession to the Community are usually very reserved when compared with statements made by politicians. See, for example, Vicente Parajón Collada, 'La industria española ante las Comunidades Europeas' and Luís Alcaide de la Rosa, 'La alternativa de España a la entrada en la CEE', *Información Comercial Española*, no. 550–1, June–July 1979.

85 Jürgen Donges, 'Toward Spain's accession into the EEC – trade growth and policy reform implications', Institut für Weltwirtschaft an der Universität Kiel, Working Paper No. 94, September 1979; *La industria española ante la CEE*, chs 6, 7 and 8.

86 *Dependencia* and centre-periphery theories, usually found in development studies,

have also been applied to Southern European countries. See Seers, Schaffer and Kiljunen, *Under-developed Europe*. Another example is the two conferences organised in Sussex and Madrid in May–June and October 1979 respectively, whose theme was 'Integration and Unequal Development'.

87 Juan Muñoz, Santiago Roldán and Angel Serrano, 'The growing dependence of Spanish industrialization on foreign investment' in Seers, Schaffer and Kiljunen, op. cit., p. 173.

88 OECD, *The Impact of the Newly Industrialising Countries*, op. cit., pp. 32–4.

89 See Tables 1.9, 1.16 and 1.23. Figures for intra-Community trade are based on OECD data.

90 See also Tsoukalis, 'The EEC and the Mediterranean: is "global" policy a misnomer?', op. cit.

91 Muñoz, Roldán and Serrano, op. cit., p. 173.

Chapter 2

1 *Eleftherotypia*, 21 January 1979.

2 *Epsilon*, April 1980.

3 See also T. A. Couloumbis, J. A. Petropulos and H. J. Psomiades, *Foreign Interference in Greek Politics* (New York: Pella, 1976).

4 Jean Siotis, 'La situation internationale de la Grèce et la démande hellénique d'adhésion aux Communautés', in *La Grèce et la Communauté* (Brussels: Institut d'Etudes Européennes, 1978), p. 51.

5 See also Roy Macridis, 'Greek foreign policy: reality, illusions, options', in Tsoukalis, *Greece and the European Community*, op. cit.

6 See, for example, New Democracy 1977 electoral programme. Speech by Karamanlis in Ioannina, 20 February 1979.

7 A. Papandreou in *Oikonomikos Tachydromós*, 7 June 1979; PASOK electoral programme 1979; *Greece and the Common Market – A Counterargument* (in Greek), March 1976.

8 J. Pesmazoglou, *To Vima*, 26 June 1977.

9 op. cit., p. 146.

10 Even the direct elections to the European Parliament were seen in this light by a leading member of PASOK. See K. Simitis, *Kyriakatiki Eleftherotypia*, 24 November 1978.

11 Loukas Tsoukalis, 'The European Community and intra-Mediterranean co-operation: two inside, three in the waiting room, and the outsiders', paper presented at the International Political Science Association round table conference in Athens, May–June 1978.

12 Andreas Papandreon at a meeting held at the Royal Institute International Affairs in London, 28 November 1980.

13 This distinction is made in Nicos Mouzelis, *Modern Greece – Facets of Underdevelopment* (London: Macmillan, 1978), pp. 149–54.

14 Speech delivered by Papandreou at the conference of Mediterranean socialist parties in Malta, June 1977.

15 K. Naupliotis, *Rizospastis* (newspaper of KKE), 1 December 1977; J. Goularas, K. Hatziargyris and I. Tobroyiannis, *Common Market and Greece* (in Greek) (Athens: Centre for Marxist Studies, 1977).

16 Quoted in *To Vima*, 17 May 1979.

17 Juan Linz, 'Europe's southern frontier: evolving trends toward what?', *Daedalus*, Winter, 1979, p. 180.

18 *Ta Nea*, 27, 28 and 29 May 1980. See also *The Times*, 4 July 1980.

19 According to a recent opinion poll 67% of the Portuguese asked knew nothing about the European Community (*Expresso*, 24 May 1980).

20 See Cândido de Azevedo, op. cit., pp. 30–44.
21 *Le Monde*, 3 December 1974.
22 Soares, in *The Times*, 23 September 1975.
23 For a detailed account of political events during this period see Richard Robinson, *Contemporary Portugal* (London: Allen & Unwin, 1979), pp. 194–275; Robert Harvey, *Portugal, Birth of a Democracy* (London: Macmillan, 1978); for the role played by European countries see Nicholas van Praag, 'European political co-operation and the southern periphery', in *The Mediterranean Challenge: I*, Sussex European Papers No. 2, 1978.
24 Soares in *Diário de notícias*, 15 February 1977; Barreto in *Expresso*, 10 September 1976. For a study of the role played by the PS see Tom Gallagher, 'Portugal's bid for democracy: the role of the socialist party', *West European Politics*, May 1979.
25 Sa Carneiro, leader of the PSD and prime minister after the 1979 elections, in the *Financial Times*, 16 January 1979; Lucas Pires (CDS) in *Diário de notícias*, 19 December 1978. See also P. Pitta e Cunha, 'Portugal and the European Economic Community' (mimeo.), June 1979; J. M. Moura and Loureiro de Miranda, 'L'impact d'adhésion sur les institutions et le droit des pays candidats: Portugal', in W. Wallace and I. Herreman (eds), *A Community of Twelve? The Impact of Further Enlargement on the European Communities* (Bruges: De Tempel/College of Europe, 1978).
26 *Financial Times*, 18 January 1980.
27 Statements made by Davignon and Natali in Lisbon. See also Commission of the European Communities, 'Opinion on Portuguese application for membership', *Bulletin of the EC*, Supplement 5/78, pp. 15–16; V. Constâncio (PS) in *Diário de notícias*, 12 March 1979.
28 *Economia*, nos. 19, 21, 22 (1979).
29 Debate in the Portuguese parliament, 18 March 1977. Soares in *The Times*, 11 February 1977.
30 op. cit.
31 Quoted in Javier Rupérez, 'Political and economic perspectives of Spain's accession to the European Communities', paper presented at a conference organised by the Danish Institute for Foreign Affairs and the Danish Society for European Studies at Helsingør, October 1979.
32 Carr and Fusi, op. cit., p. 239; Linz, op. cit., p. 200. We have also drawn on J. Romero Maura, 'The Spanish political system on the eve of Spain's probable entry into the EEC' (mimeo.), September 1975.
33 Debate in the parliament, 27 June 1979 (Cortes, *Diário de sesiones del Congreso de los Diputados*, no. 21, 27 June 1979, pp. 1049-1093).
34 M. Medina, 'Politique étrangère de l'Espagne et rélations extérieures des Communautés Européennes', paper presented at the conference on Spain's accession to the European Communities in Brussels, May 1979.
35 There have been reports that there is also a large opposition to membership of NATO inside the Spanish army, especially among junior officers (*Financial Times*, 12 June 1980).
36 See also David Bell, 'Eurocommunism and the Spanish Communist Party', in *The Mediterranean Challenge: II*, Sussex European Papers No. 4, 1979.
37 See Donald Sassoon, 'The Italian communist party's European strategy', *Political Quarterly*, July–September 1976; R. Irving, 'The European policy of the French and Italian communists', *International Affairs*, July 1977.
38 Azcarate, quoted in *Le Monde*, 2 August 1978.
39 Spanish newspapers are usually better informed than their Greek or Portuguese counterparts. This applies especially to a newspaper such as *El país*, for which there is no equivalent at all in the other two countries.

40 Quoted in Daniel de Busturia, 'Aspectos económicos de la adhesión de España a la Comunidad Europea', paper presented at the Lisbon Conference, June 1980.
41 *Le Monde*, 8–9 June 1980.

Chapter 3

1 See also Panos Tsakaloyiannis, 'The EEC and the Greek-Turkish dispute', *Journal of Common Market Studies*, September 1980. For the economic aspect of Turkey's relations with the Community see Osman Okyar and Okan Aktan (eds), *Economic Relations between Turkey and the EEC*, proceedings of a seminar held in Antalya, 11–14 October 1976 (Hacettepe Institute).
2 *Le Monde*, 7 September 1974.
3 Commission of the European Communities, 'Opinion on the Greek application for membership', *Bulletin of the EC*, Supplement 2/76.
4 *Corriere della sera*, 31 January 1976.
5 *To Vima*, 30 January 1976.
6 Beate Kohler, 'Die Süderweiterung der Gemeinschaft-Hintergrunde Motive und Konsequenzen', in Hajo Hasenpflug and Beate Kohler (eds), *Die Süd-Erweiterung der Europäischen Gemeinschaft* (Hamburg: Weltarchiv, 1977), p. 21.
7 *Financial Times*, 12 February 1976.
8 William Wallace, 'Grand gestures and second thoughts: the response of member countries to Greece's application', in Tsoukalis, *Greece and the European Community*, op. cit., p. 24.
9 *Le Monde*, 3–4 April 1977.
10 See also Michael Leigh, 'Nine EEC attitudes to enlargement', in *The Mediterranean Challenge: I*, op. cit., pp. 32–49.
11 *The Times*, 29 July 1977.
12 William Wallace, 'The reaction of the Community and of member governments', in Wallace and Herreman, op. cit., pp. 52–3.
13 Commission of the European Communities, 'Enlargement of the Community', *Bulletin of the EC*, Supplements 1–3/78.
14 Commission of the EC, 'Opinion on the Portuguese application', op. cit.
15 Commission of the EC, 'Opinion on Spain's application', op. cit.
16 *Le Monde*, 7 December 1979.
17 *The Times*, 6 June 1980; *Le Monde*, 7 June 1980.
18 *The Economist*, 21 June 1975.
19 *The Economist*, 5 July 1980.
20 For a good survey of Community attitudes to enlargement see also Leigh, op. cit.
21 Beate Kohler, 'Germany and the further enlargement of the European Community', *The World Economy*, May 1979, p. 200.
22 François Duchêne, 'Community attitudes', paper presented at the Madrid Conference in October 1979.
23 François Duchêne, 'Europe's role in world peace', in Richard Mayne (ed.), *Europe Tomorrow* (London: Fontana/Chatham House and PEP, 1972). See also David Allen, 'Foreign policy at the European level: beyond the nation-state?', in William Wallace and W. E. Paterson (eds), *Foreign Policy Making in Western Europe* (Farnborough: Saxon House, 1978); William Wallace, 'A common European foreign policy: mirage or reality?', in Bernard Burrows, Geoffrey Denton and Geoffrey Edwards (eds), *Federal Solutions to European Issues* (London: Macmillan for the Federal Trust, 1978).
24 See also Kohler, op. cit., p. 206.
25 See Ulrich Everling, 'Zehn Thesen zur Erweiterung', *EG (Europäische Gemeinschaft) – Magazin*, 5/1977. See also U. Everling, 'Possibilities and limits of European integration', and Christian Deubner, 'The southern enlargement of the

European Community: opportunities and dilemmas from a West German point of view', *Journal of Common Market Studies*, March 1980.

26 It could be argued however that there are important characteristics common to all the ancient civilisations of the Mediterranean, something which might justify including the Greeks in the same category with all Latins, as well as the Arabs. For example, all those civilisations have turned around the agora, the forum or the mosque, all of which are meeting places reproduced even in northern France in the village square. Post-Roman civilisations have no genuine concept of the village square or the forum.

27 *Le Monde*, 4 January 1974.

28 Duchêne, 'Community attitudes', op. cit.

29 Conseil National des Jeunes Agriculteurs (CNJA), *Espagne: un choc pour l'Europe* (Paris: CNJA, April 1976), pp. 9, 16.

30 *Le Monde*, 28 July 1978.

31 *Le Monde*, 12 August 1978.

32 See, for example, 'Pour une autre Europe – l'élargissement de la CEE', *Le Poing et la Rose*, supplement to no. 79 (February 1979).

33 *L'Agriculture Méditerranéenne de la France dans la CEE: problèmes et perspectives* (Rapport Desouches), May 1977; *Rapport d'information . . . sur les répercussions agricoles de la politique méditerranéenne de la CEE pour les régions du sud de la France* (Pisani–Sordel), Sénat Seconde Session Ordinaire de 1976–1977, no. 259.

34 See, for example, the statements made by M. Debatisse, president of one of the biggest farmers' organisations (FNSEA), quoted in *Le Monde*, 27 July 1978.

35 *Le Monde*, 1 February 1976.

36 *Le Monde*, 7 March 1977; 13–14 September 1978.

37 'Report on European institutions', presented by the Committee of Three to the European Council, October 1979.

38 See, for example, *L'Unità*, 2 June; 26 July 1977.

39 For a good analysis of the main issues associated with enlargement from a British point of view, see House of Lords Select Committee on the European Communities, *Enlargement of the Community* (London: HMSO, April 1978).

40 ibid., pp. 42–4.

41 Quoted in *The Times*, 13 January 1977.

42 Downing Street press statement, 2 October 1977.

43 See Garret Fitzgerald, 'A Community of Twelve? The opportunities and risks of enlargement', in Wallace and Herreman, op. cit.

44 Ernst Haas, *Beyond the Nation-State* (Stanford, Calif.: Stanford University Press, 1964), p. 111.

45 This was expressed openly by the Commission's Vice-President, Wilhelm Haferkamp, 'Chancen und Risiken der zweiten EG-Erweiterung', *Europa Archiv*, 10 October 1977, p. 620.

46 This report was made at the request of the Commission by a committee chaired by the Dutch ambassador, Dirk Spierenburg. See *Proposals for Reform of the Commission of the European Communities and its Services* (Brussels, September 1979).

47 See Leigh, op. cit., pp. 9–12.

48 *Europe, South and East: Redefining the American Interest* (Washington, DC: US Government Printing Office, 1975), p. 1.

49 See, for example, the leading article in the *New York Times*, 7 September 1974.

50 One example is a joint article written by two leading members of the PSOE and the French PS respectively, Christian Goux and Manuel Marin, 'Pourquoi la candidature espagnole?', *Le Monde*, 31 October 1978.

51 For the effects of enlargement on other Mediterranean countries see Patrick Hoguet, 'The impact of Community enlargement on the Maghreb and the Mashreq countries', paper presented at the Sussex conference in May-June 1979. See also

Alfred Tovias, 'EEC enlargement – the Southern neighbours', *The Mediterranean Challenge: III*, Sussex European Papers No. 5, 1979.

52 Reported in *Neue Zürcher Zeitung*, 8 September 1974.

53 Gian-Paolo Papa and Jean-Petit Laurent, 'Commercial relations between the EEC and the Mediterranean countries', in Shlaim and Yannopoulos, op. cit.

54 See also Wallace, 'Grand gestures and second thoughts', op. cit., pp. 24–35.

Chapter 4

1 See, for example, William Diebold Jr, *Industrial Policy as an International Issue* (New York: McGraw-Hill/Council on Foreign Relations, 1980), ch. 1; OECD, *The Aims and Instruments of Industrial Policy: a Comparative Study* (Paris: OECD, 1975).

2 Wolfgang Hager, 'Industrial policy', paper presented at the Lisbon Conference, June 1980.

3 For a study of the Schuman Plan and the creation of the ECSC see William Diebold Jr, *The Schuman Plan* (New York: Praeger for Council on Foreign Relations, 1959); Ernst Haas, *The Uniting of Europe* (London: Stevens, 1958).

4 See also Loukas Tsoukalis, *The Politics and Economics of European Monetary Integration* (London: Allen & Unwin, 1977), pp. 51–9.

5 Alexis Jacquemin and Henry de Jong, *European Industrial Organisation* (London: Macmillan, 1977), p. 243.

6 Geoffrey Denton, *Planning in the EEC – The Medium-Term Economic Policy Programme of the European Economic Community* (London: Chatham House/PEP, 1967), pp. 9–15.

7 Andrew Shonfield, 'The politics of the mixed economy in the international system of the 1970s', *International Affairs*, January 1980, p. 8.

8 For the development of industrial policy at the Community level see Michael Hodges, 'Industrial policy: a directorate-general in search of a role', in H. Wallace, W. Wallace and C. Webb (eds), *Policy-Making in the European Community* (Chichester: Wiley, 1977).

9 Wolfgang Hillebrand, 'Hypotheses concerning the future development of the European Community's industrial policy', in German Development Institute (GDI), *European Community and Acceding Countries of Southern Europe* (Berlin: GDI, 1979), pp. 31–3.

10 Raymond Vernon, 'Enterprise and government in Western Europe', in R. Vernon (ed.), *Big Business and the State* (London: Macmillan, 1974).

11 See also Alan Dashwood, 'Hastening slowly: the Communities' path towards harmonization', in Wallace, Wallace and Webb, op. cit.

12 See also David Allen, 'Policing or policy-making? Competition policy in the European Communities', in Wallace, Wallace and Webb, op. cit.; Jacquemin and de Jong, op. cit., pp. 198–242.

13 See also Steven Warnecke, 'The European Community and national subsidy policies', in S. Warnecke (ed.), *International Trade and Industrial Policies* (London: Macmillan, 1978).

14 The discussion on sensitive sectors is based on Loukas Tsoukalis and António da Silva Ferreira, 'The management of industrial surplus capacity in the European Community', *International Organization*, Summer 1980. See also Susan Strange and Roger Tooze (eds), *The Management of Surplus Capacity* (London: Allen & Unwin, forthcoming).

15 José de la Torre and Michel Bacchetta, 'The uncommon market: European policies towards the clothing industry in the 1970s', *Journal of Common Market Studies*, December 1980.

16 See, for example, Hager, op. cit. This is also one of the main arguments in Diebold, op. cit.
17 Douglas Yuill, Kevin Allen and Chris Hull (eds), *Regional Policy in the European Community* (London: Croom Helm, 1980), pp. 224–6.
18 Normalised trade balances $\left(\dfrac{X-M}{X+M} \right)$ show the ratio of the trade balance to the volume of trade and constitute an indicator of trade performance. Positive values display net export performances, becoming stronger as the figure approaches $+1$. There is exactly a corresponding relationship between net imports and negative values.
19 The conversion of monthly into hourly earnings was based on the average number of working hours per week, 53·0, 52·9, 54·6 and 55·4 respectively, for the four columns multiplied by four (data found in the ILO statistics).
20 House of Lords, *Enlargement of the Community*, op. cit., p. 37.
21 Commission of the EC, 'Opinion on Spain's application', p. 29.
22 Greece is a good example where both arguments seem to be correct. See Mitsos, 'The new role for the Greek government after accession', in *The Mediterranean Challenge: IV*, op. cit., pp. 131–4.
23 See also Tsoukalis, 'Impact on the European monetary system', op. cit.
24 Mitsos, op. cit., p. 138.
25 See George Yannopoulos, 'Sensitivity of industrial sectors to Common Market competition', in *The Mediterranean Challenge: IV*, op. cit.
26 IOVE, 'Greek industry and the EEC' (in Greek) (Athens); mimeo., 1979. This study contains the results of a research undertaken by the Institute of Economic and Industrial Research in Athens on the impact of accession on Greek industry.
27 ESADE, *La industria española ante la CEE*, op. cit., pp. 362–73; Donges, 'Towards Spain's accession into the EEC', op. cit.
28 op. cit.
29 Wilhelm Hummen, 'Small and medium industry in Greece – problems and development prospects in view of entry to the EC', in German Development Institute, op. cit., tables 1 and 2, pp. 108–9; Noelke and Cadette, *Recherche sur l'économie portugaise*, pp. 67–9; Commission of the EC, 'Enlargement of the Community – economic and sectoral aspects, pp. 11, 16.
30 IOVE, op. cit.
31 See also Vaitsos, op. cit.
32 Yuill, Allen and Hull, op. cit., p. 246.
33 Diebold, op. cit., p. 230.
34 John Pinder, 'Integrating divergent economies: the extra-national method', *International Affairs*, October 1979, p. 553.
35 Tsoukalis and Ferreira, op. cit.
36 See German Development Institute, op. cit., especially articles by Klaus Esser, Wilhelm Hummen and Wolfgang Hillebrand. The same line of argument can be found in Stefan Musto, 'Regional disparities in an enlarged EC and the problem of the intra-Community division of labour', paper presented at the Madrid Conference in October 1979.
37 John Pinder, 'A federal Community in an ungoverned world economy', in Burrows, Denton and Edwards (eds), op. cit.; Hager, op. cit.; Diebold, op. cit.
38 Hummen, op. cit., p. 87.
39 Pinder, 'Integrating divergent economies', p. 554.
40 See also Richard Stanton, 'Foreign investment and host country politics: the Irish case', in Seers, Schaffer, Kiljunen (eds), op. cit.
41 The Greek PASOK and large sections of the Portuguese and Spanish socialist parties are very reticent, not to say openly hostile, to foreign investment. See, for example, Panayiotis Roumeliotis, *The Economic Crisis and Greece's Accession to the EEC* (in Greek) (Athens: Papazissis, 1980), especially chs VI–VIII.

Chapter 5

1 For a brief history of the CAP during the 1960s see John Marsh and Christopher Ritson, *Agricultural Policy and the Common Market* (London: Chatham House/PEP, 1971), pp. 129–65. For more recent works which can serve as a good introduction to the subject see Adrien Ries, *L'ABC du marché commun agricole* (Paris and Brussels: Nathan/Labor, 1978), and Rosemary Fennell, *The Common Agricultural Policy of the European Community* (London: Granada, 1979).

2 These figures refer to 1978 (source: *The OECD Observer*, March 1980) and are therefore slightly different from those found in Table 1.3.

3 The concept of self-sufficiency has to be treated with much caution. There is first of all a practical problem in measuring self-sufficiency in terms of production and trade statistics published for each individual country. All our calculations are based on recorded domestic production, imports and exports. We therefore do not take into account changes in stocks held by intervention agencies. Thus in the case of products for which self-sufficiency is near or above 100% the figure can be quite misleading, particularly in the sense of providing an underestimate of the surplus involved. On the other hand self-sufficiency is not an absolute thing. On the contrary, it is a direct function of the level of prices.

4 A. Pepelasis, 'The Greek agriculture in the EEC', in *The Mediterranean Challenge: IV*, op. cit., table 9, p. 17.

5 The description of the Greek agricultural policy relies basically on Pepelasis, op. cit., OECD, *The Agricultural Policy of Greece* (Paris: OECD, 1979) and information provided by the EC Commission and the Greek government.

6 Pepelasis, op. cit., p. 54.

7 OECD, op. cit., p. 15.

8 Pepelasis, op. cit., p. 59. We are however sceptical about the validity or usefulness of such comparisons.

9 See also Agne Pantelouri's comment on J. Marsh's paper in Tsoukalis, *Greece and the European Community*, op. cit.

10 OECD, *Agricultural Policy in Portugal* (Paris: OECD, 1975), p. 18. For the description of the Portuguese agricultural policy we have also relied on Michael Noelke and Eduardo Maia Cadette, *Recherche sur l'économie portugaise*, Vol. 2, op. cit.; António Cortez Labão, Fernando G. Silva and Fernando Estácio, 'Agricultural policy and EEC membership', paper presented at the Lisbon Conference, September 1979; and a World Bank report.

11 Lobão, Silva and Estácio, op. cit.

12 For Spain's agricultural policy we have relied on Pedro Solbes Mira, *La adhesión de España a la CEE – los efectos sobre la protección exterior a la agricultura* (Madrid: Moneda y Crédito, 1979); OECD, *Agricultural Policy in Spain* (Paris: OECD, 1974); Denis Bergmann, 'Les voies de développement de l'agriculture espagnole', paper presented at a conference on Spain and the European Economic Community, Madrid, January 1979.

13 Quoted in Bergmann, op. cit.

14 Commission des Communautés Européennes, *Problèmes de l'agriculture Mediterranéenne* (Pizzuti Report) (Brussels), mimeo., November 1976.

15 ibid.

16 ibid.

17 Commission of the EC, *The Agricultural Situation in the Community, 1979 Report* (Brussels and Luxembourg), January 1980, p. 378.

18 For the different calendars applying for each particular agreement and product, see House of Lords, *Enlargement of the Community*, table 10, pp. 32–3.

19 op. cit.

20 See also Eric Hayes, 'La PAC – qui paye: les coûts de la PAC et leur bien-fondé, par rapport à la réforme de celle-ci; le problème de la convergence économique', in

Martin Whitby (ed.), *Doit-on réformer la Politique Agricole Commune*, (Ashford: Centre for European Agricultural Studies, Wye College, 1979). According to Saccomandi, FEOGA expenditure accounted for only 3·9% of agricultural value added in Italy as compared with 14·8% in the Netherlands, 9·4% in Belgium/Luxembourg and 5·8% in France; quoted in O. Ferro, F. Lechi and G. Ricci, 'Italian attitudes to the common agricultural policy'; in M. Tracy and I. Hodac (eds), *Prospects for Agriculture in the European Economic Community* (Bruges: De Tempel/College of Europe, 1979), p. 385.

21 G. Coda Nunziante, 'Les contradictions Nord–Sud au sein de l'Europe', *Economie Rurale*, 1 (1978).

22 Quoted in Agra Europe Special Report No. 3, *The Agricultural Implications of EEC Enlargement – Part I: Greece* (London), June 1979.

23 For a comprehensive analysis of the agricultural aspects of enlargement see John Marsh, 'The impact of enlargement on the Common Agricultural Policy', in Wallace and Herreman (eds), *A Community of Twelve?*, op. cit.

24 Short of keeping Spain out of the Community, these are the minimum conditions laid down by farmers' organisations in France (supported by their Italian counterparts) and in the various reports published in France. See, for example, the Pisani–Sordel Report to the French Senate; F. Desouches, 'L'agriculture française face à l'élargissement de la CEE vers le sud', and Roberto Pasca, 'Conflicts arising from the enlargement of the Community: an Italian perspective', in Tracy and Hodac, op. cit.

25 Silva Lopes, 'Portugal and the EEC: the application for membership', op. cit.

26 There is a complicated set of operations behind the self-sufficiency ratios for the Community of Twelve. In total there are thirty-four operations, many of them cancelling out in order to obtain the trade balance of EC–12 starting with the trade balance of EC–9. One has to exclude trade between the applicant countries and existing members as well as trade among the applicants themselves. After enlargement all this will become intra-Community trade. As with Table 5.4, self-sufficiency represents the ratio of total production divided by production minus the trade balance and multiplied by 100. No account is taken of changes in stocks. Moreover self-sufficiency ratios are directly related to the existing set of prices. Last but not least, Table 5.14 refers to only one year (1978). Thus for some products, especially the Mediterranean ones which are subject to big seasonal fluctuations, total production can vary significantly from one year to the other.

27 53·3% in 1978 (*The Agricultural Situation in the Community – 1979 Report*, op. cit., p. 234).

28 See also Tovias, 'EEC enlargement the southern neighbours', op. cit

29 Quoted in Bela Balassa, 'Portugal in face of the Common Market', paper presented at the Lisbon Conference in September 1979.

30 Pepelasis, op. cit., table 25, pp. 38–9.

31 J. J. Rodríguez Alcaide, 'Spanish agriculture and the Common Market', in *Spain, Portugal and the European Community*, op. cit., Annex 2, p. 336.

32 *The Agricultural Situation in the Community – 1979 Report*, pp. 256–8.

33 Commission of the EC, 'Enlargement of the Community – economic and sectoral aspects', op. cit., pp. 37–8.

34 Jim Rollo, 'The second enlargement of the EEC: some economic implications with special reference to agriculture', *Journal of Agricultural Economics*, September 1979.

35 House of Lords, *Enlargement of the Community*, op. cit., pp. 42–4.

36 *Le Monde*, 22 March 1980; *The Economist*, 8 March 1980. The ECU was introduced into the CAP in April 1979, thus replacing the old agricultural unit of account.

37 *The Agricultural Situation in the Community – 1979 Report*, p. 162.

38 See, for example, the article by Claude Rosenfeld in the *Financial Times*, 24 October 1979.

39 According to Commission figures Community expenditure in 1978 accounted for 41% of total agricultural expenditure in the Nine (*The Agricultural Situation in the Community – 1979 Report*, pp. 133–4). Such estimates should however be treated with much caution.
40 Tsoukalis, *The Politics and Economics of European Monetary Integration*, op. cit., pp. 59–63.
41 Quoted in *Le Monde*, 17 June 1980.
42 *Le Poing et la Rose*, op. cit., p. 15.
43 *Mediterranean Problems of the Community*, memorandum submitted by the Italian government to the Council of the European Communities, Brussels, 12 July 1977; *Memorandum on the Reform of Community Regulations Governing Mediterranean Agricultural Production*, submitted by the French government to the Council of the European Communities, Brussels, 27 July 1977.
44 Adrien Ries, op. cit., p. 169.
45 Finn Olav Gundelach, 'Prospects for the Common Agricultural Policy in the world context', in Tracy and Hodac (eds), op. cit., p. 429.
46 Quoted in *Le Monde*, 23 February 1980.
47 See, for example, D. K. Britton, 'Summary of discussions', in Tracy and Hodac (eds), op. cit.
48 John Marsh, 'Europe's agriculture: reform of the CAP', *International Affairs*, October 1977. 'Trading prices' are only part of a package of proposals put forward by Marsh in this article.
49 ibid., p. 608.

Index